INSPIRE / PLAN / DISCOVER / EXPERIENCE

DORDOGNE

BORDEAUX AND THE SOUTHWEST COAST

DORDOGNE

BORDEAUX AND THE SOUTHWEST COAST

CONTENTS

DISCOVER 6

EXPERIENCE 58

NEED TO KNOW 252

Cover: Château Castelnaud in the Dordogne valley
Left: Colourful beach tents in Biarritz
Previous page: Vineyards of Saint-Émilion

DISCOVER

Rooftops of Bordeaux, capital of Gironde

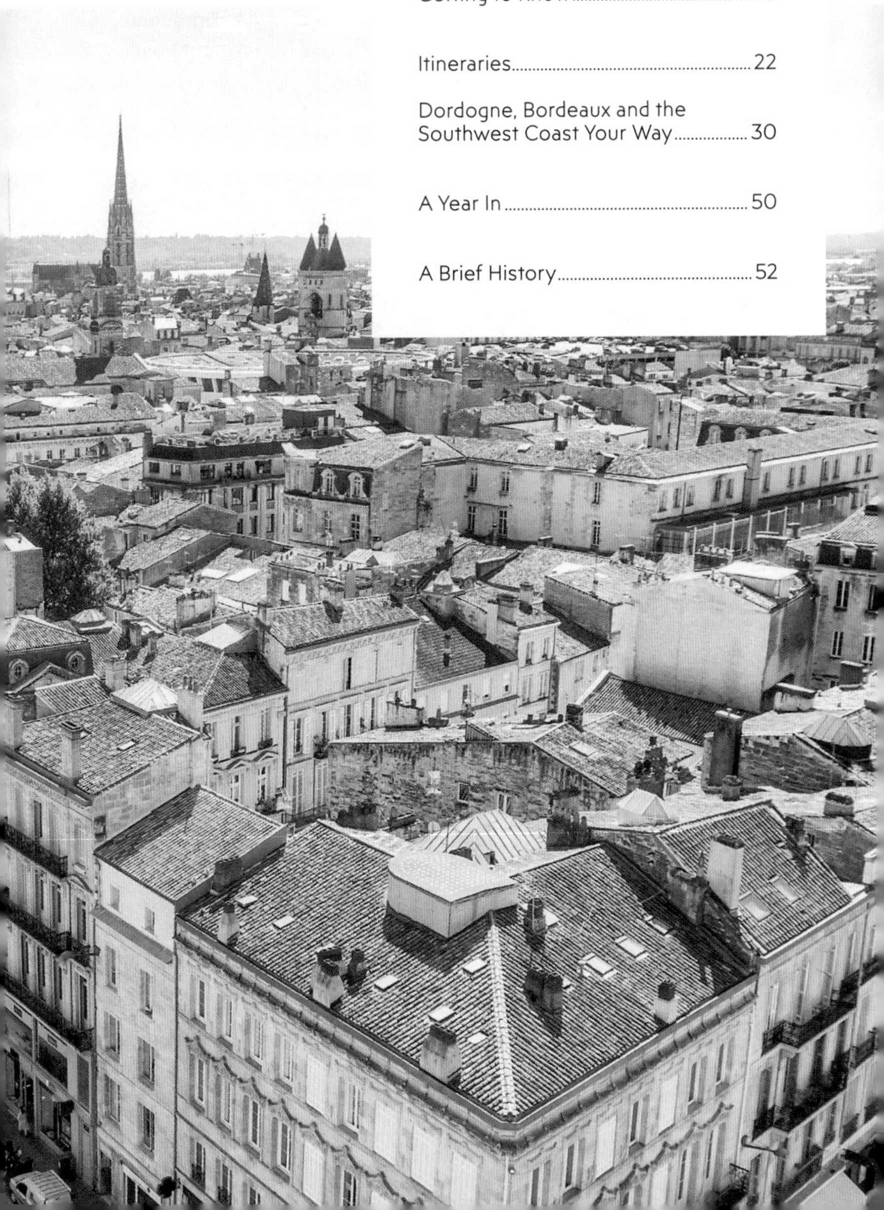

WELCOME TO
DORDOGNE, BORDEAUX AND THE SOUTHWEST COAST

The backdrop of this unhurried and delightful region of southwest France is formed of glittering coastline, emerald green hills and serene rivers. There are also fortified medieval villages carved into rocky outcroppings, historical centres of modern cities and the many châteaux that trace France's turbulent history and architectural styles. Whatever your dream trip to Dordogne, Bordeaux and the Southwest Coast includes, this DK Eyewitness travel guide is the perfect companion.

1 A sampling of regional specialities.

2 Pic du Midi d'Ossau in the Ossau Valley.

3 A lighthouse in the old port town of Capbreton.

4 Old Town in medieval Sarlat-la-Canéda.

The landscapes of southwest France offer something for everyone. History buffs will be moved by the prehistoric caves at Lascaux, where humanity's palaeolithic ancestors felt compelled to create images of the beasts that used to roam these parts. Nature lovers, cyclists and hikers will find themselves spoiled for choice between country lanes, thick forests and rolling hills, while massive dunes and soft sandy beaches on the Atlantic will keep sun-seekers and surfers content for days.

Even the urban spaces retain the relaxed, countryside atmosphere, all of them bursting with character and history. A stroll around the city of Périgueux reveals the legacy of its early Roman conquerors, whose bridges and amphitheatre are still part of the cityscape.

Bordeaux – France's elegant wine capital – is the belle of the ball, with exceptional architecture, outstanding museums and classic French cafés perfect for people-watching. Tiny rural villages are also a delight to explore, as each one is full of its own local charm, with unique festivals, speciality foods and traditional buildings surrounding old town squares.

With so much to appreciate, you won't want to miss a single thing. We've broken this region down into easily navigable chapters, with detailed itineraries, expert local knowledge and colourful, comprehensive maps to help you plan the perfect visit. Whether you're staying for a few days, weeks or longer, this Eyewitness guide will ensure that you see the very best of the region. Enjoy the book and enjoy southwest France.

REASONS TO LOVE
DORDOGNE, BORDEAUX AND THE SOUTHWEST COAST

It has a rich historical heritage. Its steeped in culture. Its cuisine and wines are world famous. Ask anyone from southwest France and you'll hear a different reason why they love this region. Here, we pick a few favourites.

WINE COUNTRY *1*

Bordeaux's wines are known around the world, bringing fame to the region since the age of the Roman Empire. Sip for yourself at one of the many vineyards throughout Gironde.

BASQUE HERITAGE *2*

The unique language, cuisine and architectural style of Pays Basque is most evident between the chic beach resort of Biarritz and the port city of Bayonne *(p46)*.

3 MOVING DUNES

Fly a kite from the top of a massive sand dune, like those in the Arcachon Basin *(p86)*. Then settle down with a picnic to watch paragliders riding the winds.

CAFÉ CULTURE 4

Lounge away an afternoon with a pastry and a coffee. Soak up the relaxed atmosphere on a rooftop terrace or choose a street-side spot to people-watch.

ROCAMADOUR 5

Dramatically etched into the cliffside, this venerated town offers a humbling climb up stairs that have been tread upon by pilgrims since the 12th-century *(p120)*.

FANTASTIC FLAVOURS 6

Fresh oysters from the ocean, black truffles from the forests and fresh farm produce. The many richly flavoured treasures here are perfect for foodies looking to indulge *(p30)*.

HISTORIC CATHEDRALS *7*
Marvel at the majesty of Gothic, Romanesque and Baroque cathedrals, whose intricate designs chart the region's changing architectural tastes across the ages.

SURF'S UP *8*
All along the coastline the sounds of the crashing waves of the Atlantic promise excitement further out to sea, where great swells challenge surfers of every level *(p48)*.

9 CLIFF-TOP CASTLES
Once standing guard over the lands of French nobles, many of these castles now have museums demonstrating life as it used to be behind those impenetrable ramparts.

PADDLING THE DORDOGNE 10

For the quintessential Dordogne experience, take to the water. Pack a picnic lunch, rent a canoe and drift along the serene river on a warm summer's day.

PREHISTORIC PAINTINGS 11

Life-size paintings of dappled horses, charging bison, and hulking mammoths are just a few of the beasts depicted on the walls of the caves at Lascaux *(p140)*.

COUNTRY ROADS 12

Take a leisurely drive or simply walk along the winding rural roads that twist through the region's most beautiful landscapes, joining picturesque hamlets and *bastide* towns.

DORDOGNE, BORDEAUX AND THE SOUTHWEST COAST

This guide divides Dordogne, Bordeaux and the Southwest Coast into seven colour-coded sightseeing areas, as shown on this map. Find out more about each area on the following pages.

Saint-Jean-d'Angély

Rochefort

CHARENTE-MARITIME

Saintes

Royan

Gémozac

Soulac-sur-Mer

Jonzac

Lesparre-Médoc

La Gironde

Hourtin

Lac de Hourtin et de Carcans

Blaye

Lacanau

Étang de Lacanau

GIRONDE
p72

Bordeaux

BORDEAUX
p60

Bassin d'Arcachon

Arcachon

Hostens

Biscarrosse

Mimizan

Sabres

Saint-Julien-en-Born

LANDES
p186

Mont-de-Marsan

LANDES

Dax

Tartas

Hossegor

Biarritz

Bayonne

Saint-Jean-de-Luz

Orthez

PYRÉNÉES-ATLANTIQUES

Zarautz

Pau

San Sebastian

PAYS BASQUE
p204

Oloron-Sainte-Marie

Durango

Tolosa

BÉARN
p232

SPAIN

Roncesvalles

0 kilometres   40

0 miles   40

N

Pamplona

GETTING TO KNOW
DORDOGNE, BORDEAUX AND THE SOUTHWEST COAST

A region for any season, southwest France is a land of stunning natural beauty and ancient townscapes. Amid its mountain peaks, languorous valleys and endless golden beaches stand beautiful towns and villages that are alive with culture and tradition.

BORDEAUX

A port city on the Garonne River, Bordeaux has been attracting visitors for centuries, most notably wine-lovers who come to sample the exquisite reds and whites that have been produced here since Roman times. Outside the wine bards, the magnificent architecture makes the city a great place to explore on foot. Stroll along the grand boulevards lined with UNESCO Heritage-listed medieval and Neo-Classical buildings. On the way, dip into one of the old riverside warehouses that have been turned into welcoming cafés, and take some time to explore the city's museums.

Best for
Architecture, wine and fine cuisine

Home to
Grand-Théâtre

Experience
Exploring the world of wine at the ultra modern La Cité du Vin, ending with a tasting session and views over the river

GIRONDE

PAGE 72

A wealth of vineyards makes this a must-see destination for oenophiles, who can enjoy wine tastings at stately château all over Gironde. But there's far more to this *département* than its grapes. The verdant country-side is dotted with old *bastide* towns bursting with history and a relaxed, rural atmosphere that makes southwest France such a rejuvenating leisure spot. If you want to get active, or simply enjoy the out-doors, head to the Arcachon Basin inland sea, home to Europe's highest dune, or to the nearby resort town of Arcachon for seaside fun and oysters.

Best for
Wine country tours
and watersports

Home to
Saint-Émilion, Château de
Cazeneuve, Arcachon Basin,
Phare de Cordouam

Experience
Kiteboarding, paragliding and
surfing at Arcachon Basin

→

PAGE 108

DORDOGNE AND LOT

The *départéments* of Dordogne and Lot are two of the most beautiful areas in the country, replete with all the experiences you could ask for on a dream vacation in France. Hop in a canoe and drift along the Dordogne river; take a road trip down country lanes to sample fine wines and cheese in *bastide* towns and old châteaux; stroll through the medieval city centres of Périgueux and Bergerac. Adventurous travellers can explore ancient caves while culture and history lovers admire ethereal, larger-than-life prehistoric paintings gracing the walls inside.

Best for
Nature, prehistoric cave paintings and medieval towns

Home to
Périgueux, Gardens of the Manoir d'Eyrignac, Les Eyzies-de-Tayac, Rocamadour, Château de Hautefort, Figeac, Château de Castelnaud, Bergerac, Grotte du Pech-Merle and Sarlat-la-Canéda

Experience
Cruising the Dordogne in a traditional wine cargo boat

PAGE 156

LOT-ET-GARONNE

The scenery throughout Lot-et-Garonne is built upon its limestone plateaux, then framed by some of France's most alluring towns and countryside vistas. It's impossible to pass through without making detours to explore some of the many wonderful old *bastide* towns such as Villeréal, enjoy the verdant valleys of the Pays du Dropt, or visit a historic castle like the Château de Bonaguil. Wherever you find yourself, make sure to stop and enjoy all the local delicacies on offer, including truffles, foie gras and fine wines from local vineyards.

Best for
Countryside, bastide *towns and indulgent food*

Home to
Château de Bonaguil and Agen

Experience
Feasting on truffles on a café terrace in Agen

PAGE 186

LANDES

Known primarily for its beautiful landscapes, Landes' outdoor adventures are bursting with an exciting array of holiday fun. The inland region is dominated by vast pine forests criss-crossed with routes for hiking and cycling, while the coastline is paradise for surfers and sunseekers, who come here for the rolling waves and sweeping sandy shores of Europe's longest string of beaches – the Côte d'Argent. Picturesque villages such as Labastide d'Armagnac appear like a tableau from a storybook, and their markets and restaurants offer up gastronomic treasures like seafood and goat cheese.

Best for
Beaches, forests and spas

Home to
Parc Naturel Régional des Landes de Gascogne

Experience
Relaxing in the thermal springs of Dax

$\rightarrow$

PAGE 204

PAYS BASQUE

There's a bit of everything on offer to entertain you in Pays Basque, whether you're after the perfect waves for surfing, a pristine beach for sun lounging or a glamorous casino for an evening of thrills. This is also France at its most proudly independent, with unique traditions, festivals and food that make the region's towns fascinating places to explore. Take in trendy Bayonne or stay a while in the chic surf city of Biarritz with its six golden sand beaches. Absorb its culinary and cultural influences from Gascony and Spain – a blend of traditions and history that makes this region unique.

Best for
Basque culture, seaside resort towns and regional cuisine

Home to
Bayonne

Experience
Sampling the famous jambon de Bayonne *(melt-in-your-mouth cured ham)*

PAGE 232

BÉARN

One of the most sparsely inhabited parts of the country, Béarn contains some of southwest France's most magnificent natural sights. At its centre are the three valleys of Barretous, Ossau and Aspe, with their endless opportunities for biking, hiking, climbing and soaking up breathtaking mountain views in summer. In winter the region becomes a popular place for off-piste skiing. There's even more to see in Béarn's urban landscapes, such as the capital city of Pau, whose grand château, inspiring art museums and grand villas will delight culture and history lovers.

Best for
Mountain views, outdoor adventures

Home to
Pau and Ossau Valley

Experience
Taking the Train d'Artouste up the valley for vews of the distinctive Pic du Midi d'Ossau mountain peak

←

1 Splashing in the Miroir d'Eau at place de la Bourse.

2 La Cité du Vin.

3 Inside the Grand Théâtre.

4 Dessert at Le Bouchon Bordelais.

Spend some time in southwest France and you'll find the very best of the country's landscapes, food and culture all in a single region. These itineraries will inspire you to make the most of your visit.

2 DAYS
in Bordeaux

Day 1

Morning Start at the majestic Cathédrale Saint-André *(p68)* where Eleanor of Aquitaine (one of the most powerful French women of her time) married her first husband, French King Louis VII. Climb its bell tower, the Tour Pey-Berland *(p69)* for beautiful views of the city below. Stroll north along grand boulevards lined with fine 18th-century buildings, passing by the imposing stone Porte Cailhau *(p67)*, the city's historic gate built in 1495. Continue on, with the 14th-century Église Saint-Pierre on your left and stop at place de la Bourse, Bordeaux's most popular square *(p66)*, with its famed *Miroir d'Eau* (Water Mirror) sitting beside the Garonne River's edge - a lovely place for a rest and a few photos.

Afternoon After a morning admiring the city's magnificent historic sights, immerse yourself in contemporary art at CAPC, Bordeaux's modern art museum, stunningly located in a former wine warehouse. Treat yourself with a typical Bordelais sticky treat, *canelés*, at the rooftop terrace Café du Musée *(www. cafedumusee-capc-bordeaux.com)*. Walk or take the tram line up to La Cité du Vin *(p69)* for one of their themed tours to learn all about the region's famous wines.

Evening Return south via the tram to the columned, 18th-century Grand Théâtre *(p64)* for a dinner of fine regional French cuisine at the on-site Le Quatrième Mur *(www.quatrieme-mur.com)*, followed by an opera or ballet performance.

Day 2

Morning Wander around the ruins of Palais Gallien *(p66)*, left behind by the Romans who took over Bordeaux in the first century BC. Grab a picnic breakfast from one of the supermarkets nearby and then walk to place des Quinconces, a grand city square,to take part in the quintessential French pastime of people-watching. Continue your history lesson of Bordeaux and the surrounding region at the Musée d'Aquitaine *(p67)*, which has exhibits dating back to the city's ancient Gaulish inhabitants.

Afternoon To get even betteer acquainted with Bordeaux wine, book a tour or drive out to one of the many beautiful wineries around the city. The historic Château Pape Clément is a great spot for both its wonderful red and white wines *(www.chateau-pape-clement.fr)*.

Evening Dine at Le Bouchon Bordelais *(www.bouchon-bordelais.com)*, the perfect Bordeaux bistro to round off your visit, offering a diverse menu of local dishes in a friendly and cosy atmosphere (reservations are recommended). If you're up for a nightcap, head to place du Parlement, a lovely square in the historic heart of Bordeaux, brimming with lively bars and cafés.

←

① Colourful houses in the Bayonne's Old Town.

② Shale cliffs at Pointe Sainte Barbe, outside St-Jean-de-Luz.

③ Bayonne ham market stall.

④ Espelette peppers.

3 DAYS

in the Basque Country

Day 1

Morning Start your Basque adventure in Bayonne *(p208)*, beginning with the area around 13th-century Cathédrale Sainte-Marie known as Grand Bayonne. Stop for a glass of hot chocolate at one of the many *chocolateries*. Then cross the River Nive to Petit Bayonne to visit the Musée Basque, where you can learn about this vibrant cross-border culture.

Afternoon Enjoy a light lunch at bustling Tarte Julie *(18 rue Thiers)* then spend the afternoon at the Jo Moiraz surf school on the Grande Plage *(www.jomoraiz.com)*.

Evening Sample Bayonne ham at the Auberge du Cheval Blanc *(www.au-cheval-blanc.fr)*. Then head to the pier to stay in one of the spacious cabins aboard Péniche Djebelle *(www.djebelle.com)*, a small bed and breakfast in a barge.

Day 2

Morning Arrive in St-Jean-de-Luz *(p214)*, and browse the buzzing market (held Tuesday and Friday) for its charcuterie, cheese and seafood, then wander to the Église St-Jean-Baptiste to admire its glittering altar. Take care to look up – the wooden ship hanging from the ceiling is a witty nod to the town's seafaring tradition.

Afternoon Cross the Charles de Gaulle bridge to the village of Ciboure *(p228)* and wander its narrow, hilly streets lined with red-and-white Basque architecture.

Evening Walk up to Pointe de Sainte-Barbe for sensational sunset views, then on to dinner at La Réserve *(1 rue Gaëtan de Bernoville)*. Spend the night in one of its luxurious rooms overlooking the water.

Day 3

Morning Pass through Aïnhoa *(p218)* – one of France's official Most Beautiful Villages – on your way to the lively village Espelette *(p218)*, which is famous for its eponymous red peppers.

Afternoon Visit St-Jean-Pied-de-Port *(p224)* – the last French town on the Camino de Santiago de Compostela pilgrimage route before the route crosses into Spain. Climb the town's old ramparts for panoramic views and to see pilgrims trouping up towards the mountains.

Evening Linger in St-Jean-Pied-de-Port for a sunset aperitif and then dine at Café Ttipia *(2 place Floquet)*.

←

1 Medieval Rocamadour.

2 Dining al fresco in Bergerac.

3 Cave paintings at Lascaux.

4 Charcuterie at a market stand in Sarlat-la-Canéda.

5 DAYS
in Dordogne

Day 1

Morning There's no more dramatic way to start a tour of Dordogne than at the stunning town of Rocamadour *(p120)*. Climb all 216 steps of the Grand Escalier to explore the cliff-side Cité Religeuse.

Afternoon Make your way to Gouffre de Padirac *(p142)*, where a boat trip takes visitors along a stream to the sub-terranean Lac de la Pluie (Lake of Rain).

Evening Drive to the hilltop town of Domme. The terrace at L'Esplanade hotel-restaurant *(www.esplanade-perigord.com)* affords wonderful countryside vistas.

Day 2

Morning Set off early to Sarlat-la-Canéda, where each Saturday, the town square fills with market stalls laden with foie gras, walnuts and truffles *(p31)*.

Afternoon Travel into the tranquil Vézère Valley *(p138)*, famed for its prehistoric art. Marvel at spectacular cave paintings of horses, bison and deer in Lascaux *(p140)*.

Evening Find a tasty dinner and cosy bed at Les Glycines *(www.les-glycines-dordogne.com)*, a bijou hotel in glorious countryside on the way to your next stop.

Day 3

Morning Just a short drive northwest lies Périgueux *(p112)*, where you can strike out on foot to explore Roman remains and a Byzantine-style cathedral.

Afternoon Sample regional favourites at Pierrot Gourmet *(6 rue de l'Hôtel de Ville)*,

a delicatessen just steps from the Musée d'Art et d'Archéologie du Périgord.

Evening Follow the River Isle northeast to Sorges and sample sumptuous truffles, a local delicacy, at Auberge de la Truffe *(www.auberge-de-la-truffe.com)*.

Day 4

Morning Drive west to Brantôme *(p136)*, the "Venice of Dordogne". Wander the leafy banks of the river Donne and lunch on seafood at the waterside Au Fil de l'Eau *(www.fildeleau.com)*.

Afternoon Leave the car behind and take to the water – an absolute must for any trip to the Dordogne region. Canoe downriver to Bourdeilles, and stop for lunch at a café in this lovely old village.

Evening Catch a taxi back to Brantôme and dine at Les Freres Charbonnel *(www.lesfrerescharbonnel.com/restaurant)*, a hotel restaurant with regional dishes.

Day 5

Morning Journey south to the market town of Bergerac *(p128)*, surrounded by vineyards. The Maison des Vins can tell you more about the local wine industry.

Afternoon Drive south to sample more fine wines at the idyllic 16th-century Château de Monbazillac *(www.chateau-monbazillac.com)*.

Evening Return to Bergerac and Restaurant L'Imparfait *(www.imparfait.com)* for *café liégois* (coffee ice cream topped with chantilly cream) – a delicious and indulgent house speciality.

1

2

3

5 DAYS
on the Coast

Day 1

Drive up the Gironde estuary past the fabled vineyards and grand Châteaux of the Médoc *(p106)*, stopping at Château Lamothe Bergeron *(www.lamothe bergeron.com)*, a fairy-tale-like castle dating from the 18th century. Ask for the tasting and picnic option for a tour of the castle followed by a delicious lunch to be savoured right on this lovely estate. Drive north to Le Vedon-sur-Mer and take a boat out to the remarkable 17th-century Phare de Cordouan *(p88)*, a lighthouse known as the "Versailles of the Sea". Head to Soulac-sur-Mer *(p90)* and visit the Romanesque Basilique-Notre-Dame-de-la-Fin-des-Terres. End the day with a seafood dinner and ocean views at Le Grill Océan *(www.legrillocean.com)*.

Day 2

Tour around the charming 19th-century villas in the Ville d'Hiver in Arcachon *(p96)* and catch a trans-basin boat to see the fascinating birdlife, oyster huts and huts on stilts in the Arcachon Basin *(p86)*. Take food with you as you climb the golden Dune du Pilat *(p97)* and join the other picnickers on the top for lunch. Drive south down the country roads to enjoy the view along the "Silver Coast", named for its long line of beaches. As well as the glittering ocean to the west, this region is criss-crossed by many water-ways – known as *courants* – making their way to the sea. Stop for a while at the Étang de Léon *(p193)* and take a tour along this maze of rivers on a *galupe*, a traditional flat-bottomed boat propelled by punt *(www.batelierscourant-huchet.fr)*. End your day at surf-loving Hossegor *(p192)*, where annual surf competitions take place out on the great waves of the Atlantic. Watch the sunset and slurp up fresh oysters at one of the shacks on the northern end of Lac d'Hossegor.

Day 3

Double back and head up north again for a relaxing morning in Mimizan *(p192)*, which has beautiful woodlands with miles of cycling routes for a refreshing morning ride, as well plenty of pristine beaches for some swimming and sunbathing

1 Château Lamothe Bergeron.

2 Seaside terrace at the Arcachon Basin.

3 Les Halles market in Bayonne.

4 Surfing in Hossegor.

5 Rocher de la Vierge, Biarritz.

6 Port at Saint-Jean-de-Luz.

afterwards. When you've soaked up some sun, head down to Bayonne *(p208)* and enjoy a leisurely tea or coffee along with a sweet pastry at Mokofin *(www.mokofin. com)*. Bayonne is a great place to explore on foot, with pockets of history and character to be found all over, from the ruins of Château-Vieux to the cosmopolitan Quartier Saint-Esprit. Tapas and drinks at riverside Le Bistrot Itsaski *(www.lebistrotitsaski.com)* complete the evening in this attractive port city.

Day 4

The covered market of Les Halles along the river is overflowing with Basque Country goods for breakfast. Walk off a full belly along the old city ramparts which have been turned into pretty gardens. Next, head south to explore the Art Deco splendours and beautiful coastline in glitzy Biarritz *(p216)* – one of Europe's most popular resort towns since the days of Napolïon III. Take a stroll along the beachfront promenade to see L'Église Sainte-Eugénie, the casino, chic boutiques and oceanside cafés for a

lunch of *fruits de mer*. End your walk at the Phare de Biarritz, a lighthouse in the middle of a park that makes the perfect setting for a gorgeous sunset view. For an indulgent Basque dinner – such as lobster-stuffed pasta with a truffle sauce – try Iqori at the Regina Biarritz hotel *(www.hotelregina-biarritz. com)*, which has direct views of the lighthouse nearby.

Day 5

Start your day with a morning walk from the Rocher de la Vierge, a rocky point reached via a metal footbridge. Then surf the waves at Biarritz's famous Grand Plage – or pretend to with a virtual reality headset at Cité de l'Océan *(www.citede locean.com)*. Then hop in the car and carry on south along the coast to Hendaye *(p214)*, and the spectacular Château d'Abbadia, which is open late in the summer and hosts regular evening events. Join the queue of locals at Grillerie du Port *(www. restaurantlasardinerie.com)* in Saint-Jean-de-Luz *(p214)*, for grilled sardines freshly caught that morning.

TOP 3 FARM VISITS

Caviar de Neuvic
⌂ La Grande Veyssiere
ⓦ caviar-de-neuvic.com
Tours of the sturgeon-breeding facilities and caviar tastings.

Ferme de Cor
⌂ Saint-Avit-Sénieur
ⓦ fermedecor.e-monsite.com
A hundred-year-old, family-run organic farm specialising in saffron and walnuts.

Terre d'Escargots
⌂ Puybazet ⓦ terre-d-escargots.fr
A farm tour dedicated to the quintessential French delicacy: snails.

Fresh oysters, a delicacy of the Arcachon Basin ↑

FLAVOURFUL FOOD

Southwest France might be famous for its wines, but for foodies it is a gastronomic paradise. Whether it's a rustic farmhouse or a sumptuous Michelin-starred dining room, you'll find delectable dishes and regional specialities to indulge in for every meal of the day.

From the Farm

It's true farm-to-table dining in this region, with vast green pastures making up a huge portion of the landscape. Lamb often comes from Pauillac *(p93)* and is slowly braised and stewed; ducks and geese, mostly for foie gras and confit de canard, are raised in Landes; and *jambon de Bayonne* is produced from pigs that roam around the Adour River basin in the Basque country.

←

Thinly-sliced *jambon de Bayonne* (Bayonne ham), a speciailty from Pays Basque

Fruits de Mer

"Fruits of the sea" is the perfect description of the ocean and freshwater harvests from this region. All the French classics are in abundance, but keep an eye out for menus offering local delicacies. Oysters are gathered from the pure, clear waters of the Arcachon Basin (p86). Sturgeon, which thrive in the estuaries, are farmed for eggs to produce caviar. And in Pays Basque, small squid are stuffed with spicy sweet red peppers.

💬 INSIDER TIP
Truffle Hunting

Sarlat-la-Canéda's truffle market is held on Saturday mornings from December to early March. Here you can shop and enquire about good recipes, but the vendors keep the truffle locations a closely guarded secret.

Black Diamonds

The black Périgord truffle, a native species of the forests of the Dordogne, is a highly prized aromatic mushroom coveted by chefs and locals alike. Its complex flavours are used to enhance local dishes such as roasted meats or omelettes topped with truffle shavings. During truffle season, from November to March, these little black treasures are sold at markets in villages such as Lalbenque (p151) and Sarlat (p132), and at astronomical prices.

←

Truffles at a market in the village of Lalbenque

Room for More

While the region is best known for its savoury dishes, there are plenty of sweet treats on offer, too. Local desserts include *canelés de Bordeaux* - small fluted cakes with a soft, moist centre and caramelized shell, and ewe's milk cheese from the Ossau valley (p240) served with black cherry jam.

→

Delicious and moist *canelés de Bordeaux* cakes

Did You Know?

Research suggests that spotted horses, painted at Pech-Merle, were alive during the Ice Age.

PREHISTORIC ART

Southwest France is home to some of the best preserved prehistoric art on the continent, especially in the Vézère valley. The paintings and sculptures on display at Lascaux an Les-Eyzies-de-Tayac offer a remarkable insight into the way these early artists viewed their place in the world.

Incredible Carvings and Sculptures

Discovered in 1909, the rock shelter of Abri du Cap Blanc, just outside Les Eyzies-de-Tayac *(p118)*, is home to a life-size frieze of horses sculpted in the rock. A display of the flint tools found at the site are on display at the on-site museum, which also shows a replica of the Magdalenian Woman and several "Venuses". Nearby in Laugerie-Basse, the visitor's centre displays finely carved throwing spears found in the area, and children can borrow a tablet to have a virtual "excavation" as they roam the site.

←

Frieze of a grazing horse, Abri du Cap Blanc

Inspiring Cave Paintings

Southwest France boasts an extraordinary concentration of prehistoric art, some around 20,000 years old. Visit a reconstruction of the Lascaux IV cave *(p140)*, where interactive displays recreate the original decorated cave's atmosphere and paintings. At Grotte du Pech-Merle *(p130)*, the "spotted horses" and handprints make the artists seem spine-tinglingly close. Learn the context at the Musée National de Préhistoire *(p118)*.

←

Exploring wall paintings in the lit-up Lascaux IV cave replica

ART FOR ART'S SAKE?

No one knows the exact significance of the cave paintings. They were once believed to be part of a ceremony to invoke a successful hunt, but the common view now is that they were painted in a trance as part of a shamanic ritual. Or they may simply have been attempts to capture fleeting beauty.

→

A room of reconstructions of Lascaux IV cave

Epic Etchings and Sketchings

Etchings, carvings and sketchings, created by the stroke of a few lines, are seen in stunning detail at Grotte de Pech-Merle *(p130)*. Another chamber also contains etchings of female silhouettes and mammoths, and footprints chiselled into the rock. Children in particular enjoy a visit to Grotte de Rouffignac in the Vézère Valley *(p138)*, and the journey into the cave on an underground electric train, stopping at various points to marvel at the 13,000-year-old engravings, many depicting mammoths. The highlight is the final chamber, the ceiling of which is decorated with animals.

↑ Line drawing of a woolly mammoth drawing at the Grotte de in Rouffignac

▷ Tranquil Rivers

More than 3,000 km (1,860 miles) of rivers and streams crisscross the region, so take to the water for a fun way to see the countryside from a new perspective. The Dordogne stretches through some of the most beautiful villages in France, and the Vézère tributary forms a valley that includes some famous prehistoric sites (p138).

STUNNING LANDSCAPES

Vast forests stretching out beside pristine beaches, broad rivers meandering through sleepy valleys, and medieval villages clinging to the slopes of the Pyrénées – observing the ever-changing scenery is one of the real pleasures of a stay in southwest France.

◁ Verdant Forests

This region is renowned for its beautiful, peaceful forests. Soak up the greenery under the dappled sunlight with a simple picnic lunch or – even better – a full-blown camping trip. For truly unspoiled nature, visit the Parc Naturel Regional des Landes de Gascogne (p190), a vast protected area of forest, wetlands and coastline.

Did You Know?

The Forêt des Landes is the largest man-made forest in Western Europe.

▷ Windswept Dunes

The sand dunes along the Atlantic coast stretch over 200 km (124 miles), rising and falling past sandy beaches, marshy basins and lush forests. The most prominent among them is the Dune du Pilat *(p97)*, the highest and largest dune in Europe. Picnic on the peak and watch how the sea breeze moulds the ever-shifting sands.

◁ Small-Town Charm

The towns dotted across the landscape seem just as much a natural part of the land as the rivers and forests. The weathered stone buildings and cobblestone streets feel organic and alive with history and personality. Some, such as Les Eyzies-de-Tayac *(p118)*, look like they're formed right out of the surrounding stone cliffs, while others, including Pujols *(p168)*, are recognized as some of France's "Plus Beaux Villages" (Most Beautiful Villages).

▷ Beckoning Coastline

The Atlantic Ocean meets France along a diverse coastline. The Cap Ferret headland curls around the Arcachon Basin *(p86)*, creating an inland bay surrounded by tiny towns, marshes and oyster farms. An almost unbroken line of white sandy beaches runs from Biscarrosse *(p192)* to Capbreton *(p195)* – some of them deserted, and others bustling with surfers, bathers and world-class resorts built in the dunes.

◁ Breathtaking Mountains

Adventurous travellers can hike up into the Pyrénées for incredible views across the Ossau Valley landscape *(p240)*. But for those who don't want the trek, the mountains' distinctive peaks can be seen from as far away as Pau *(p236)*, and there are hilltop views all over the region, with castles such as Château de Castelnaud *(p126)* perched high above the valleys they once ruled.

Rainy Day Fun

If the weather lets you down, there's still plenty of fun to be found indoors. The Aquarium du Périgord Noir (p141) and L'Aquarium Biarritz (p216) are excellent choices, tying in exhibits on local geography and wildlife with all the fun of an aquarium. The region's many fascinating prehistoric sights are also a highlight in any weather, as are accompanying museums such as the cliff-hugging Musée National de la Préhistoire (p118) with its life-size mammoths displays.

→

L'Aquarium Biarritz, with exhibits on local marine life

FAMILY FUN

It might be all wine tastings and fine art museums for the grown-ups, but kids can have just as much fun in southwest France. With a mild climate, fascinating history and beautiful natural environments to explore, this region is packed full of adventures to discover together.

Time to Unwind

When you're exploring the towns of southwest France and your little ones need a break, you'll have a choice of beaches, green riverbanks, public gardens and old town squares where they can let off some steam. Even in the busy city of Bordeaux, the Miroir d'Eau on place de la Bourse (p67) is great for splashing around in on a hot day, while the Jardin Public has lakes and a vintage carousel.

→

Relaxing in Bordeaux's Jardin Public

> 💬 INSIDER TIP
> ### Market Meals
>
> Evening summer markets like those in Sarlat-la-Canéda are great for picking up family meals of fresh local food – just be sure to bring your own utensils, plates and cups to enjoy your feast.

Exciting History Lessons

Fabulous castles from every era are perched on hilltops across southwest France. While adults can enjoy the architecture, furnishings and history, there's also lots to entertain the kids – such as knights in shining armour and live catapult demonstrations at Château de Castelnaud *(p126)*. For an even earlier history immersion, Préhisto Parc in the fascinating Vallée de l'Homme *(p137)* has giant dioramas of Neanderthals and ancient beasts, as well as hands-on workshops in constructing stone tools.

← Catapults on the ramparts at Château de Castlenaud

TOP 3 FAMILY CAMPSITES

Cabanes de la Romaningue
🏠 Pompignaci
🌐 cabanes.laromaningue.fr
Glamp in a wooden caravan, zipline-accessed treehouses and bubble tents.

Camping le Paradis
🏠 Saint-Léon-sur-Vézère
🌐 le-paradis.fr
Luxury safari-style tents and cosy cottages set around a swimming pool by the Vézère River.

Camping Aux Couleurs du Ferret
🏠 Lege-Cap-Ferret
🌐 campingcapferret.com
A forested campsite with stilted cabins near the Atlantic coast and the Arcachon Basin.

Back to Nature

The Dordogne is wonderful for wading, with safe, accessible beaches to be found up and down the river. There are also many boat companies in the area if you want to head out on the water. For seaside destinations, you'll be spoiled for choice, but for something picturesque with local character visit Hossegor *(p192)*.

↑ Bathers enjoying the pristine sandy beach and calm ocean at Hossegor

↑ La Cité du Vin in the wine capital Bordeaux

Celebrating the Wine Region

When touring the wine country in southwest France, you'll come across many old estates, such as the Château Lanessan *(p92)*, where the historic and prosperous story of the wine industry is evident in the beautiful old buildings that overlook local vineyards. But for a modern twist on the region's wine legacy, visit the jaw-dropping La Cité du Vin *(p69)*. Home to tasting laboratories and workshops, this building on the Garonne river looks like a slosh of wine poured into a champagne flute.

AMAZING ARCHITECTURE

Encompassing chateaux, grand cathedrals, Art Deco icons and modern masterpieces, the architecture of southwest France embodies the heart and soul of the region, and an architecture tour is both an adventure through history and an introduction to local life and culture.

Lords of the Castles

This region is full of beautifully preserved castles perched on hilltops high above the lands over which they once presided. The châteaux here are a unique blend of both English and French styles and history, as the region changed hands between the two throughout the Middle Ages. Château de Bonaguil *(p160)* was the last fortified castle built during the region's English era, while Château de Hautefort *(p122)* is a classic French design. In both cases, the fairy-tale-like feel is evocative of the history and splendour behind each estate.

↑ The French garden around Château de Hautefort

18th-Century Bordeaux

In 2007, Unesco protected almost half of Bordeaux *(p61)* because of its intrinsic architectural value – the world's first city of its size to be awarded this distinction. The city is full of remarkable structures, meaning a straightfoward stroll can end up feeling like a photo shoot as you try to snap the perfect picture of each sight. The Pont de Pierre bridge is a good place to start, before enjoying the Quays, the Port de la Lune and the shopfronts of the old town. Visit the Grand-Théâtre *(p64)* in the evening to see it illuminated in a golden glow.

←

The Neo-Classical Grand-Théâtre, a highlight of Bordeaux

The Art Deco City

When it comes to early 20th-century architecture, few places capture the imagination like Biarritz *(p216)*. It may have a fabulous string of beaches, but the real pull is in the stylish hotels and venues constructed in the late 19th century. To enjoy the city's Art Deco magic, check in to Le Regina Biarritz *(www.hotelregina-biarritz.com)* for a Belle Époque vibe.

→

Art Deco buildings along the coast in Biarritz

Bastide Towns

Southwest France is scattered with old fortified towns known as *bastide* towns. Locals are passionate about preserving their medieval townscapes, so there are dozens of examples still to be found across the region – such as Monflanquin *(p172)* and Eymet *(p149)* which have ramparts, arcades, half-timbered houses and picturebook-pretty cobblestone squares.

←

Traditional half-timbered around an old town square in Monflanquin

Listen Up

For many, Nouvelle-Aquitaine nightlife revolves around music. There are concerts to be discovered almost every night at big city venues such as Pau's modern temple to the arts, Zénith de Pau *(www.zenith-pau.com)*. But you'll also find events popping up everywhere from small churches to the gardens of the Médoc's wine estates. For festivals, don't miss Le Grand Pruneau Show in Agen *(p162)*, a music festival to honour the plum harvest, and Nuits Lyriques de Marmande, a grand singing competition in Marmande *(p176)*.

→

Florent Pagny performing at Zénith de Pau

CAPTIVATING CULTURE

Never mind the history and outdoor pursuits – this is region is just as great for exciting nightlife and cultural events. Head to the vibrant coastal casinos or explore a stunning art gallery. There are myriad bars and nightclubs, of course, but it's also a hotbed of fun festivals, concerts and live music venues.

Hey, Big Spender

Casinos here are different to the glorified arcades of Las Vegas. The chic and glamorous venues on the Atlantic coast evoke the atmosphere of the 1920s when these resorts began to boom, and also showcase some of the area's finest buildings. Come to Arcachon *(p96)* for a casino inside a 19th-century seafront castle, and stop by Casino Barrière in Biarritz *(p216)* for Art Deco glamour.

→

The seafront Casino D'Arcachon

The World's a Stage

There are so many performing arts festivals in this region that it's hard to know how to make time for all the highlights. Some of the biggest and best events are held in July, such as Le Festival des Jeux du Théâtre in Sarlat-la-Canéda (p132) – a hotbed of amateur dramatics. Mimos (p51), also in July, is Périgueux's fun, contemporary mime festival, with circus and clown acts for people of all ages. Likewise, Le Festival Arte Flamenco in Mont-de-Marsan (p199) welcomes first-timers and wannabe dancers with open arms. Check online before you go to find out what events are taking place near you during your stay.

← Mimes at the Mimos festival in Périgueux

DRINK

Le Plus Que Parfait
A retro old-town hangout. Cosy up on a sofa and listen to live music from local regulars.

Ⓐ E3 Ⓐ 12 rue des Fontaines, Bergerac Ⓒ 05 53 61 95 11

Thélonious Café Jazz Club
An atmospheric club meets fusion diner north of Bordeaux's historic centre.

Ⓐ C3 Ⓐ 18 rue Bourbon, Bordeaux Ⓦ thelonious-jazz-club-bordeaux.com

Glorious Galleries

France's artistic legacy is world famous, and no trip here would be complete without some time spent perusing its incredible galleries. For some of the best, you'll want to visit Bordeaux. Here, the Musée des Beaux-Arts (p68) provides a wonderful overview of art from the Renaissance to the modern era, while Musée d'Aquitaine (p67), celebrates the region's ancient art scene, with Roman statues and prehistoric sculptures.

↑ Admiring classical paintings in Bordeaux's Musée des Beaux-Arts

TOP 3 HISTORY TOURS

Bordeaux
W bordeaux-guided-tours.com
Splurge on this guided tour of the city's viticulture history and beautiful architecture.

Les Eyzies-de-Tayac
There are archaeological sites here dating back 400,000 years, and many of them offer tours (p118).

Lascaux
The most dazzling prehistoric art in Europe, with tours offered at Lascaux II and Lascaux IV (p140).

Magnificent Museums

No matter what era of French history sparks your curiosity, you'll undoubtedly find a museum to enjoy somewhere in the region. Castles often include exhibits and original decor from their heyday, while even rural towns may have a venue to regale visitors with stories of local history and culture, such as the Musée du Béret in Nay (p247). For a great all-encompassing history tour, Périgueux's Musée d'Art et d'Archéologie du Périgord (p113) underlines the region's rich prehistoric legacy.

→

Artists sketching replica tombs at the Musee d'Aquitaine in Bordeaux

FOR HISTORY BUFFS

History is all around you in southwest France, so take some time to delve a little deeper into its captivating story. Whether it's prehistoric caves, medieval villages or old battle sites – no matter where you turn, inspiring sights attest to the region's long and colourful history.

War-time Memorials

Southwest France has seen more than its fair share of wars over the centuries (p52), and there are many battlefields and memorials for those with an eye on military history. One of the most poignant is the Croix de Mouguerre near Bayonne, dedicated to the soldiers who fought with Napoléon in 1813. For World War II sights, BETSOM in Bordeaux was one of five submarine bases built by the Axis Powers along the Atlantic coast (www.bordeaux.fr/o271/base-sousetmarine).

→

Commemorating a tragic World War II massacre in Oradour-sur-Glane

↑ Navarrenx, a *bastide* town in the southern region of Béarn

Step Back in Time

History in southwest France isn't limited to museum displays. Head outside and walk along the streets of a fortified medieval town such as Navarrenx (p245) to get a feel for what the region was like in the Middle Ages. You may find Roman ruins popping up unexpectedly in modern city streets, as at the Palais Gallien in Bordeaux (p66). Prehistoric cave paintings abound in the valleys of Dordogne, and further south on Monte Argibel (p222) there's a stone circle whose purpose is shrouded in mystery.

Red-wine tasting in a beautiful vineyard setting ↑

WINE LOVERS' PARADISE

Southwest France is famous for its wines, with Bordeaux widely regarded as the wine capital of the world. Oenophiles will have plenty to discover here, as each area produces a unique character and flavour according to the blend of grapes, the soil, the climate, and local processes.

Brilliant Whites

Complex and full of character, with both dry and sweet options, the crisp, white wines produced in this region come from a blend of Sémillon, Sauvignon Blanc, Muscadelle and Sauvignon Gris grapes. White Bordeaux are served cool but not too cold, and are often sipped as an aperitif or to accompany fresh seafood dishes. To learn more, there's no better starting point than Chateau Haut Brion *(www. haut-brion.com)*, which has been involved in wine production since Roman times.

→

A glass of Chateau Carbonnieux, from the Pessac-Léognan sub-region of Graves

Legendary Reds

Intense and bold, with rich aromatic bouquets, the reds produced in the Bordeaux region come from a blend of several grape varieties whose names are now world famous, including Cabernet Sauvignon, Merlot and Malbec. The blend varies depending on whether the winery is located on the left bank or the right bank of the Garonne estuary. Red Bordeaux are decanted for about half an hour, served slightly below room temperature, and are perfect companions to roasted lamb and duck dishes, or even just with a slice of Ossau-Iraty cheese. For a lesson in Bordeaux reds, book a tour and wine tasting at Château Pichon Baron (www.pichonbaron.com). This grand estate, complete with a turreted castle, has been producing some of the finest red wines since the 17th-century.

← A vineyard of Cabernet Sauvignon grapes in Bordeaux

A WINE LOVER'S ITINERARY OF GIRONDE

A tour of some of Gironde's top wineries will leave you with a better understanding of these world-famous wines. Start at the historic Neo-Gothic Château Pape Clément (216 Avenue Dr Nancel Penard, Pessac) for their 5 Senses Tour, which will take you all around the stunning winery and vineyard. In the afternoon, pay a visit to the 16th-century Château de Reignac (38 Chemin de Reignac, Saint-Loubès) to complete your first lessons in oenology. Tastings are held here in a greenhouse built by Gustav Eiffel, the designer of the Eiffel Tower in Paris..

And for Dessert

Produced from Sémillon, Sauvignon Blanc and Muscadelle grapes, Sauternes is the region's famous sweet white wine. A type of fungus causes the grapes to shrivel and sweeten, and notes of apricot, caramel and citrus can be expected. Enjoy after a meal with fruit tarts and cheeses.

→

A classic French dessert of cheese, ham and fruit, accompanied by a glass of white wine

BASQUE CULTURE

The Basque people possess an intriguing blend of culture, tradition and language that's utterly their own. In a region long squabbled over by their Spanish and French neighbours, red is the colour of their spirit of independence, and you'll see it everywhere.

Fêtes de Bayonne

The capital of the French Basque country is Bayonne (p208), and each July the city comes alive with five days of festivals that see the red-and-white-clad locals party hard. Join the throngs lining the streets to watch parades through the city, dance and sing along at concerts, cheer on *pelota* matches (a Basque ball game) and light up at the eruption of fireworks each night.

←

Locals celebrating the Fêtes de Bayonne

Bastions of Everyday Basque Life

For a true Basque experience, start with Bayonne *(p208)*, the capital of Basque culture and home to the Musée Basque for an overview on local tradition and history. Then dip into one of the border towns such as Aïnhoa *(p218)*, or visit one of the fishing villages that dot the coast, such as St-Jean-Pied-de-Port *(p224)*, to dine on bowls of *marmitako* (fish stew, typically tuna), eaten to the sound of *pelota* balls being smacked across a court. If there is only time to visit one Basque town, make it St-Jean-de-Luz *(p214)*. This proud fishing port, with its red timber-framed architecture set against the breathtaking backdrop of the Pyrénées, is a quintessential Basque gem.

←

Fishing and pleasure boats bobbing in front of St-Jean-de-Luz's charming and colourful harbourfront

PELOTA

A traditional Basque ballcourt game, *pelota* pits players against each other using their bare hands, different kinds of bats or a *chistera* – a narrow curved basket on the end of a glove. It can be played in a number of ways, generally against a wall, like a cross between squash and handball; you'll see a high-walled court or *fronton* in most Basque towns and villages.

→

Axoa aux piments d'Espelettes, a typically spicy Basque veal stew

Zingy Cuisine

The food in this region is distinctly different from the rest of French cuisine. Basque dishes are generally spicy, with their central ingredient being the *piment d'Espelette*, a mild red pepper. You'll see strings of these peppers adorning buildings throughout the region, but most evidently in the village of Espelette *(p223)*, from which they take their name.

→

Stringing Espelette peppers into *ristras* (chains) to dry

Hit the Road Jacques

With more than 100 hiking trails and around 80 pilgrimage routes, it's well worth packing your hiking boots when you head for south-west France. For hardened hikers, there are four soul-stirring stages of France's cross-country GR10, taking those with an unbendable spirit from the Pays Basque to Béarn. Easier routes along the coast include a hike from Hendaye *(p214)* to Saint-Jean-de-Luz, or ambling along the cape around the Arcachon Basin *(p86)*.

Pic du Soum Couy on the cross-country GR10 footpath in the Pyrénées ↑

THE GREAT OUTDOORS

To make the most of this region's sweeping beaches, mountain peaks and river-streaked forests, you'll need to get active. Be it surfing, backcountry skiing, cycling or paddling the languid turns of the Dordogne, it's never been easier or more fun to head back to nature.

The Alternative Tour de France

With an enviable backdrop of epic hills and deep valleys to discover, it's no surprise the French have a love affair with mountain biking and road touring in southwest France. A stand-out for those seeking a lesser-known playground is the Aspe Valley *(p248)* in the Pyrénées, where rental shops and self-catering *gîtes* are particularly well set up for those on cycling holidays. Other highlights include a trip from Pau *(p236)* to the Col du Tourmalet (a Tour de France favourite) and from Bordeaux *(p62)* to Pauillac *(p93)*, with a well-earned break in Médoc's vineyards.

→

Cycling the Col du Tourmalet, a mountain pass in the Pyrénées

Mountain Heights

While the rest of France descends upon Mont Blanc and the Alps, savvy locals keep the Pyrénées to themselves. Climbers, hikers, skiers and stargazers all have reasons to adore the Pic du Midi d'Ossau *(p241)*, home to one of the world's highest observatories and accessible by cable car from La Mongie. Surprises lie in store elsewhere, particularly for off-piste skiing at lesser-known La Pierre-Saint-Martin or Artouste, and at Gourette for cycle tours, trail running and via ferrata climbing in summer.

> **INSIDER TIP**
> ### Hiking Trails
>
> Be sure to plan ahead before exploring new terrain. Local tourist offices are a great resource, so ask there for trail maps, route ideas and advice on weather and terrain.

↑ Off-piste skiing on the Pic du Midi d'Ossau

On the Water

There's a perfect marriage of expert thrills and beginner excitement on Nouvelle-Aquitaine's coastline, where you can hop from scuba kit or sea kayak to surf gear or kiteboard. For those who don't want to deal with the Atlantic waves, the massive Arcachon Basin *(p86)* has calmer waters for enjoying a bit of seaside fun.

←

Surfing on the Atlantic coast in Gironde

The River Less Travelled

Rent a canoe for a few hours and it's easy to see why there's an obsession in Dordogne with getting out for a paddle under the dappled shade of the riverbanks. Upstream is far wilder than the more mellow, châteaux-strewn curves towards Beynac-et-Cazenac. For a guided tour, book a trip on a traditional *gabarre* (flat-bottomed cargo boat) – particularly around Bergerac *(p128)*.

→

Paddling on the Dordogne past the town of La Roque-Gageac

A YEAR IN
DORDOGNE, BORDEAUX AND THE SOUTHWEST COAST

JANUARY

△ **Maskarada** *(1st Sun in Jan–1st Thu in Lent).* The Pays Basque's odyssey of drama, dance and poetry.

Truffle Festival *(mid–late Jan).* The black Périgord truffle is celebrated in its home town of Sarlat-la-Canéda with huge feasts.

FEBRUARY

△ **Jumping International de Bordeaux** *(early Feb).* Top-level equestrianism, show jumping and plenty of horsing around.

Fête des Boeufs Gras *(last Thu before Lent).* A cattle beauty contest in Bazas, followed by a 13th-century-style feast before Lent.

MAY

Festival Jazz Pourpre Périgord *(early–mid-May).* Get ready for a string of concerts, dinners and dancing at this jazzathon in Bergerac.

△ **Fête de l'Agneau** *(mid-May).* Wine by the barrel, award-winning grilled lamb and sheep dog demos in Pauillac.

JUNE

Pride *(mid-Jun).* Cities around the region, including Biarritz and Bordeaux, host LGBT+ pride events.

△ **Fête du Fleuve** *(late Jun).* Ships ahoy on Bordeaux's Garonne river, with fireworks, concerts and masted brigs to explore.

SEPTEMBER

△ **Jurade** *(late Sep).* A festival of wine in Saint-Émilion, celebrating harvest vintages chosen by the town's wine council.

OCTOBER

△ **Foire au Fromage** *(1st weekend in Oct).* Tastings, competitions and street banquets dedicated to Laruns' zingy sheep cheese.

Fête du Piment *(late Oct).* Espelette goes all out for its sweet chili pepper during this two-day feast.

MARCH

△ **Fest' Oie à Sarlat** (early Mar). Expect noisy gaggles of geese and honking birds during this foodie celebration of France's beloved fowl, with banquets using local produce.

Bi Harriz Lau Xori (late Mar). Film, music and theatre, all delivered in the Pays Basque's unique tongue — Euskara.

APRIL

△ **Bayonne Ham Fair** (week before Easter). Expect four days of feasting on one of France's most famous hams.

Fête des Soufflaculs (after Easter). The Nontron carnival sees nightgown-wearing locals chase spirits away – using medieval bellows.

Festival des Vallées et des Bergers (late Apr–early May). Concerts in Oloron-Sainte-Marie to celebrate the Béarnese dialect.

JULY

Festival d'Art Flamenco (early Jul). Mont-de-Marsan embraces its Spanish influence with classical guitar jams and moonlight dance-offs.

Mimos (Jul–Aug). Circus acts, clowning and puppetry at the Périgueux mime festival.

△ **Fêtes de Bayonne** (late Jul–early Aug). France's largest festival, with five days of dances, parades and fireworks.

AUGUST

Féria de Dax (mid-Aug). Parades and concerts in Dax, plus plenty of red scarf waving (a local festival tradition).

△ **Caraïbos Lacanau Pro** (mid-Aug). Surf's up! The five-day World Surf League drops in to Lacanau.

NOVEMBER

△ **Festival du Film de Sarlat** (early Nov). A cinema celebration focusing on the next generation of film-makers.

Festival International du Film d'Histoire à Pessac (mid-Nov). Films, documentaries, debates and discussions all focused on one thing: history.

DECEMBER

Journée Portes Ouvertes en Jurançon (mid-Dec). Join 50 estates, 50 winemakers and 50 parties for this annual Pyrénées spectacle.

△ **Olentzero** (24th Dec). The festive figure of Olentzero drops off gifts for children – an inseparable part of Basque Christmas culture.

A BRIEF
HISTORY

This region's history can be traced back to its first settlers in 400,000 BC. There are many places where history lives on, existing side-by-side with the 21st century: the ancient cave paintings of Lascaux, medieval fortified towns, and the millennia-old Basque culture and language.

Early Years

In the early 3rd century BC, the Celtic Gauls began to settle in southwest France, in a region known as Aquitana. Their leaders established trade links with a Roman province in southern Gaul, but in 52 BC the Romans took over after winning the Battle of Alesia, marking the beginning of their dominance in the region.

Invasions and Unrest

The end of the 3rd century AD saw the first of many invasions by Germanic tribes from the east. The citizens of Aquitaine took refuge behind hastily constructed town ramparts, and a turbulent

Did You Know?

Under English rule, Aquitaine was known as Guyenne.

Timeline of events

c 107 BC
The Gauls defeat the Romans in the Battle of Burdigala (the early name for Bordeaux).

c 300 BC
The first Celtic group (the Gauls) settle in southwest France.

52 BC
More conflict between the Romans and Gauls; the Romans are victorious, and take control of Aquitania.

284–305
Ramparts are built to defend Bordeaux and Périgeux from invasion by Germanic tribes.

481
A series of invasions leads to the Visigoths making the region part of their kingdom.

period of history began in the region as a succession of groups attacked from the 3rd century through to the late 9th century. Some of these groups only had short-lived victories, but others were more successful, claiming land or ravaging existing towns. After centuries of turmoil in the region, the Gallo-Roman civilization was broken and gradually withered away.

The Middle Ages

During the 11th and 12th centuries, political stability returned. Christianity spread, and more land was cleared in order to build abbeys and monasteries. For much of the Middle Ages, Aquitaine was under English rule, after Eleanor of Aquitaine – a duchess and former wife of King Louis VII of France – married Henry II of England. Defending this position against French claims to the territory led to almost continuous conflict, and the construction of many castles. Each of these great fortresses belonged to a lord, who was either under the protection of the king of France or the king of England. At the same time, the rapid population expansion that occurred in the 13th and 14th centuries caused towns and cities to double in size.

1 Map of France showing Aquitaine during the Carolingian Empire.

2 A depiction of the Battle of Alesia between the Romans and Gauls.

3 Ilustration of the Visigoth's invasion in the early 5th century.

4 Eleanor of Aquitaine, one of the most powerful woman in France during the Middle Ages.

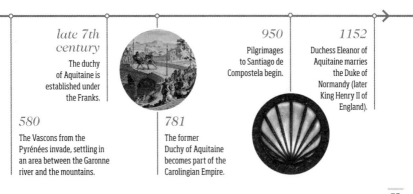

late 7th century
The duchy of Aquitaine is established under the Franks.

950
Pilgrimages to Santiago de Compostela begin.

1152
Duchess Eleanor of Aquitaine marries the Duke of Normandy (later King Henry II of England).

580
The Vascons from the Pyrénées invade, settling in an area between the Garonne river and the mountains.

781
The former Duchy of Aquitaine becomes part of the Carolingian Empire.

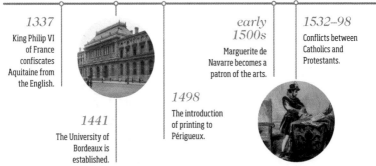

French Rule

During the Hundred Years' War (1337–1453), the kings of England and France fought over French territory, and Aquitaine was eventually seized by King Louis VI of France. This marked the beginning of the *Ancien Régime*, an administrative system through which the monarchy ruled with absolute power across the Kingdom of France. After many years of relative calm, strife broke out in the mid-17th century, first among peasants who revolted against rising taxes and excessive authority, followed by a rebellious movement led by aristocrats seeking to gain independence from the grip of royal power. The trouble was suppressed by the ruling powers, and the first half of the 18th century was an era of enlightenment rather than rebellion.

The French Revolution

Members of Bordeaux's parliament were the first to question royal power in the late 18th century, so, in August 1787, King Louis XVI ordered them to be exiled to Libourne. In Bordeaux, this decision marked the first stirrings of the French Revolution (1789–99) which brought an end to the *Ancien Régime*. A

↑ King Louis XVI, the last king of France before the French Revolution

Timeline of events

1337
King Philip VI of France confiscates Aquitaine from the English.

1441
The University of Bordeaux is established.

1498
The introduction of printing to Périgueux.

early 1500s
Marguerite de Navarre becomes a patron of the arts.

1532–98
Conflicts between Catholics and Protestants.

4

political faction of Aquitaine deputies, known as the Girondins, became instrumental in campaigning for the end of the monarchy. When the Revolution began to spiral away from their initial goals, the Girondins tried to bring it to an early end, but found themselves the target of other politicians who supported to the ongoing Revolution. When power passed to their opponents, many Girondins were arrested or guillotined, ushering in the Reign of Terror (1792–4).

Aquitaine Against Napoléon

Although the political situation stabilized during the subsequent era of the French Empire (1804–14), the upper classes remained hostile to its ruler – Napoléon Bonaparte – as his blockade against Britain made trading from Bordeaux difficult. In March 1814, English troops arriving to combat Napoléon's forces were favourably received by Bordeaux's inhabitants, who welcomed the end of the Napoleonic Wars. When Napoléon attempted to return to power during the Hundred Days period (20 March–8 July 1815), the Duchess of Angoulême made a stand against him in Bordeaux.

1 French troops during the Hundred Years' War.

2 Bordeaux in 1750.

3 Monument to the Girondins, Bordeaux.

4 Duchess of Angoulême rallying the citizens of Bordeaux.

Did You Know?

The Duchess of Angoulême was the eldest child of King Louis XVI and Marie Antoinette.

1637–53
Rebellions among peasants, aristocrats and parliamentarians.

1743–57
Marquis de Tournylays out Bordeaux's elegant squares.

1789–99
Aqutiaine's economy collapses during the French Revolution.

1792–4
The Reign of Terror during the French Revolution.

1815
The Duchess of Angoulême rallies the troops of Bordeaux against Napoléon Bonaparte, who is seeking to regain power.

Rise of Aquitaine

Although the economy of the southwest struggled after the French Revolution, the region blossomed during the Second French Empire (1852–70). In line with the huge increase in the region's wine exports, the ports of Bordeaux and Bayonne expanded and, with the development of the coastal resorts of Arcachon and Biarritz, tourism grew. Aquitaine become a magnet for an elite who sought to emulate the Emperor and Empress, who came to visit the region several times.

Early 20th Century

During the Franco-Prussian War (1870–1), fears of a German invasion led the seat of government to be moved from Paris to Bordeaux. The city became the capital of France again under similar circumstances during World War I (1914–18) and World War II (1939–45). After the Armistice of June 1940, southwest France was bisected by a demarcation line and, until 1942, Bordeaux and the whole Atlantic coast were occupied by Germany. The French Resistance gradually came together, but the Gestapo and the French militia harshly cracked down on it.

① Empress Eugénie, who brought fame to Biarrtiz.

② Parliament in session in Bordeaux's Grand Théâtre.

③ A World War II-era submarine base, Bordeaux.

④ The beach at Hendaye.

Did You Know?

Wine was introduced to Bordeaux by the Romans in the 1st century.

Timeline of events

1852–70
Empress Eugénie visits the Basque coast and Pyrénéan spa resorts.

1871
Bordeaux's Grand-Théâtre is requisitioned as a makeshift parliament.

1914
The French government once again moves to Bordeaux.

1939
France and the UK declare war on Germany, marking the start of World War II.

1940
A young man discovers prehistoric cave paintings at Lascaux while walking his dog.

Fearing an Allied landing, the Germans installed a string of military bunkers, known as the Atlantic Wall, all along the coast. World War II eventually drew to a close in 1945, but political and economic unrest continued to plague southwest France until the mid-1970s, when tourism took off once again and brought new life to the region of Aquitaine.

Dordogne, Bordeaux and the Southwest Coast Today

The area's natural beauty and historic towns are a source of local pride that continue to charm millions of tourists every year. Faster trains from Paris and beyond are also introducing this mesmerizing region to more visitors than ever before. The region underwent signifcant change in 2014, when three *departéments* merged together to form Nouvelle-Aquitaine, the southern half of which contains Dordogne, Bordeaux and the southwest coast. Given this revitalization and renewed interest in the area, the renaming and birth of a new, larger region feels particularly symbolic, and a positive omen ushering in a new era of this region's long and storied past.

↑ Wines from Bordeaux, one of the best wine regions in the world

1954
The discovery of natural gas at Lacq and of oil deposits at Parentis helps to boost the southern economy.

2014
Aquitaine merges with two other regions to form Nouvelle-Aquitaine.

2019
Biarritz hosts the G7 summit.

1942
The Atlantic coast is occupied by Nazi Germany.

1997
France declares Pays Basque an official *pays* - a special cultural territory.

EXPERIENCE

Sunset at the Capbreton coast

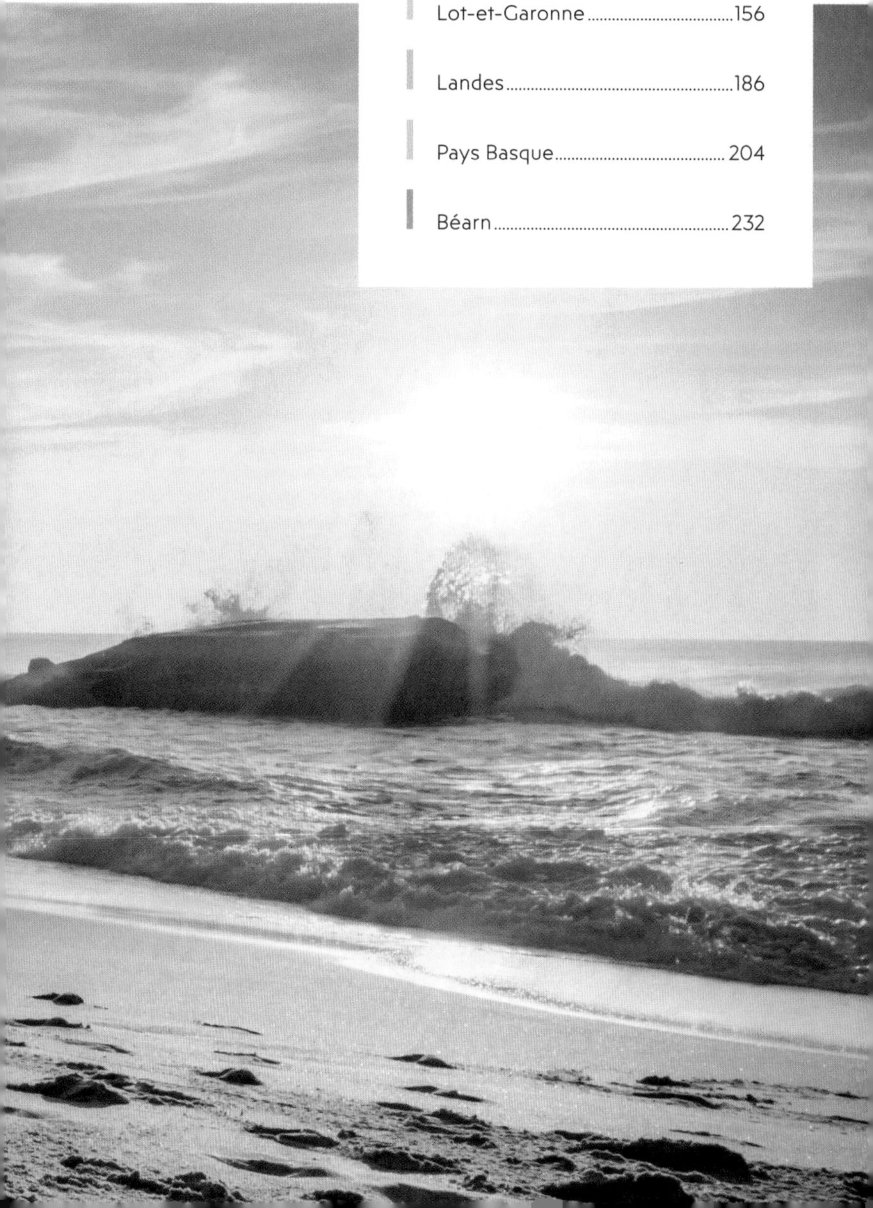

BORDEAUX

With its strategic location at the Garonne River, Bordeaux – once known as Burdigala – has been a major hub of trade since the 3rd century BC. Along with its prosperity, Bordeaux's prominence also made it a key setting during turbulent periods of French history – being torched by Normans in 848, passing from English to French rule in the Middle Ages and suffering under Napoléon's Continental blockade. Yet through these difficult periods, Bordeaux's busy port, and its influential politics, culture and art, made the city the crowning jewel of Aquitaine.

Meticulous restoration has enhanced the many splendours of Bordeaux: the richly decorated façades of its majestic buildings; the glorious Gothic churches that hint at its importance in medieval Europe; entire quarters that have been pedestrianized; and quays that offer long riverside walks. All these invite the visitor to explore the city's riches, and with modern trams and a network of bike lanes to aid travel, it's a pleasure to seek out the highlights of this captivating city.

BORDEAUX

Must See

① Grand-Théâtre

Experience More

② Palais Gallien
③ Centre National Jean-Moulin
④ Quartier Saint-Pierre
⑤ Musée National des Douanes
⑥ Porte Cailhau
⑦ Musée d'Aquitaine
⑧ Musée des Beaux-Arts
⑨ Basilique Saint-Michel
⑩ Cathédrale Saint-André
⑪ Quartier des Chartrons
⑫ Cité du Vin
⑬ Palais Rohan
⑭ Musée des Arts Décoratifs

Eat

① Le Quatrième Mur
② La Brasserie Bordelaise
③ Bordeaux River Cruise
④ Le Chapon Fin

Drink

⑤ La Comtesse

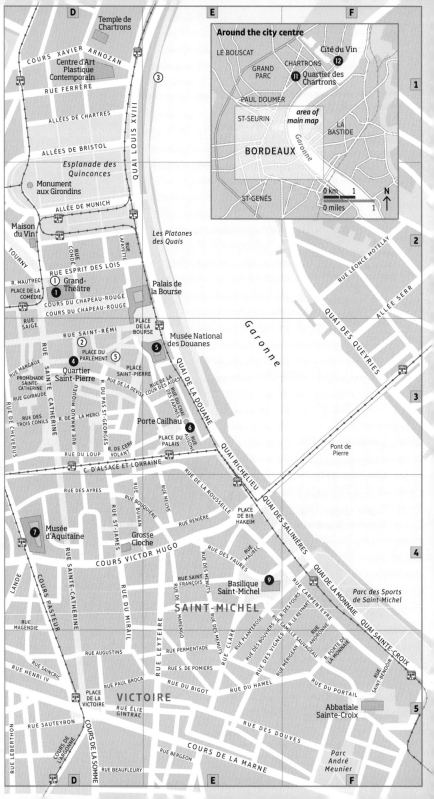

D

Temple de
Chartrons

COURS   XAVIER   ARNOZAN

Centre d'Art
Plastique
Contemporain

RUE FERRÈRE

③

ALLÉES DE CHARTRES

ALLÉES DE BRISTOL

QUAI LOUIS XVIII

*Esplanade des
Quinces*

Monument
aux Girondins

ALLÉE DE MUNICH

Maison
du Vin

*Les Platanes
des Quais*

TOURNY

RUE LAFAYETTE

RUE CONDÉ

R. MAUTREC

RUE ESPRIT DES LOIS

PLACE DE LA
COMÉDIE

① Grand-
Théâtre

RUE SAIGE

COURS DU CHAPEAU-ROUGE

COURS DU CHAPEAU-ROUGE

Palais de
la Bourse

RUE SAINT-RÉMI

②

PLACE DE
LA BOURSE

Musée National
des Douanes

PLACE DU
PARLEMENT

④ ⑤

⑤

Quartier
Saint-Pierre

PLACE
SAINT-PIERRE

RUE MARGAUX

PROMENADE
SAINTE-
CATHERINE

RUE GUIRAUDE

RUE SAINTE   CATHERINE

RUE ARNAUD MIQUEU

R. DU PAS ST-GEORGES

RUE DE LA DEVISE

RUE DE LA
COUR DES AIDES

RUE DU HAN
DES FAURES

Garonne

QUAI DES QUEYRIES

QUAI DE LA DOUANE

RUE DES
TROIS CONILS

RUE DE
LA MERCI

RUE DE CHEVERUS

Porte Cailhau ⑥

PLACE DU
PALAIS

RUE DU LOUP

R. DE CERF
VOLANT

RUE
DE L'AUSONE

C. D'ALSACE ET LORRAINE

Pont de
Pierre

RUE DES AYRES

RUE BOUQUIÈRE

RUE NEUVE

RUE DE LA ROUSSELLE

Musée
d'Aquitaine ⑦

RUE ST-JAMES

RUE BUHAN

RUE RENIÈRE

PLACE
DE BIR
HAKEIM

COURS VICTOR HUGO

Grosse
Cloche

RUE DES FAURES

QUAI RICHELIEU

QUAI DES SALINIÈRES

LANDE

COURS PASTEUR

RUE SAINTE-CATHERINE

RUE DU MIRAIL

RUE SAINT
FRANÇOIS

RUE DE

RUE DES MENUTS

Basilique
Saint-Michel ⑨

RUE
MAUBEC

RUE CARPENTEYRE

Parc des Sports
de Saint-Michel

RUE MAGENDIE

RUE AUGUSTINS

RUE LEYTEIRE

RUE DE
MARENGO

RUE PERMENTADE

RUE CLARE

RUE PLANTEROSE

RUE DES BOUVIERS

RUE DES VIGNES

RUE DES TOURS

R. CAMILLE SAUVAGEAU

RUE MÉRIGNAN

RUE
ANDRONNE

R. E RETAN

RUE DU PORTAIL

QUAI SAINTE-CROIX

QUAI DE LA MONNAIE

SAINT-MICHEL

RUE SAINCRIC

RUE HENRI IV

RUE S. DE POMIERS

RUE DU BIGOT

RUE DU HAMEL

R. PORTE DE
LA MONNAIE

RUE SAINT-BENOÎT

PLACE
DE LA
VICTOIRE

RUE PAUL BROCA

VICTOIRE

RUE LEBERTHON

RUE SAUTEYRON

COURS DE
L'ARGONNE

RUE ÉLIE
GINTRAC

COURS DE LA SOMME

Abbatiale
Sainte-Croix

RUE DES DOUVES

RUE BEAUFLEURY

COURS DE LA MARNE

RUE BERGEON

Parc
André
Meunier

D   **E**   **F**

1   2   3   4   5

Around the city centre

LE BOUSCAT

GRAND
PARC

CHARTRONS

Cité du Vin ⑫

⑪ Quartier des
Chartrons

PAUL DOUMER

ST-SEURIN

*area of
main map*

LA
BASTIDE

BORDEAUX

Garonne

ST-GENÈS

0 km   1

0 miles   1

N

1 M3

GRAND-THÉÂTRE

D2 ☐ Place de la Comédie 🚌 B, C 🚍 Many buses ⊙ Times vary, check website 🖥 opera-bordeaux.com

At the center of Bordeaux stands the Grand-Théâtre, one of the oldest and most beautiful 18th-century concert halls in the world. Designed by Victor Louis, the building's dramatic architecture and brilliant colors enhance the venue's stunning performances.

The theatre was comissioned by the maréchal-duc de Richelieu, who was governor of Guyenne (the former name for Aquitaine). A fine example of the Neo-Classical style, it was constructed between 1773 and 1780 on the site of a Gallo-Roman temple, known as the Piliers de Tutelle. Built to a rectangular plan, the building is surrounded by vaulted galleries and faced with 12 Corinthian columns. Inside, the grand Foyer is a homogeneous example of the style of the Second empire (1852–70). The auditorium, which is renowned for its acoustics, is still decorated in its original colours of blue, white and gold. A host of productions are held throughout the year, including both classic and contemporary ballet, operas and jazz concerts.

Did You Know?

In World War II, the theatre was used by the National Assembly for the French Parliament.

EAT

Le Quatrième Mur

A decadent restaurant inside the theatre, featuring beautifully plated local dishes such as grilled seafood.

D2 ☐ Place de la Comédie 🖥 quatrieme-mur.com

€€€

DRINK

La Comtesse

Snug and characterful cocktail bar near the theatre, perfect for after-show drinks. Best known for its mojitos

D3 ☐ 25 rue Parlement Saint-Pierre
📞 05 56 51 03 07

The façade is surmounted by statues of the goddesses Juno, Venus and Minerva, and the nine Muses, carved by Pierre-François Berruer (1733–1797).

Grand Foyer

The building is faced with 12 Corinthian columns. The arcaded galleries on either side once housed small shops.

Atrium

The theatre bathed in gold lighting and *(inset)* the auditorium ↑

An allegorical painting by François Roganeau (1883–1974), executed in 1917, fills the dome. above the auditorium

Crystal chandelier, with 400 lights

Unusually large for the time it was built, the stage area takes up over a third of the theatre's interior.

Laid out to a horseshoe-shaped plan, the auditorium can seat 1,114 people. The majestic sweep of the three upper tiers is broken up by 12 ornate Classical columns.

The extensively decorated staircase inspired Garnier's design for the staircase at the Paris Opéra.

Ticket office

↑ Illustration of the Grand-Théâtre in central Bordeaux

EXPERIENCE MORE

❷
Palais Gallien

◉ B1 **⌂ Rue du Docteur-Albert-Barraud** **☎ 05 56 00 66 00** **◷ 24 hours daily**

The late 2nd-century Palais Gallien is the only vestige of ancient Burdigala, as Bordeaux was known in Gallo-Roman times. About 130 m (425 ft) long and 110 m (360 ft) wide, this ancient amphitheatre could seat 15,000 people. Gutted by fire during the barbarian invasions of 276, it was also partly destroyed during the French Revolution (1789–99).

The ruins are free during the day, with an atmospheric evening tour available in summer (call for details).

❸
Centre National Jean-Moulin

◉ C3 **⌂ Place Jean Moulin** **☎ 05 56 10 19 90** **◷ For renovations until 2022**

This war museum, established in 1967, is devoted to the French Resistance, the deportation of France's Jews and the wartime role of the Free French.

❹
Quartier Saint-Pierre

◉ D3 **⌂ Place Pey-Berland** **🚋 Place du Palais**

Located between the Garonne river and the city centre, this quarter was once enclosed by walls, which were demolished in the 18th century. Now beautifully restored, it is a pleasant area to explore on foot. What is now place de la Bourse was laid out by the Gabriels, a father-and-son team of architects, in 1729–55. On its north side is the Palais de la Bourse (now the Chamber of Commerce) and on the south is the Hôtel des Fermes, its upper storey set with columns on ornate pediments. Decorative carving covers the majestic façades here, with masks and ironwork on the balconies. In the square's centre is the Fontaine des Trois-Grâces, erected in 1864. Lined with restaurants and cafés, place du Parlement – commissioned by Tourny in 1754 – is a masterpiece of architectural harmony. Louis-

---

MASKS OF STONE

Many of the façades of Bordeaux's houses are decorated with carved masks. While the earliest date from the 16th century, they are more typical of the 18th century. Legendary gods and mythological beings are chosen to tie in with the location they watch over. Mercury, the ancient Roman god of trade, surveys the harbour traffic from place de la Bourse, while Bacchus, the Roman God of the grape harvest, evokes the wealth that wine brings to the city.

XV townhouses surround a paved courtyard, containing a Neo-Rococo fountain that dates from 1867. On place Saint-Pierre is the Église Saint-Pierre, built in the 14th–15th centuries and remodelled in the 19th century.

5

Musée National des Douanes

Q E3 **⌂** 1 place de la Bourse
⏰ 10am–6pm Tue–Sun
w musee-douanes.fr

Occupying a part of the Hôtel des Fermes that formerly served as a customs house, this museum – the only one of its kind in France – traces the history and work of French customs officers up to the present day. Exhibits

---

> 📷 PICTURE PERFECT
> **Miroir d'Eau**
>
> Between the Garonne River and ornate 18th-century façades sits the largest reflecting pool in the world, the Miroir d'Eau (Water Mirror), at place de la Bourse. It's an ideal location for photos, day or night.

---

include a fine painting by Monet, *La Cabane du Douanier, Effet d'Après-midi* (1882).

6

Porte Cailhau

Q E3 **⌂** Place du Palais
🚇 Place du Palais **⏰** 10am–1pm & 2–6pm daily

This city gate offers lovely views of the north bank of the Garonne. The gate was built in 1495 to honour a victory won by the French king in Italy. Its design is a beautiful and unique mixture of decorative features (such as the conical roofs) and defensive elements (including a portcullis and a crenellated gallery).

7

Musée d'Aquitaine

Q D4 **⌂** 20 cours Pasteur
🚇 Musée d'Aquitaine
⏰ 11am–6pm Tue–Sun
w musee-aquitaine-bordeaux.fr

The museum's Prehistory and Protohistory collections highlight the region's fascinating ancient legacy. Among the

↑ The fairy-tale-looking Porte Cailhau, a defensive city gate

Gaulish items include an outstanding hoard of gold from Tayac *(p118)* and Roman pieces include a bronze figure of Hercules.

Also on display is a varied collection of pieces dating from the Middle Ages, while the Modern Era collection explores Bordeaux's own history through the 18th century, with a focus on its prosperous port. Tied in with the topic of maritime commerce are detailed exhibits focusing on the history of slavery in the Bordeaux region, from the organization of the slavery system in the Caribbean to the political, social and cultural impact that remains to this day.

←

The Miroir d'Eau pool on place de la Bourse, in Quartier Saint-Pierre

↑ 19th century paintings © Bordeaux, Musée des Beaux-Arts de Bordeaux

EAT

La Brasserie Bordelaise

Choose from over 700 wines to pair with a delicious Bordelais meal.

📍 D3 🏠 50 rue Saint-Rémi 🌐 brasserie-bordelaise.fr

€€€

Bordeaux River Cruise

Dine on regional dishes on board a boat while cruising the Garonne River. Includes stops along the way and exceptional views.

📍 D1 🏠 2 Quai des Chartrons 🌐 bordeaux-river-cruise.com

€€€

Le Chapon Fin

Dating back to 1825, this fine-dining spot has a fabulous interior, and an extensive and excellent wine cellar.

📍 C2 🏠 5 rue Montesquieu 🕐 Sun-Mon 🌐 chapon-fin.com

€€€

8

Musée des Beaux-Arts

📍 C3 🏠 20 cours d'Albret 🚇 Hôtel de Ville, Palais de Justice, Château de Hâ 🕐 11am-6pm Wed-Mon 🌐 musba-bordeaux.fr

The north and south wings of the city hall – added to the building by Charles Burguet in 1878–81 – now house this museum. Almost the entire history of Western art, from the Renaissance to the late 20th century, is covered by the collection on display. Represented are the Italian and Flemish Schools, Romantic painting, Impressionists, and modern works.

9

Basilique Saint-Michel

📍 E4 🏠 Place Cantaloup 🚇 Saint-Michel 🕐 10am-5:30pm Mon & Sat, 2-5:30pm Tue–Fri, 11am-3pm Sun

The Basilique Saint-Michel is in a colourful antiques dealers' district, where there is also a lively market on Mondays and Saturdays and a flea market on Sundays.

Begun in the 14th century, the church was completed 200 years later in the Flamboyant Gothic style. The Chapelle Saint-Jacques within

---

> **The Basilique Saint-Michel is in a colourful antiques dealers' district, where lively markets are held Saturday through to Monday.**

was built for the use of the city's brotherhood of pilgrims.

10

Cathédrale Saint-André

📍 C3 🏠 Place Pey-Berland 🚇 Hôtel de Ville 🕐 Times vary, check website 🌐 cathedrale-bordeaux.fr

A UNESCO World Heritage Site, this is the finest of all Bordeaux's churches. The nave, built in the 11th and 12th centuries, was altered in the 1400s. Depictions of the apostles, bishops and martyrs, and of the Last Judgment, adorn the west and north doors and the entrance to the southern wing of the transept (built in the 13th–14th centuries). The cathedral was restored in the 19th century, having been used to store animal feed during the French Revolution (p54).

11

Quartier des Chartrons

🚇 Many stops

This is the historic hub of Bordeaux's wine trade, which dates back to Roman times. Here the city's wealth was amassed and dynasties of wine merchants were established. **Musée du Vin et du Négoce de Bordeaux** is

→

The dynamic design of the Cité des Civilisations du Vin and a display of wine (inset)

located in three 18th-century vaulted cellars not far from the quai des Chartrons. The multimedia exhibits relate the history of the wine trade at the Port of Bordeaux.

Musée du Vin et du Négoce de Bordeaux

 🏛 41 rue Borie 🕙 10am–6pm daily 🌐 museeduvinbordeaux.com

12

Cité du Vin

📍 Esplanade de Pontac, 134 Quai de Bacalan 🚊 & 🚌 La Cité du Vin 🕙 Times vary, check website 🌐 laciteduvin.com

Housed in a striking contemporary building on the riverbank, this excellent museum explores the history and traditions of viticulture around the world, with a focus on the Gironde region. The visit culminates with wine tasting on the eighth floor, offering spectacular views across the city and river.

13

Palais Rohan

📍 C3 🏛 Place Pey-Berland 🏛 Hôtel de Ville 📞 05 56 10 20 30 🕙 8:30am–5pm Mon–Fri, 9am–noon Sat

Dating from 1771–83, this was built as the residence of Archbishop Mériadec de Rohan. Since 1937, it has housed the city hall. Features of particular note are the lavishly decorated dining room and grand staircase.

---

14 🔖 🍵 🛍

Musée des Arts Décoratifs

📍 C3 🏛 39 rue Bouffard 🕙 11am–6pm Sun–Mon 🌐 madd-bordeaux.fr

This museum is housed in the Hôtel de Lalande, a refined townhouse built in 1775–9. Several rooms evoke the opulence typical of Bordeaux townhouse interiors in the 18th century. On display are paintings, miniatures, prints, sculpture and furniture.

TOP **3**

CHURCH TOWERS

La Flèche
The belfry at Basilique Saint-Michel. Built in the 15th century, it was restored in the 19th century and separated from the basilica.

Tour Pey-Berland
The bell tower at Cathédrale Saint-André was built in the mid-15th century in the Flamboyant Gothic style.

Église Saint-Croix
This church has two imposing squared bell towers. While they look similar, they were built around 800 years apart.

A SHORT WALK
BORDEAUX

Distance 2.5 km (1.5 miles) **Time** 30 minutes
Nearest tram stop Grand Théâtre

Built on a curve of the Garonne river, Bordeaux has been a major port since pre-Roman times, although you'll see little evidence of this era history as you walk around the city. Always a forward-looking place, Bordeaux underwent a radical transformation in the 18th century. Today, its industrial and maritime sprawl is scattered around a mix of grand boulevards and noble, Neo-Classical squares that are a joy to explore on foot. Facing directly onto the waterfront lies the place de la Bourse, flanked by a row of elegant wine merchants' houses, originally built to mask the medieval slums that once lay behind. The magnificence of the Esplanade des Quinconces sweeps down to the river, offering a fine view of the lavishly decorated Monument aux Girondins from the quayside. Also striking is the place des Grands-Hommes, a rare example of town planning in Bordeaux at the time of the Revolution.

Did You Know?

Many of Bordeaux's buildings were once black from pollution.

The stunning Baroque **Église Notre-Dame** *was completed in 1707.*

START

COURS DE L'INTENDANCE

RUE MAUTREC

The façade of the **Grand-Théâtre** *(p64) is decorated with statues of the nine Muses, and the goddesses Juno, Minerva and Venus.*

RUE SAINTE-CATHERINE

PL. DE LA COMÉDIE

FINISH

RUE SAINT-RÉMI

COURS DU CHAPEAU ROUGE

RUE ESPRIT DES LOIS

A masterpiece of architectural harmony, **place de la Bourse** *is flanked by two buildings, the Bourse – old Stock Exchange – and the Hôtel des Fermes – now the Musée des Douanes (p67).*

PL. DE LA BOURSE

← Outside the elegant Neo-Classical Grand-Théâtre in the heart of Bordeaux

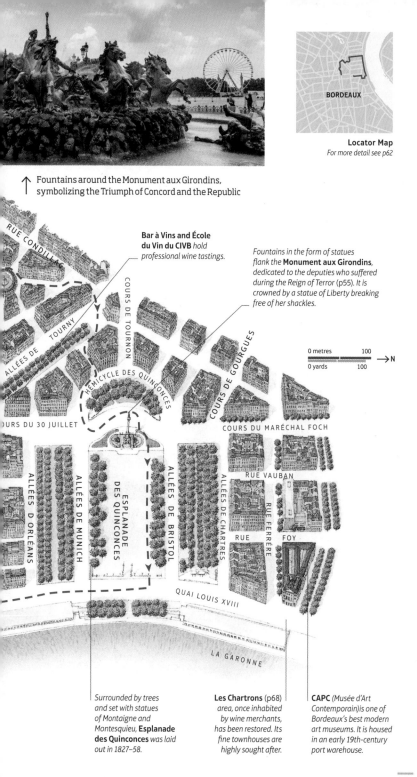

Fountains around the Monument aux Girondins, symbolizing the Triumph of Concord and the Republic

Locator Map
For more detail see p62

BORDEAUX

Bar à Vins and École du Vin du CIVB hold professional wine tastings.

Fountains in the form of statues flank the **Monument aux Girondins**, dedicated to the deputies who suffered during the Reign of Terror (p55). It is crowned by a statue of Liberty breaking free of her shackles.

RUE CONDILLAC

COURS DE TOURNON

ALLÉES DE TOURNY

COURS DE GOURGUES

HÉMICYCLE DES QUINCONCES

0 metres 100
0 yards 100
→ N

COURS DU 30 JUILLET

COURS DU MARÉCHAL FOCH

RUE VAUBAN

ALLÉES D'ORLÉANS

ALLÉES DE MUNICH

ESPLANADE DES QUINCONCES

ALLÉES DE BRISTOL

ALLÉES DE CHARTRES

RUE FERRÈRE

RUE FOY

QUAI LOUIS XVIII

LA GARONNE

Surrounded by trees and set with statues of Montaigne and Montesquieu, **Esplanade des Quinconces** was laid out in 1827–58.

Les Chartrons (p68) area, once inhabited by wine merchants, has been restored. Its fine townhouses are highly sought after.

CAPC (Musée d'Art Contemporain) is one of Bordeaux's best modern art museums. It is housed in an early 19th-century port warehouse.

Paragliders soaring over the Dune du Pilat

GIRONDE

The Romans were among the first to exploit
the Gironde's potential. They laid out vineyards
on the hillsides, where they built sumptuous villas.
Pioneering medieval monks erected prestigious
abbeys and English rulers established the *bastide*
towns such as Monségur and Sauveterre-de-
Guyenne. The late 19th century witnessed the
discovery of the health-giving benefits of the
sea air at Arcachon and Soulac, and the coming
of the railways, making the region accessible.

Today Gironde has plenty to tempt travellers.
The great waves crashing on to the sandy beaches
of Gironde's Atlantic seaboard offer surfers and
other water sports enthusiasts near perfect
conditions. Similarly, the banks of the Gironde
Estuary are a paradise for anglers, and are also
lined with a succession of prestigious wine-
producing châteaux and some magnificent
Romanesque and Gothic architecture.

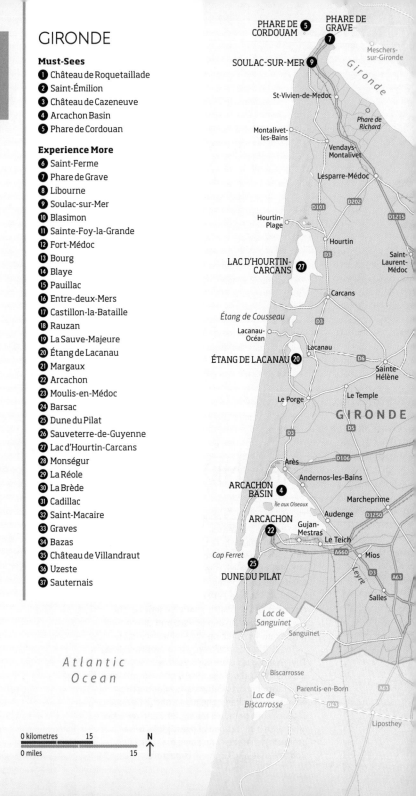

GIRONDE

Must-Sees

1. Château de Roquetaillade
2. Saint-Émilion
3. Château de Cazeneuve
4. Arcachon Basin
5. Phare de Cordouan

Experience More

6. Saint-Ferme
7. Phare de Grave
8. Libourne
9. Soulac-sur-Mer
10. Blasimon
11. Sainte-Foy-la-Grande
12. Fort-Médoc
13. Bourg
14. Blaye
15. Pauillac
16. Entre-deux-Mers
17. Castillon-la-Bataille
18. Rauzan
19. La Sauve-Majeure
20. Étang de Lacanau
21. Margaux
22. Arcachon
23. Moulis-en-Médoc
24. Barsac
25. Dune du Pilat
26. Sauveterre-de-Guyenne
27. Lac d'Hourtin-Carcans
28. Monségur
29. La Réole
30. La Brède
31. Cadillac
32. Saint-Macaire
33. Graves
34. Bazas
35. Château de Villandraut
36. Uzeste
37. Sauternais

Atlantic
Ocean

0 kilometres   15
0 miles   15
N ↑

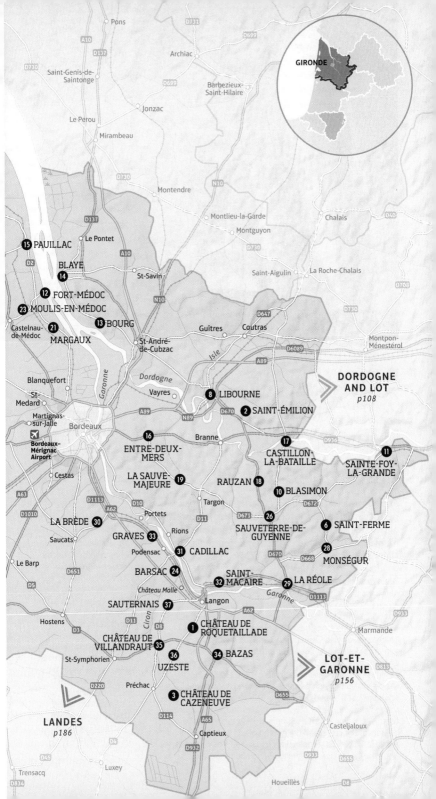

CHÂTEAU DE ROQUETAILLADE

C3 ⬛**Mazères** ⬛**For tours only; times vary, check website** ⬛**roquetaillade.eu**

An imposing fortress built by Charlemagne once perched here above the forest. The estate now consists of two castles and a chapel, family by the same family for over 700 years, and exquisitely decorated in the Neo-Gothic style of Viollet-le-Duc.

Set in extensive parkland full of centuries-old trees, this is one of the most astonishing castles in the Gironde *département*. It perches high over a series of troglodyte caves, a perfect position for striking at would-be invaders. The castle consists of two main parts, one being the ruins of the12th-century Château-Vieux (Old Castle), with its fortified gatehouse, guardroom and keep. The other is the better preserved Château-Neuf (New Castle), built by Cardinal Gaillard de La Mothe – nephew of Pope Clement V – in 1306, with the permission of King Edward I of England (then ruler of Aquitaine). Still owned by the Cardinal's family after more than seven centuries, it boasts six towers and an impressive central keep that give it the air of a true storybook castle.

Tours of the castle and the grounds must be booked in advance. As well as stunning interiors to admire in Château-Neuf, the estate is also home to a farm and a vineyard.

THE FATHER OF NEO-GOTHIC

The Mauvesin family commissioned Eugène Viollet-le-Duc (1814-79) to restore the Château-Neuf in the 19th century. A great exponent of Neo-Gothic architecture, Viollet-le-Duc turned the castle into a highly romanticised medieval jewel. Work began on the exterior in 1865, but the elaborate interiors - in a style that anticipated Art Nouveau - were sadly never finished.

← The fabulous Pink Room, deocrated by Viollet-le-Duc and Edmond Duthoit; the 14th-century Château-Neuf (inset)

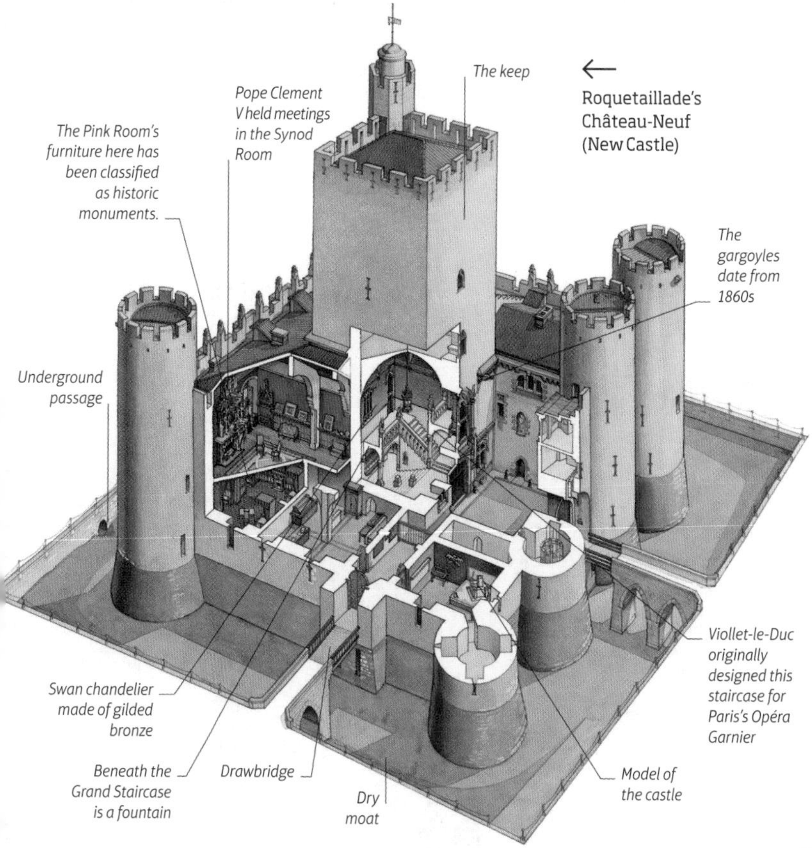

← Roquetaillade's Château-Neuf (New Castle)

The Pink Room's furniture here has been classified as historic monuments.

Pope Clement V held meetings in the Synod Room

The keep

The gargoyles date from 1860s

Underground passage

Swan chandelier made of gilded bronze

Beneath the Grand Staircase is a fountain

Drawbridge

Dry moat

Model of the castle

Viollet-le-Duc originally designed this staircase for Paris's Opéra Garnier

②

SAINT-ÉMILION

🅐D2 🚌🚆 *ⓘ* **Doyenné (Deanery), place des Créneaux;**
www.saintemilion-tourisme.com

Saint-Émilion traces its past back to the Romans, who introduced wine to the region, and to the monks who built extraordinary underground churches here. The UNESCO designation "Cultural Landscape" perfectly describes the charming medieval architecture and heritage that is displayed here.

①

Église Monolithe

🅐 Place de l'Église-Monolithe
📞 05 57 55 28 28 **🕐 Sat & Sun**

This incredible church sits at the heart of Saint-Émilion in the place de l'Église-Monolithe, with its ancient covered market and many restaurants. A troglodyte building, it was dug directly out of the surrounding limestone rock in the 12th century, and is unique in Europe. With a nave 12 m (39 ft) high and decorated with relief carvings, it has a 14th-century Gothic doorway with a tympanum containing depictions of the Last Judgment and the Resurrection of the Dead.

🔺 **GREAT VIEW**
Tour du Roy

A symbol of royal power in Saint-Émilion, this fortress was built in the 13th century. From the top (a 180-step climb), there is a magnificent view. The Fêtes de la Jurade (a committee of wine tasters that release Saint-Émilion wine for global export) takes place here.

Excavations have brought to light drainpipes that the monks installed to enable the rainwater to be rerouted.

One of the finest sights in Saint-Émilion is the **tower** of the medieval Église Monolithe. The church's tall bell tower rises 68 m (223 ft) above place du Marché. Climbing the 196 steps to the top is certainly a challenge but the breathtaking views of Saint-Émilion and its surrounding vineyards is reward enough.

Beyond the entrance to the Église Monolithe is an underground passage, which leads to a space containing several burial niches, which are dug directly into the rock. Its dome above forms the base of a well whose walls enclose a spiral staircase. Archeologists studying this area have documented that these **catacombs** may have been originally used as an underground graveyard.

Tower and Catacombs

♿♿ **🅐 Place de l'Église-Monolithe**
📞 05 57 55 28 28
🕐 By appointment (call ahead)

A distant landmark, the Monolithic church of Saint-Émilion and its bell tower ↑

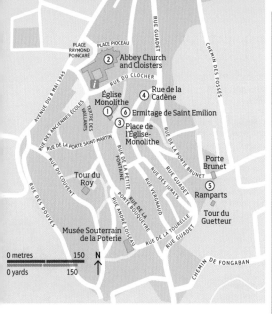

consider their patron saint. The Romanesque cloister was modified in the 14th century.

③

Place de l'Église-Monolithe

Once place du Marché, this central square is lined with restaurants. The original Tree of Freedom, planted in the centre during the Revolution, died and has been replaced.

④

Rue de la Cadène

From place de l'Église-Mono-lithe, this road leads to Porte de la Cadène, once the access point between the upper and the lower town. A 15th-century wooden house is built onto it, with charming features such as turrets, mullioned windows and a polygonal tower.

⑤

Ramparts

Surrounded by a dry moat, the ramparts encircled the upper part of the town. They were pierced by six gates. The Romanesque Porte Brunet, on the southeastern side, the Tour du Guetteur, to the south, and L'Éperon, a lookout tower at Porte Bouqueyre, still stand.

⑥

Ermitage de Saint-Émilion

🏠 Place de l'Église-Monolithe 📞 05 57 55 28 28 🕐 By appointment (call ahead)

The Ermitage de Saint-Émilion is supposed to be where the monk Émilion spent his days. The spring water that flows from the rock nearby is said to have therapeutic powers.

②

Abbey Church and Cloisters

🏠 Church: rue des Écoles; Cloisters: via tourist office 📞 05 57 55 28 28 🕐 Daily

The church's 12th-century nave, in the Romanesque style, has Byzantine-style domes that are supported by stone pillars. Traces of frescoes remain, including an image of the Madonna and the martyrdom of St Catherine. The choir dates from a later phase of construction in the 14th century. By the vestry door is a statue of St Valéry, who local vinegrowers

A SHORT WALK
SAINT-ÉMILION

Distance 1.5 km (1 mile)   **Time** 15 minutes
Nearest station Gare de Saint-Émilion

In the 8th century, a hermitage was set up here by Émilion, a monk from Brittany. Fortifications began to be built there in the 12th century, and throughout the Middle Ages, houses, chapels and monasteries were added. This rich history, along with is famous vineyards, have earned Saint-Émilion and its outlying villages a place on UNESCO's World Heritage list, making it a fascinating place to stop for a walk. The town's architectural heritage is almost without equal, and the ochre-coloured stone buildings, complete with pinkish-red roof tiles, make Saint-Émilion a picturesque place for a stroll.

*The cloisters of the **abbey church** (p79) are 30 m (98 ft) square. Built originally in the Romanesque style, they were rebuilt in the Gothic period.*

↑ Sunlight filtering through the cloisters of the abbey church

*One of the finest sights in Saint-Émilion is the bell tower of the **Église Monolithe** (p79). It is the second highest in the Gironde after the spire of the Église Saint-Michel in Bordeaux.*

*Once known as place du Marché, **place de l'Église-Monolithe** is lined with restaurants. The original Tree of Freedom, planted in the centre during the Revolution, died and has been replaced.*

AVENUE DE VERDUN

PLACE POINCARÉ

PLACE PIOCEAU

START

PLACE P. MEYRAT

FINISH

RUE DU CLOCHER

R DES ANCIENNES ÉCOLES

LACE D

L'ÉGLISE MONOLIT

RUE DE LA GRANDE FONTAINE

RUE DE LA PETITE FONTAINE

Hôtel de Ville

RUE GUADET

PLACE MARCADIEU

RUE DE L'ABBÉ BERGEY

RUE MME BOUQUEY

RUE GUADET

RUE DES GIRONDINS

Moat

PL. DU MARCHÉ

RUE DE LA CAD ÈNE

RUE DE LA PORTE BRUNET

RUE DU THAU

MARCHÉ

Cloître des Cordeliers

Porte de la Cadène

Gothic house

Locator Map
For more detail see p79

↑ Dining in place de l'Église-Monolithe in Saint-Émilion

Did You Know?

The monk Émilion is said to have performed miracles, earning him many disciples over the years.

0 metres   20   N
0 yards   20   ↑

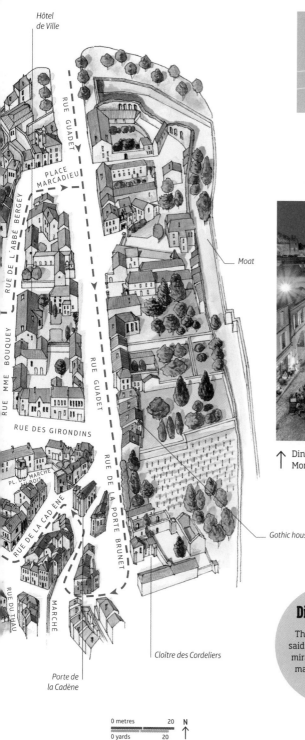

A DRIVING TOUR
SAINT-ÉMILION

Length 100 km (60 miles) **Starting point** Saint-Émilion
Stopping-off points Wine-tastings abound in this area,
so pick up some brochures from the St-Émilion tourist office

The Saint-Émilion area is dotted with picturesque
villages that have fallen under the town's jurisdiction
since 1289. In 1999 the whole area was declared a
UNESCO World Heritage Site, and there are historic
towns and beautiful architecture to admire on your
drive. The land itself is crossed by winding country
roads, and with colours that change with the
seasons it is a strikingly beautiful place for a
drive at any time of year. Beyond the natural
beauty and pretty towns, it is the vineyards of
Saint-Émilion that are the highlight for many
tourists. Viticulture was brought here by the
Romans, and the exceptionally favourable
climate and vine-growing soil have
resulted in it becoming one of the
most prestigious wine regions
in the world.

*At **Pierrefitte**, near the
village of Saint-Sulpice- de-
Faleyrens, is a prehistoric
menhir (standing stone). At
5-m- (16-ft-) high, it is made of
limestone, widely found on
the Saint-Émilion plateau.*

GIRONDE

Saint-Émilion

Locator Map

Saint-Émilion
*(p78) is one of the
oldest wine-growing
areas in France.*

START

*Vignonet's economy
is based entirely on
vine-growing, with
vineyards right up to
the banks of the
Dordogne river.*

← Vineyards growing
around the town of
Saint-Émilion

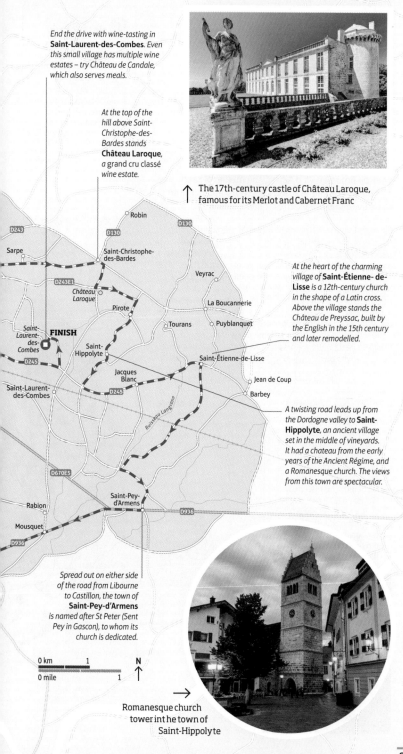

End the drive with wine-tasting in **Saint-Laurent-des-Combes**. *Even this small village has multiple wine estates – try Château de Candale, which also serves meals.*

At the top of the hill above Saint-Christophe-des-Bardes stands **Château Laroque**, *a grand cru classé wine estate.*

The 17th-century castle of Château Laroque, famous for its Merlot and Cabernet Franc

At the heart of the charming village of **Saint-Étienne-de-Lisse** *is a 12th-century church in the shape of a Latin cross. Above the village stands the Château de Preyssac, built by the English in the 15th century and later remodelled.*

A twisting road leads up from the Dordogne valley to **Saint-Hippolyte**, *an ancient village set in the middle of vineyards. It had a chateau from the early years of the Ancient Régime, and a Romanesque church. The views from this town are spectacular.*

Spread out on either side of the road from Libourne to Castillon, the town of **Saint-Pey-d'Armens** *is named after St Peter (Sent Pey in Gascon), to whom its church is dedicated.*

Robin
D243
D130
D130
Sarpe
Saint-Christophe-des-Bardes
D243E1
Veyrac
Château Laroque
Pirote
La Boucannerie
Saint-Laurent-des-Combes
FINISH
Tourans
Puyblanquet
Saint-Hippolyte
Saint-Étienne-de-Lisse
D245
Jacques Blanc
Saint-Laurent-des-Combes
D245
Jean de Coup
Barbey
Ruisseau Langrane
D670E5
Saint-Pey-d'Armens
Rabion
D936
Mousquet
D936

0 km   1
0 mile   1

N
↑

→ Romanesque church tower in the town of Saint-Hippolyte

3 (icons)

CHÂTEAU DE CAZENEUVE

C4 **Préchac** **Easter-May & Oct: 2-6pm Sat & Sun; Jun-Sep: 2-6pm daily** **chateaudecazeneuve.com**

The 11th-century Château de Cazeneuve was once a place of exile for Margaret of Valois – wife of King Henry IV and queen consort of Navarre and France. Built by Amanieu VII d'Albret, the medieval castle was completely rebuilt in the 17th century and continues to be lived in by the same family.

Set high above the deep, picturesque gorge carved by the Ciron river, the castle is fronted by vast acres of wooded parkland. Although this elegant building has a unified look, its appearance today is the result of several successive phases of building. The castle grew out of a simple keep built on a motte in the 11th century. Three hundred years later it had become a fortress and in the 17th century it was converted into a sumptuous residence. The buildings, which are still inhabited, are arranged round the main courtyard. An extensive tour takes visitors through the castle's various stages of development and brings to life famous visitors and inhabitants, including Henri IV of France, who owned it, and his queen, Margaret of Valois.

HIDDEN GEM
Historic Park

The park surrounding Château de Cazeneuve is well worth exploring after the castle. The grounds feature a bamboo forest, pond and waterfall, and a cave system known as the Queen's Cave.

QUEEN MARGARET

An intelligent and cultivated woman, Margaret of Valois' life was torn between duty and family, politics and art. Despite her many accomplishments, she was banished to Cazeneuve by her husband Henri IV when he was unable to produce an heir. She later moved to Paris, where she died in 1615.

Light streams into the large, vaulted chapel through the seven windows. The nave is flanked by aisles.

Dating from the Middle Ages, the cellars are stacked with barrels of highly prized Bordeaux wines.

Merovingian tombs

The lower courtyard leads to the pool and to the medieval wine cellars.

← Château de Cazeneuve set in beautiful grounds

→ Barrels in the wine cellar below the château

Study

The foot of Henri IV's bed is inscribed with an H (for Henri) and two opposed Fs (for the alliance of France and Navarre).

Queen Margaret's bedroom is hung with a fine Aubusson carpet and has an imposing Louis XIII style wardrobe.

Queen Margaret's drawing room has a fine Renaissance chimneypiece and furniture mostly in the Louis XV style.

Troglodytic caves

Did You Know?

After being banished to Cazeneuve by Henri, Margaret was imprisoned in the Château d'Usson.

← Illustration of Château de Cazeneuve and inner courtyard

④

ARCACHON BASIN

Ⓐ B3 🚌🚆 **ℹ 21 avenue du Général-de-Gaulle, Arcachon; www.bassin-arcachon.com**

Only 50 km (31 miles) from Bordeaux, the Atlantic Ocean leaps and creeps into France through the Arcachon Basin. Oyster-farming ports, sandy beaches, pine forests, and a string of towns and villages surround the basin to create a unique maritime culture.

Between the Dune du Pilat and the tip of Cap-Ferret, the Arcachon Basin forms a triangle more than 100 km (60 miles) long. Being almost completely enclosed, it is like the Gironde's inner sea. At high tide, it holds 370 million cu m (1,300 million cu ft) of water, with a surface area of 156 sq km (60 sq miles). At low tide, only about a quarter of this remains, as the water recedes to reveal sandbanks, mudflats and salt meadows. The basin is an important sanctuary for many birds, including the pied oystercatcher, the common curlew and the great cormorant, as well as for migratory birds that pass through the nature reserves at the Banc d'Arguin and the Parc Ornithologique du Teich. All around the basin are small oyster-farming communities.

① 🚲 🅼

Parc Ornithologique du Teich

ℹ Maison de la Nature du Bassin d'Arcachon **Ⓒ Daily** **Ⓦ reserve-ornithologique-du-teich.com**

This 1 sq km (0.5 sq miles) nature reserve, sitting on the basin's wildest shores along the Eyrre Delta, was created around the brackish waters of abandoned salt meadows. Up to 260 species of migratory birds can be seen here throughout the year. Herons, wild ducks, egrets, storks, swans and bluethroats may be observed in a natural setting, with salt-loving plants such as false willow and tamarisk growing nearby.

②

Gujan-Mestras

ℹ 37 avenue de Lattre-de-Tassigny; 05 56 66 12 65

This small town with seven harbours produces 55 per cent of all the oysters farmed in the basin. The **Maison de l'Huître**, an information centre, is located in Larros harbour. *Pinasses*, long slender boats made of Landes pine, are anchored in the channels here.

Maison de l'Huître

Ⓐ Rue du Port de Larros **Ⓒ 05 56 66 23 71** **Ⓒ Jul & Aug: daily; Sep-Jun: Mon-Sat**

EAT

Pinasse Café

Indulge in an array of seasonal dishes and an extensive wine list at this waterfront spot. The venue also has a sushi bar and small café for lighter meals.

Ⓐ 2Bis, avenue de l'Océan, Lège-Cap-Ferret **Ⓦ pinasse-cafe.com**

€€€

← Houses on the sandy coastline stretching along the Arcachon Basin

③ Île aux Oiseaux

Lying 3 km (2 miles) north of Arcachon, this island is named for the many seabirds that flock here. The island is also an oyster-farming centre, and is popular with hunters, who lie in wait for their prey in hides. Raised on stilts, these wooden huts are known as *cabanes tchanquées*, from the Gascon word *tchanque*, meaning "stilt".

④ Lège-Cap-Ferret Peninsula

🛈 1 avenue du Général-de-Gaulle; 05 56 03 94 49

Sandy beaches stretch for 22 km (14 miles) along the western side of this thickly wooded peninsula. On its eastern side there are beaches at Claouey, Grand-Piquey, Petit-Piquey and Pirailan. At the oyster farming villages of Canon and L'Herbe, most of the tiny cottages are now second homes. The Moorish-style chapel at L'Herbe is all that remains of the grand Villa Algérienne. The peninsula's smartest resort is at **Phare du Cap-Ferret**, where the lighthouse has a curious red lantern.

Phare du Cap-Ferret
⊗ **🏠** Rue de la Poste **📞** 05 56 03 94 49 **🕐** Apr-Sep: daily; Oct-Mar: Wed-Sun

⑤ 🅜 Domaine de Certes

🛈 Audenge; 05 57 70 67 56

The fish-farming shallows at Certes consist of large expanses of fresh and salt water interconnected by the odd patch of dry land. Sea bass, grey mullet and sea bream are farmed here. A footpath runs along the coast, and bird-watchers can see a variety of species in their natural habitat.

⑥ Andernos-les-Bains

🚂🛈 Esplanade du Broustic; 05 56 82 02 95

This family-oriented resort nestles on the northeastern shore of the basin. There is no water here at low tide, but when the tide is in, its many small beaches are ideal for relaxing and swimming. The resort also has an oyster farm and a marina at Le Bétey.

Did You Know?

— *Pinasses* boats are designed to safely navigate the waters concealing the basin's sandbanks.

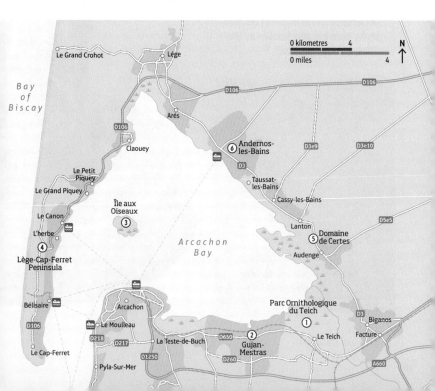

5 🏊 🏍

PHARE DE CORDOUAN

🅰B1 🚤Le Verdon-sur-Mer, Royan ℹ️Le Verdon-sur-Mer;
05 56 09 61 78 🕐Apr & Oct: Sat & Sun; May–Sep: Sat–Thu
(mid-Jun–mid-Sep: daily); times depend on the tides

Originally manned by a religious hermit, the Phare de
Cordouan has been watching over the Gironde estuary
and its turbulent tidal waves for over four centuries.
The "King of Lighthouses", with its domed chapel, is
a UNESCO World Heritage site.

The lighthouse's elegant silhouette rises up
against the skyline to the west of Pointe de
Grave. A boat can take you part of the way, but
you must wade the last part of the journey to visit
the lighthouse and explore the beautiful tower
interiors. Work began in 1584, although 10 years
later Henri IV had the original plans altered. In
1611, a Renaissance-style tower was added. The
lighthouse was declared a historic monument in
1862 and, because of its restrained classical style,
soon became known as the "Versailles of the Sea".

> **The lighthouse was declared a
> historic monument in 1862 and,
> because of its restrained classical
> style, soon became known as the
> "Versailles of the Sea".**

↑ The Phare de
Cordouan at low tide

The beam from the
lantern can be seen
from 40 km (25 miles).

Stairwell

The stained-glass
windows of the
Chapelle Royale
date from the
19th century.

The
Renaissance-
style King's
Apartments

Doric columns
frame the
monumental
portico.

Parapet

↑ The spiralling staircase inside the Phare de Cordouan

301

The number of steps to get to the top of the lighthouse tower.

Entrance

Outer stairway

↑ Illustration of the Phare de Cordouan showing inside the tower

EXPERIENCE MORE

6 Saint-Ferme

🅰B1 🛈 Place de l'Abbaye; 05 56 61 69 92

This small town is almost overwhelmed by the great Abbaye de Saint-Ferme, which was founded in the 11th century. Being near the Dropt – the river marking the border between French and English territory – it was fortified. The wealthy abbey was run by enterprising monks, who took in pilgrims on the road to Santiago de Compostela (p226). It was sacked during the Hundred Years' War (1337–1453) and again during the Wars of Religion (1562–1598).

The 12th-century **abbey** church is crowned by a small dome, and its Romanesque capitals have magnificent carvings of Daniel in the Lions' Den and other biblical scenes. The old **monastery** buildings now house the town hall. Entrance is free, but there is a fee for guided tours.

Abbey and monastery
🕥 🏠33580 Saint-Ferme 🕐Daily ☒abbayesaint ferme.jimdo.com

7 Phare de Grave

🅰B1 🏠2 allée du Sémaphore, 33123 Le Verdon sur Mer 📞05 56 09 00 25 🕐Apr-Jun & Sep-Nov: 2pm-6pm Fri-Mon; Jul & Aug: 11am-7pm daily

This lighthouse has a museum, with exhibits illustrating the daily life of a lighthouse-keeper. The 108 steps to the top of the 28-m- (92-ft-) tall lighthouse lead to a platform with panoramic views of the Phare de Cordouan out at sea and the port at Le Verdon.

↓ The little fishing harbour and marina at Pointe de Grave

8

Libourne

🅐C2 🚉🚌 🅸 40 place Abel-Surchamp; www.tourisme-libournais.com

Lying at the confluence of the Isle and the Dordogne, this *bastide* town still has portions of the old ramparts. The 15th-century town hall houses the **Musée des Beaux-Arts**.

Libourne is a great base from which to explore other interesting towns in the area, many of which are known for their wines. In Périssac, 17 km (10 miles) northwest of Libourne is **Domaine de la Chataignière** which houses a wine museum. The collection documents the workings of the vineyards at Fronsac, which produce robust, full-bodied red wines. (Call ahead to make a reservation.) To the north lie the vineyards of Pomerol. The fine wines that are produced here owe their smoothness to the iron oxides in the local soil. This is particularly true of Château Pétrus, the most highly prized of them all.

At Guîtres, 15 km (9 miles) north, is the **Abbatiale de Guîtres**, a Romanesque abbey, dating from the 11th to the 15th centuries. At the

Musée Ferroviaire, which has a small railway, visitors can relive the age of steam and diesel trains. The **Train Touristique de Guîtres** operates a steam-train service that covers a 14-km (9-mile) circuit of the countryside between Guîtres and Marcenais and stops off at a pleasant rural café-restaurant. Visitors can also explore the town using the marked walks or indulge in a little wine-tasting at a wine *chai* (warehouse).

Musée des Beaux-Arts

🅐 42 place Abel-Surchamp
☎ 05 57 55 33 44 🕑 Tue–Sat

Domaine de la Chataignière

🅐 1 les Grandes Terres, Périssac ☎ 06 85 52 26 88

Abbatiale de Guîtres

🅐 Guîtres ☎ 05 57 69 10 34
🕑 Jul–mid-Sep: daily; mid-Sep–Jun: by appointment

Musée Ferroviaire

🅐 Gare de Guîtres ☎ 05 57 69 10 69 🕑 May–Oct: Sun

Train Touristique de Guîtres

♿ 🅐 Gare de Guîtres ☎ 05 57 69 10 69 🕑 May–Oct: Sun; Jul–mid-Sep: Wed

9

Soulac-sur-Mer

🅐B1 🚉🚌 🅸 68 rue de la Plage; www.medoc-atlantique.com

Soulac-sur-Mer developed during the Second Empire (1852–70), when a resort served by the railway line was built here. Attractive villas sprang up in the late 19th and early 20th centuries. Soulac has fine sandy beaches, Plage Amélie and Plage la Négade, the latter of which is a nudist beach.

A UNESCO World Heritage Site, the **Basilique Notre-Dame-de-la-Fin-des-Terres** lies on the route taken by pilgrims travelling from Britain to Santiago de

Fronsac vineyards near Libourne, renowned for their excellent red wines ↑

Did You Know?

Soulac's basilica is named after its proximity to "the end of the earth" at Pointe de Grave.

←

Soulac's beautifully austere
Basilique Notre-Dame-
de-la-Fin-des-Terres

of Louis IX. After 1271, it stood in English territory, but was retaken by the French in 1453. By the 16th century, it had become a centre of trade and was one of the most dynamic of all Huguenot towns.

Of the medieval town, only four towers survive, now converted into houses. There are also several half-timbered dwellings from the 15th–17th centuries and a number of fine 18th-century town-houses. In the same building as the tourist office, the **Musée Charles-Nardin** is a small museum devoted to prehistory and archaeology.

At Port-Sainte-Foy, on the opposite bank of the river, is the **Musée de la Batellerie**, a fascinating museum of river craft, with models of *gabares*, wide flat-bottomed boats that sailed down the river as far as the Atlantic.

Musée Charles-Nardin

🏠 Tourist office 🕒 Jul & Aug: daily; Sep–Jun: Mon–Sat

Musée de la Batellerie

♿ 🏠 6 rue Notre-Dame 📞 05 53 22 24 10 🕒 Mid-Jun–mid-Sep: Tue–Sun; Oct–May: by appointment

Compostela (*p226*). This great 12th-century church has superb modern stained-glass windows and carved capitals.

The nearby **Musée d'Art Contemporain de Soulac** contains modern and contemporary paintings and sculptures by Aquitaine artists. The museum's archaeological exhibits are closed for renovation, reopening in 2020.

Basilique Notre-Dame-de-la-Fin-des-Terres

🏠 33780 Soulac-sur-Mer 🕒 Daily

Musée d'Art Contemporain de Soulac

♿ 🏠 1 avenue El-Burgo-de-Osma 📞 05 56 09 83 99 🕒 Apr–Jun: Fri–Sun; Jul & Aug: daily; Sep: Wed–Sun

---

🔟

Blasimon

🅐 D3 🛈 Mairie; 05 56 71 52 12

Founded in 1273, Blasimon became a *bastide* town in 1322 on the orders of King Edward II of England, when

the area was under his rule.

Nestling in a small wooded valley washed by the Gamage river is Blasimon's stately **Benedictine abbey**. Built in the 12th and 13th centuries, it was owned by the abbey of La Sauve-Majeure. The two-tier façade looks particularly beautiful at sunset, when it is bathed in golden light. The doorway and the arches that frame it are decorated with some of the most delicate of all Romanesque carvings in the Gironde.

On Wednesday evenings in July and August, there is a market, with local craft items and locally grown produce.

Benedictine Abbey

🏠 Quai Pascal Elissalt 🕒 Inner courtyard: all year

Sainte-Foy-la-Grande

🅐 D3 🚉 🛈 102 rue de la République; 05 57 46 03 00

This 13th-century *bastide* town on the banks of the Dordogne was founded by Alphonse of Poitiers, brother

12

Fort-Médoc

C2 **Avenue du Fort Médoc, Cussac-Fort-Médoc** **Feb & Mar: daily** **bordeaux-tourisme.com**

This fort was built by prolific military engineer Vauban in the late 17th century and, together with the citadel at Blaye and Fort-Paté, it formed part of the Gironde Estuary's defences. The Porte Royale, a gateway whose pediment is filled with a relief of the sun, symbolizing Louis XIV, leads through to a courtyard. Beyond are the surviving elements of the fort, which include the guardroom and the battery platform. Based on a rectangular plan, the building is set with four corner bastions. One of these, overlooking the Gironde, offers wide views of the estuary and opposite bank.

The **Château Lanessan**, 2 km (1 mile) away, welcomes visitors to its wine cellars, where Haut-Médoc wines are matured. It also has a Musée du Cheval devoted to horses.

Château Lanessan

Cussac-Fort-Médoc **05 56 58 94 80** **Daily (by appointment)**

13

Bourg

C2 **Hôtel de la Jurade, place de la Libération; www.tourisme. bourg-en-gironde.fr**

Built from local limestone, Bourg was a fortified town in the Middle Ages. Set on a steep slope, the town offers fine views over the Gironde river below, and can only be visited on foot. Today it is known for its local Côtes-de-Bourg wines.

In the upper part of the town is the **Château de la Citadelle**. This elegant folly, built to an elongated plan and surrounded by formal gardens, was once the summer residence of the archbishops of Bordeaux. It now houses the **Musée des Calèches**, a museum devoted to the horse-drawn carriage. The upper and lower town are separated by Porte Batailleyre, a 13th-century gate carved out of the surrounding rock.

A prehistoric cave, **Grotte de Pair-non-Pair**, lies 4.5 km (3 miles) east of Bourg on the D669. Discovered in 1881, its walls are covered with engravings of animals, including mammoths, ibexes and horses. It is the only decorated cave in the Gironde open to the public.

Château de la Citadelle

Parc du Château **Daily**

Musée des Calèches

05 57 68 23 57 **Mar-May & Oct: Sat & Sun; Jun-Sep: daily** **Nov-Feb**

Grotte de Pair-non-Pair

⊛⊛ 🚫 🏠 Prignac-et-Marcamps 🕐 Tue–Sun (book ahead) 🕸 pair-non-pair.fr

---

14

Blaye

🅰C2 🚌🚢 🛈 Rue Couvent des Minimes, La Citadelle; www.tourisme-blaye.com

Blaye is of interest chiefly for its citadel, which was made a UNESCO World Heritage Site in 2008. It was built in 1689 and is set with star-shaped bastions. Overlooking the Gironde, the citadel offers breathtaking sunset views, especially from the Tour de l'Aiguillette. Guided tours of the citadel's old underground tunnels are available from the tourist office. In summer, the citadel is filled with artisans selling arts and crafts, as well as local produce and wine.

Next to place d'Armes, the Manutention – which was once a prison and later a bakery – houses the **Musée d'Histoire et d'Archéologie du Pays Blayais**, tracing the history of Blaye and its citadel.

Just south of Blaye lies the **Villa Gallo Romaine de Plassac**. Three villas, built from around the 1st to 5th centuries, have been carefully excavated and reveal details

←

The main street in the Citadelle de Blaye and *(inset)* views over the Gironde

of the prosperous people once had here. Imported marble was used for much of the construction and floors had underground heating.

Musée d'Histoire et d'Archéologie du Pays Blayais

⊛ 🏠 5 place d'Armes 📞 05 57 42 13 70 🕐 Daily

Villa Gallo Romaine de Plassac

⊛⊛ 🏠 5 allée de la Mairie, Plassac 🕐 Times vary, check website 🕸 villagallo romaine-plassac.com

---

15

Pauillac

🅰C2 🚌🚢 La Verrerie; www.pauillac-medoc.com

The marina at Pauillac is very popular in summer and a common stopping-place for sailing boats to de-mast before taking the river to the Canal du Midi.

While Pauillac is well known for its lamb, which is enjoyed all over France, it is more famous as the capital of Médoc wine-making. Three of the five Bordeaux *grands crus* vineyards (the highest level of red wine classification) lie around Pauillac - Lafite Rothschild, Mouton Rothschild, and Latour. The **Maison du Tourisme et du Vin** here sells local *grands crus* wines and organizes tours of the region's châteaux, with opportunities to meet the growers.

Northwest of Pauillac is Vertheuil. The Abbaye des Prémontrés was founded here in the 11th century, but all that remains is an 18th-century building. The abbey church, the **Église Saint-Pierre**, which also dates from the 11th century, is a Romanesque church with a nave flanked by aisles. It has two bell towers, one dating from the Middle Ages. On the north side, the moulding round a restored

↑ Sailing boats jostling for space at the marina in Pauillac

doorway is carved with scenes from the life of Christ.

The Gironde estuary is dotted with a number of islands. One of them, the Île Patiras, lies just off Pauillac and can only be visited through a boat trip with **Bordeaux River Cruise**. They offer a range of different trips, such as wine cruises and a visit to the island's restored lighthouse. The Refuge de Patiras, located next to the lighthouse, is the former caretaker's home and is now a restaurant, also accessible via the boat cruise.

Maison du Tourisme et du Vin

🏠 Vinothèque La Verrerie 🕐 Daily 🕸 pauillac-medoc.com

Église Saint-Pierre

🏠 Vertheuil 🕐 Daily 🕐 Sun

Bordeaux River Cruise

🕸 bordeaux-river-cruise.com

Did You Know?

Pauillac's lamb pairs well with the local claret.

← The vineyards of medieval Château de Montbadon, near Castillon-la-Bataille

16 Entre-deux-Mers

🗺 C2 ℹ 4 rue Issartier, Monségur; www.entredeuxmers.com

In spite of its name, the area known as Entre-deux-Mers ("Between Two Seas") lies in fact between two rivers, the Dordogne and the Garonne. It consists of a large plateau cut by small valleys that are covered with meadows, fields and woodland. Human settlement here goes back far into prehistory. Entre-deux-Mers also boasts a rich heritage of *bastide* towns, Romanesque churches and fortified mills.

Vayres, set high above the Dordogne, is the gateway to the region. The 13th–17th-century **Château de Vayres**, with its beautifully landscaped formal gardens, was owned by Henri IV.

Entre-deux-Mers' vineyards cover 15 sq km (6 sq miles), with 250 vine growers producing a fruity dry white wine. Visitors can enjoy tastings at the **Maison des Vins de l'Entre-deux-Mers**.

Château de Vayres

⊗ 🏠 63 avenue de Libourne ⏰ Easter–Jun & mid-Sep–1 Nov: Sun & hols; Jul–mid-Sep: daily 🌐 chateaudevayres.com

Maison des Vins de l'Entre-deux-Mers

🏠 16 rue de l'Abbaye, La Sauve ⏰ Jun–Sep: Mon–Sat; Oct–May: Mon–Fri 🌐 vins-entre-deux-mers.com

17 Castillon-la-Bataille

🗺 D3 ℹ 5 allée de la République; www.tourisme-castillonpujols.fr

Castillon-la-Bataille is named after the decisive battle fought between the French and the English on the Plaine de Colly in July 1453. General Talbot was killed by Charles VII's troops, under the command of the Bureau brothers, and his 8,000-strong army was decimated. This defeat of the English marked the end of the Hundred Years' War and led to Aquitaine and the southwest being restored to the French Crown.

Vestiges of this eventful past include the town's 11th–12th-century gate, the Porte de Fer, a 17th–18th-century Baroque church and the Église Saint-Symphorien. The town hall, a former inn in the form of a rotunda, was built in 1779 with funds provided by Maréchal de Turenne.

The Côtes-de-Castillon wine *appellation*, created in 1989, covers 30 sq km (12 sq miles) of vineyards and includes about 366 vine growers. Visitors can sample around sixty different wines from Castillon and around at the **Maison des Vin de Castillon Côtes de Bordeaux**.

At Petit-Palais-et-Cornemps, some 17 km (10 miles) north of Castillon-la-Bataille, is the beautiful Église Saint-Pierre. It is located just behind the cemetery and its façade is one of the best examples of Romanesque architecture in southwestern France. It has three super-imposed arcatures supported by four sets of double columns. The doorway has spectacular carvings of lions and human figures, including a Spinario (a boy removing a thorn from his foot), based on the famous Roman statue.

Maison des Vin de Castillon Côtes de Bordeaux

🏠 6 allée de la République 📞 05 57 40 00 88

Did You Know?

In the summer, the Battle of Castillon is re-enacted at Château Castegens, in Belvès de Castillon.

Rauzan Castle

Although the Rauzan castle is now in ruins, visitors can still climb to the top of the keep, which stands at 30 m (98 ft) high and offers a wide panorama of the town and the surrounding countryside.

18

Rauzan

D3 **12 rue Chapelle; 05 57 84 03 88**

Rauzan is best known for the atmospheric ruins of its fortified medieval **castle**. The castle in its present form was built by the Plantagenets in the 14th century. Restored in Gothic style after the Hundred Years' War, it then passed to the Durfort de Duras family. It was acquired by the municipal authorites of Rauzan in 1900. Built on a limestone plateau, the castle still has some impressive features, such as the keep, the main living quarters and the central tower. Access is over a bridge that leads to a massive gateway.

The **Grotte Célestine**, an underground river, which was discovered in about 1845, is open to visitors. Boots, protective clothing and helmets with headlamps must be worn and are provided.

Castle

⊘ 12 rue de la Chapelle
Jul & Aug: daily; Sep-Jun: Tue-Sat

Grotte Célestine

⊘ 8 rue de Lansade
Jul & Aug: daily; Sep-Jun: Tue-Sat (by appointment)
grotte-celestine.fr

→

The graceful arches of the Romanesque abbey at La Sauve-Majeure

19

La Sauve-Majeure

C3 **62 boulevard Victor-Hugo, Créon; 05 56 23 23 00**

The Benedictine **abbey** of La Sauve-Majeure was founded by Gérard de Corbie in 1079, in an area that the monks gradually cleared of trees. Located on the pilgrim route to Santiago de Compostela, the abbey became a dynamic centre of religion and trade, and counted 70 priories in its sphere of influence.

Reduced to ruins by wars and the unrest during the French Revolution, the abbey has undergone several phases of restoration since 1952 and was made a World Heritage Site in 1988.

The abbey's majestic Romanesque and Gothic ruins stand in beautiful, mostly open countryside. The choir has Romanesque capitals carved with strikingly expressive biblical scenes. Next to the church are the remains of the 13th-century cloister, the chapter room and the refectory. A museum displays pieces found during excavations of the abbey.

Fine 13th-century frescoes can be seen in the Église Saint-Pierre, in the village.

The **Maison de la Poterie** in Sadirac, 10 km (6 miles) west of La Sauve-Majeure, displays a range of pottery, made in a style that has been traditional in Sadirac since antiquity. The museum is built around an old 19th-century kiln. Two hundred archaeological pieces are on display, while temporary exhibitions focus on more contemporary ceramics.

Abbey

⊘ ⊘ 05 56 23 01 55
Jun-Sep: daily; Oct-May: Tue-Sun

Maison de la Poterie

⊘ 2–6pm Tue-Sat
maisonpoteriesadirac.fr

↑ Étang de Lacanau's natural lake, its calm waters, perfect for boating and watersports

20 Étang de Lacanau

B2 Place de l'Europe, Lacanau-Océan; www.medoc-atlantique.com

Covering 20 sq km (8 sq miles), this lake in between the coast and the town of Lacanau is ideal for sailing and sailboarding. For over 20 years, this "Lacanau-Océan" has hosted a stage of the world surfing championship. It also has a large number of early 20th-century seaside villas.

The **Étang de Cousseau**, 5 km (3 miles) northeast of Lacanau, is a serenely tranquil lake with a nature reserve.

21 Margaux

C2 Route du Port, 33460 Lamarque; www.margaux-tourisme.com

The charming village of Margaux on the banks of the Gironde river is a portal to one of this area's best wine regions. Together, the vineyards around the villages of Arsac, Cantenac, Labarde, Margaux and Soussans produce the wines officially classed as "Margaux". Wine-lovers should make a point to stop at **Château Margaux**, which produces one of the great *premier grand cru classé* wines. Its fine oak-beamed cellars are open to the public, although sadly tastings are not available. The **Maison du Vin**, on the edge of Margaux, is an informative visitor centre for those interested in the great local wines.

Château Margaux

33460 Margaux Mon-Fri, by appointment only Public hols, Aug & grape harvest chateau-margaux.com

Maison du Vin

7 place la Trémoille Jun-Sep: daily; Oct-May: Mon-Sat maisonduvindemargaux.com

22 Arcachon

B3 21 avenue Général de Gaulle; www.arcachon.com

It was thanks to Napoléon III, who fell in love with the place, that Arcachon began to develop as a coastal resort. This process was completed by the arrival of the railway in 1857. Arcachon is one of the most spread-out towns in France, covering 200 sq km (77 sq miles) and almost merging with the neighbouring La Teste-de-Buch. A marina was built in the 1960s, and the long pier on the busy seafront serves as the town's central meeting place.

Looking down onto the coast road above Arcachon is the Ville d'Hiver, an area of 19th-century villas, set in exquisitely kept gardens. They were originally built for the visitors who came to Arcachon for health cures. Surrounded by pines and sheltered from the wind, the Ville d'Hiver comprises 300 villas, each one different. Visitors can do a self-guided tour of the area with a map from the tourist office.

→

The ever-shifting Dune du Pilat, one of France's most impressive natural wonders

At the **Musée-Aquarium**, beside the beach and near the casino, there are exhibits on the local marine life.

Musée-Aquarium

⊗ 🏠 2 rue du Professeur-Jolyet 🕒 Feb–Nov: daily 🌐 musee-aquarium-arcachon.com

---

㉓

Moulis-en-Médoc

🅰 C2 🚹 La Verrerie, Pauillac; 05 56 59 03 08

This village has a 12th-century Romanesque church with a Gothic bell tower and sculpted capitals. The **Maison du Vin de Moulis** here organizes tours of the châteaux within the Médoc *appellation* area.

By taking the D5 northwards, you will come to **Port de Lamarque**, on the Gironde. From here you can take a ferry to Blaye (*p93*).

Maison du Vin de Moulis

📞 05 56 58 32 74 🕒 Jul–mid-Sep: Tue–Sat; mid-Sep–Jun: Mon–Fri 🌐 moulis.com

Port de Lamarque

📞 05 57 88 08 08

㉔

Barsac

🅰 C3 🚌 🚆 11 allée Jean-Jaurès, Langon; 05 56 63 68 00

From the 18th century, Barsac, on the west bank of the river Ciron, was an important centre of trade. It owed its wealth not only to wine, but also to the local limestone that was used for building throughout the Bordeaux area. The church, which is dedicated to St Vincent, patron saint of Gironde vine growers, was rebuilt in the 18th century by the architect who designed the Château de Malle, a Louis XIV-style wine estate in the Graves region (not open to the public).

The Barsac *appellation* applies to several châteaux, including **Château Climens** and Château Coutet, *premiers crus classés*. The Barsac white wines are slightly lighter and a little less sweet than the Sauternes wines.

Château Climens

🏛 🏠 33720 Barsac 🕒 Mon–Fri, by appointment only 🌐 chateau-climens.fr

🏔 GREAT VIEW
Dune du Pilat

From the top of the Dune du Pilat, you can enjoy splendid views of the Atlantic Ocean to the west. Turning inland, you can see the Forêt Domaniale de la Teste, an ancient woodland that crosses Gironde and Landes.

㉕

Dune du Pilat

🅰 B3 🚹 Route de Biscarrosse, Pyla-sur-Mer; 05 56 54 02 22 or 05 56 22 12 85 (summer)

This is, quite literally, France's most moving monument. About 3 km (2 miles) long, 610 m (2000 ft) wide and 110 m (360 ft) high, the Dune du Pilat is the highest sand dune in Europe. It overlooks the Banc d'Arguin and is covered with beachgrass, sea holly, gilly flowers and convolvulus. It was formed partly by the action of westerly winds, which lift and blow the sand from the banks along the valleys. In 1855, it was only 35 m (114 ft) high, but grows by 1–4 m (3–13 ft) a year. There are wonderful sweeping views from the top of the dune.

A tree-lined road leading to the Château Margaux wine estate

26 Sauveterre-de-Guyenne

D3 **Place de la République; 05 56 71 53 45**

In 1283, Edward VII, king of England, founded the *bastide* town of Selva-Terra. Later known as Sauveterre, it stood on the site of Athala, a small town founded in the 9th century. With its strategic location at the junction of roads running between Libourne and La Réole, and between Bordeaux and Duras, Sauveterre was long an object of dispute between the French and English, until it finally fell to the French in 1451. Sited at the heart of Entre-deux-Mers (*p88*), the town no longer has its ramparts, which were destroyed in the early 19th century, though the four gates at the corners of the town remain. A vestige of Sauveterre's days as a defensive town is Tour Saubotte, on its west side, a tower with arrow-slits and a rampart walk.

The village of Castelviel, situated 7 km (4 miles) southwest of Sauveterre,

has a church with a beautiful Romanesque doorway. The barrel vaulting is decorated with carvings of allegorical figures of the Virtues and Vices.

About 7 km (4 miles) southeast is Castelmoron-d'Albret. With 52 inhabitants, this is one of the smallest villages in France. This former seneschal town (the seat for royally-appointed governors) used by the House of Albret is set on a rocky outcrop with sheer cliffs 80 m (260 ft) high.

27 Lac d'Hourtin-Carcans

B3 **Place de l'Europe, Lacanau Océan ; www.medoc-atlantique.com**

Some 17 km (11 miles) long and with a vast surface area, the Lac d'Hourtin-Carcans is one of the largest lakes in France. Its shores are a good place to spot wildlife, such as herons, foxes, rabbits and hares. Plants include the rare aquatic flower *Lobelia dortmanna* and insect-devouring species, such as pitcher plants and sundews. The nearby resort of Carcans-Maubuisson offers tennis, cycling, horse riding and water sports. It also has a museum of local culture, the **Maison des Arts et Traditions Populaires de la Lande Médocaine**.

Maison des Arts et Traditions Populaires de la Lande Médocaine

129 avenue de Maubuisson, Carcans **Jul & Aug: Mon–Fri**

28 Monségur

D3 **3 rue Porte de la Réole; 05 56 61 39 44**

This *bastide* town was founded in 1265 by a charter granted by Eleanor of Provence, wife of Henry III of England, who was also Duc d'Aquitaine. It was built on a promontory overlooking the valley of the river Dropt, and its strategic position gave the town its name (*Monségur* means "hill of safety"). The surviving medieval buildings include some half-timbered houses, a narrow alley known as the Ruelle du Souley, and a Gothic tower, the Tour du Gouverneur. In the northeast corner of the arcaded square stands the Église Notre-Dame, a late Gothic building that was restored in the 19th century. The cast-iron and glass

↑ An old stone church peeking above grapevines in the bastide town of Sauveterre-de-Guyenne

← Fishing on the Lac d'Hourtin-Carcans, one of the largest lakes in France

market hall dates from the late 19th century. It was large enough to store 700 to 800 tonnes of *pruneaux d'Agen*, the famous local prunes. Today it is the setting for weekly markets and various festivals such as the food and wine festival, the Foire au Gras, which takes place on the second Sunday of December and February. In July the town hosts the 24 Heures du Swing jazz festival.

A substantial amount of the town's original fortifications remains intact. The 2-km (1.2-mile) walk around the ramparts rewards you with views of the lush Dropt valley.

29

La Réole

🅰D3 🚉 ℹ52 rue André Bénac; 05 56 61 13 55

Because of its strategic location on the banks of the Garonne, not far from the opening of the Dropt valley, this ancient walled town grew rich in the Middle Ages.

The town hall, founded by Richard the Lionheart in about 1200 and superbly restored, is one of the oldest in France. The 13th-century Château des Quat'Sos is now privately owned.

The town's Benedictine priory is now home to municipal offices. The grille over the central doorway of this jewel of 18th-century architecture was made by the master ironworker Blaise Charlut, who also made the banister of the inner staircase. The building is fronted by an elegant stone double staircase. The Église Saint-Pierre has a Romanesque apse and Gothic vaulting, which was rebuilt during the 17th century. A signposted walk around the town, with explanatory boards, lets visitors explore its architectural heritage. The town's ramparts were dismantled in 1629 by order of Cardinal Richelieu, but some remains can still be seen.

Did You Know?

La Réole's suspension bridge was built by Gustave Eiffel when he was still a little-known public servant.

↑ The elegant cloisters of Saint Pierre de La Réole dating from the 18th century

30
La Brède

C3 **7** 3 place Marcel Vayssière, Martillac; 05 56 78 47 72

A wide avenue leads up to the **Château de la Brède**, where the philosopher and writer Charles de Montesquieu was born and lived. This rather austere Gothic building is surrounded by a man-made lake and moats. While the keep dates from the 13th century, the circular towers, chapel and other buildings date from the 15th century. Inside, Montesquieu's bedroom/study has been preserved. It was here that he wrote *De l'Esprit des Lois (The Spirit of Laws)*. His great library, with a barrel-vaulted ceiling, holds 7,000 books. The landscaped grounds in which the château stands were laid out by Montesquieu after a visit to England. Since 2011, they have also made wine, a fitting tribute to Montesquieu, who was a keen promoter of the merits of Bordeaux wines.

Château de la Brède

⊘ ⊘ **Avenue du Château** **O** Easter–May & Oct–mid-Nov: times vary, check website; Jun–Sep: Wed–Mon **W** chateaulabrede.com

CHARLES DE MONTESQUIEU

Charles-Louis de Secondat, later Baron de La Brède et de Montesquieu, was born in La Brède in 1689. He became a lawyer but also had a keen interest in philosophy and science, and was also a tireless promoter of the merits of Bordeaux wines. In 1721, his *Persian Letters* - a political satire on the reign of Louis XIV and a brilliant critique of social mores - were published in Amsterdam, bringing him lasting fame. Elected president of the Parlement de Bordeaux, he also kept in touch with Parisian literary circles. He travelled widely, drawing on his observations to write *The Spirit of Laws* (1748), which laid the foundations of political science.

31
Cadillac

C3 **7** 2 rue du Cros; 05 56 62 12 92

Set on the banks of the Garonne, the *bastide* town of Cadillac was established in 1280 to halt the progress of French troops, at a time when the Aquitaine region was ruled by the British. A surviving town gate, the Porte de la Mer, is a reminder of those warlike times.

The town is dominated by the **Château de Cadillac**. It was founded in 1599 by one of Henri III's favourites, who demolished the medieval fortress that stood on the site and built a sumptuous residence. Notable features of the interior include the decorated ceiling and eight monumental chimney pieces. The building was looted during the French Revolution, then in 1818 it served as a women's prison. From 1890 to 1952, it was used as a school for young offenders.

Rions, 5 km (3 miles) north of Cadillac on the D10, is a small town of Gallo-Roman origin and with medieval fortifications. A further 5 km (3 miles) northwest on the D10 is the impressive **Forteresse de Langoiran**.

Château de Cadillac

⊘ ⊘ **4 place de la Libération** **O** Jun–Sep: daily; Oct–May: Tue–Sun **W** chateau-cadillac.fr

← The idyllically set Château de la Brède, home of writer and philosopher, Montesquieu

Forteresse de Langoiran

👁 🕐 🏠 Le Château 🕐 Mid-Jul–Aug: 11am–noon & 2-7pm daily; Sep–mid-Jul: 2-6pm 🌐 chateaudelangoiran.com

---

32
Saint-Macaire

🅰C3 🚌🚏ℹ️ 8 rue du Canton; 05 56 63 32 14

This medieval village on the edge of the Bordeaux region has some attractive buildings in ochre-coloured limestone. The priory church of Saint-Sauveur, in the form of a Latin cross, contains 14th-century frescoes, as well as a gilded wooden statue of the Madonna and Child. Place du Mercadiou, the ancient market square, is lined with fine 15th- and 16th-century merchants' houses. In summer, the village hosts Les Médiévales, with plays and concerts.

About 6 km (4 miles) northeast of Saint-Macaire is the wine-producing **Château Malromé**, built in late Middle Ages. It was the home of the artist Henri de Toulouse-Lautrec, who died there in September 1901. He is buried in the cemetery at Verdelais, 3 km (2 miles) north of Malromé. The inside of the château is open to the public and also houses a restaurant.

Around 3 km (2 miles) to the northwest is Saint-Maixant. The **Centre François-Mauriac de Malagar** here is devoted to the life and work of this French author and journalist (1883–1970) and Nobel laureate.

Château Malromé

👁 🕐 🏠 Saint-André-du-Bois 🕐 Apr, May & Oct: Fri-Sun; Jun-Sep: Wed-Sun 🌐 malrome.com

Centre François-Mauriac de Malagar

👁 🕐 🏠 Domaine de Malagar, Saint-Maixant 🕐 Mar-Nov: daily (guided tours only) 🌐 malagar.fr

---

> Podensac is also one of the best places to see the funnel-like steep wave, or tidal bore *(mascaret)*, that sweeps up the Gironde Estuary with each incoming tide.

33
Graves

🅰C3

This area stretches along the south bank of the Garonne, south of Bordeaux on the Pessac and Léognan side. The Graves is the oldest wine-producing area in the Bordeaux region. The soil here is gravelly *(graveleux)*, hence its name. There are no fewer than 350 vine-growing estates in the Graves. Both red and white wines are produced, sometimes on the same estate, as at **Château Haut-Brion**. The Graves *appellation* covers an area of 31 sq km (12 sq miles), which produces about 18,200,000 litres (over 4 million gallons) of wine a year.

Podensac, a major port on the Garonne in the 18th century, has some fine houses of this period. Lillet, a mixture of wine, fruit liqueur and cinchona bark, is the traditional apéritif here. The town's **Maison des Vins de Graves** illustrates the history of local winemaking and sells around 300 different Graves wines, both white and red. Podensac is also one of the best places to see the funnel-like steep wave, or tidal bore *(mascaret)*, that sweeps up the Gironde Estuary with each incoming tide.

At Portets, in the heart of the Graves, is Château Lagueloup. Its vast wine cellars have wine presses and other devices that seem impressively sophisticated for their time. There is also a **Musée de la Vigne et du Vin** here.

↑ Cadillac's Porte de la Mer, a vestige of its medieval *bastide* walls

Château Haut-Brion

🏠 Pessac 🕐 By appointment 🌐 haut-brion.com

Maison des Vins de Graves

🕐 🏠 61 cours du Maréchal-Foch, Podensac 🕐 Times vary, check website 🌐 vins-graves.com

Musée de la Vigne et du Vin

👁 🏠 Château Lagueloup, Portets 🕐 Daily 🌐 chateaudemongenan.com

---

DRINK

Maison du Lillet

This 19th-century distillery is the best place to discover Lillet – a regional aperitif that blends wine and liqueur, and is a component of the Vesper cocktail. The distillery offers Lillet tastings and has its own shop.

🅰C3 🏠 8 cours du Maréchal Foch, Podensac 🕐 Sun & Mon 🌐 lillet.com

③④
Bazas

⚐ C4 🚌 ℹ 1 place de la
Cathédrale; www.tourisme-
sud-gironde.com

Founded over 2,000 years
ago, the town of Bazas later
became a bishopric on the
pilgrim route to Santiago
de Compostela (p226). Its
magnificent Gothic cathedral
was built between the 13th
and 17th centuries, and has
been restored. Particularly
striking are the beautiful rose
window and a triple Gothic
doorway embellished with
intricate carvings, both dating
from the 13th century. Behind
this majestic building lie the
chapterhouse gardens. Place
de la Cathédrale is a gently

sloping square on which a
market has been held for
centuries. It is lined with
arcaded 16th- and 17th-
century houses, which have
finely decorated façades.

The **Musée Historique
de Bazas** is devoted to the
archaeology and history of
the town. The **Apothicairerie
de l'Hôpital Saint-Antoine
de Bazas** contains a fine
collection of pottery and
glassware. For a pleasant
tour of the town, a waymarked
walk allows visitors to explore
its picturesque old streets.

Did You Know?

In Bazas, the speciality
on the dinner menu is
local Bazadaise beef,
also celebrated in an
annual festival.

↑ The magnificent
Gothic cathedral of
Bazas and its soaring
vaulted roof *(inset)*

The town of Captieux, 17 km
(10 miles) south of Bazas, is
one of the overwintering sites
of the migratory common
crane. For information about
these birds, contact the Ligue
de Protection des Oiseaux
Aquitaine in Audenge (tel:
05 56 26 20 52).

Musée Historique
de Bazas

⚐ 2 place de la Cathédrale
📞 05 56 25 25 84 🕐 Mid-Jun-
Aug: Sat; Sep-mid-Jun:
by appointment

Apothicairerie de
l'Hôpital Saint-Antoine
de Bazas

♿ ⚐ 1 place de la Cathédrale
📞 05 56 25 25 84 🕐 By
appointment

36
Uzeste

🅐 C3 **ℹ** 1 place de la Cathédrale, Bazas; 05 56 25 25 84

Consecrated in 1313 on the orders of Pope Clement V, the **Collégiale d'Uzeste** is one of the Gironde's finest Gothic buildings. Large in relation to the size of the village, this abbey church was probably built to house the Pope's tomb (sited in the choir). The bell tower, in the Flamboyant Gothic style, stands at the east end.

Collégiale d'Uzeste
🅰 place de l'Église
📞 06 09 92 20 23 🕑 9am–7pm daily

37
Sauternais

🅐 C3 **🚌ℹ** 7 rue Principale, Sauternes; 05 56 76 69 13 (Jun–Sep)

Lying along the south bank of the Garonne, the Sauternais area has a mix of siliceous, limestone and gravelly soil. The Ciron river, which flows through the area, gives it a favourable climate. The Sauternais is also dotted with prestigious châteaux, the most famous of which is the **Château d'Yquem**. Rated *premier cru supérieur*, the Sauternes wines produced there are some of the finest and most expensive in the world. Dating from the Middle Ages, Yquem is also one of the oldest wine estates in the area. Its vineyards cover just over 1 sq km (0.4 sq miles).

The Sauternes *appellation* covers five villages: Sauternes, Bommes, Fargues, Preignac and Barsac. These *grands crus* can be tasted and purchased at the **Maison du Sauternes**.

About 4.5 km (3 miles) west of Sauternes is the fortress at **Budos**, one of

35
Château de Villandraut

🅐 C3 **🅰** Rue Lafon Isoré 🕑 Times vary, check website 🌐 chateaude villandraut.fr

This impressive château was built in 1305, both as a residential palace and for defensive purposes, on the orders of Pope Clement V (c 1264–1314) who was born in Villandraut. A huge building with an interior courtyard, it was – like the Château de Roquetaillade (*p76*) – defended by a rectangular line of ramparts set with six towers. From the top of these, there are fine views of the surrounding landscape. In July and August, torchlit explorations of the château are held on Wednesday evenings, and an atmospheric escape game can be reserved throughout the year.

SAUTERNES WINE

The grapes used for Sauternes must have been infected by a form of fungus known as noble rot. This causes them to shrivel and have a very high sugar content, resulting in the sweetness of the wine. The Sauternes grape harvest is a long and painstaking process, with every grape picked by hand. After fermentation, the wine matures in barrels for two years before being bottled. Sauternes is served well chilled, but it is not only a dessert wine. It can also be enjoyed as an apéritif, or sipped alongside rich food such as foie gras or Roquefort cheese.

Pope Clement V's castles, built in 1308. Ruins of another of his castles lie at **Fargues**, 5 km (3 miles) east.

Château d'Yquem
🅰 rue Château d'Yquem
🕑 By appointment
🌐 yquem.fr

Maison du Sauternes
🕑 🅰 14 place de la Mairie, Sauternes 📞 05 56 76 69 83 🕑 Daily

↑ Wine-tasting at Château Guiraud in the Sauternais, an area known for its sweet white wines

A DRIVING TOUR
THE MÉDOC REGION

Length 25 km (15 miles) **Starting point** Château Margaux **Stopping-off points** Join a Bordeaux River Cruise at Pauillac and dine on Île Patiras

This riverside drive takes in some of the most beautiful countryside of southwest France, as well as the Médoc vineyards, which produce some of the world's finest wines. The area sits between the Gironde Estuary and an extensive forest, with the Atlantic Ocean to the west. It therefore enjoys a mild, humid climate that is ideal for grapevines. There is also a good mix of gravel, sand and clay soils. All this, combined with the expertise of local growers, accounts for the subtle wines created from traditional grape varieties, such as Cabernet-Sauvignon.

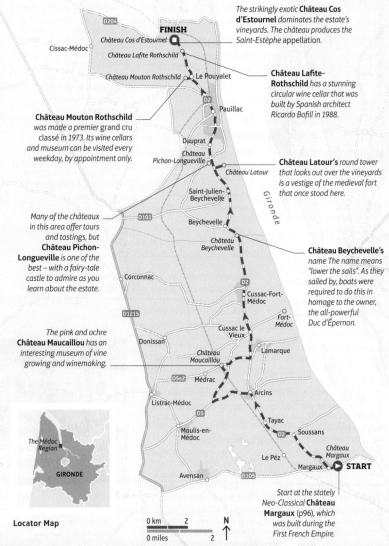

*The strikingly exotic **Château Cos d'Estournel** dominates the estate's vineyards. The château produces the Saint-Estèphe appellation.*

Château Lafite-Rothschild *has a stunning circular wine cellar that was built by Spanish architect Ricardo Bofill in 1988.*

Château Mouton Rothschild *was made a premier grand cru classé in 1973. Its wine cellars and museum can be visited every weekday, by appointment only.*

Château Latour's *round tower that looks out over the vineyards is a vestige of the medieval fort that once stood here.*

*Many of the châteaux in this area offer tours and tastings, but **Château Pichon-Longueville** is one of the best – with a fairy-tale castle to admire as you learn about the estate.*

Château Beychevelle's *name The name means "lower the sails". As they sailed by, boats were required to do this in homage to the owner, the all-powerful Duc d'Épernon.*

*The pink and ochre **Château Maucaillou** has an interesting museum of vine growing and winemaking.*

*Start at the stately Neo-Classical **Château Margaux** (p96), which was built during the First French Empire.*

Locator Map

The Médoc Region

GIRONDE

0 km 2
0 miles 2

N

↑ A glowing sunset over the vineyards of the Médoc region

DORDOGNE AND LOT

The *départements* of Dordogne and Lot form a region known as Périgord-Quercy. Humans have left their mark here in a legacy going back to prehistoric times. The Vézère valley caves, Gallo-Roman sites, great castles that bore witness to centuries of war, and the many medieval *bastide* towns are just a few aspects of a local heritage that covers tens of thousands of years. Marrying the history with the region's famous natural beauty, the region's architecture sits in perfect harmony with the scenery – through stony fortress towers perched on rocky spurs, elegant Romanesque chuches built of golden sandstone and troglodytic cliff-dwellings decorated with ancient artwork.

With the pride of local citizens tied to their history and serene landscapes, it's no wonder that this region is also home to no less than 16 of France's official Plus Beaux Villages (Most Beautiful Villages), over 10 per cent of the entire list. The mix of landscapes offers something for everyone: to the north, meadows and forests; to the east, rugged limestone plateaus; to the south, vineyards, running down almost seamlessly into those of Bordeaux.

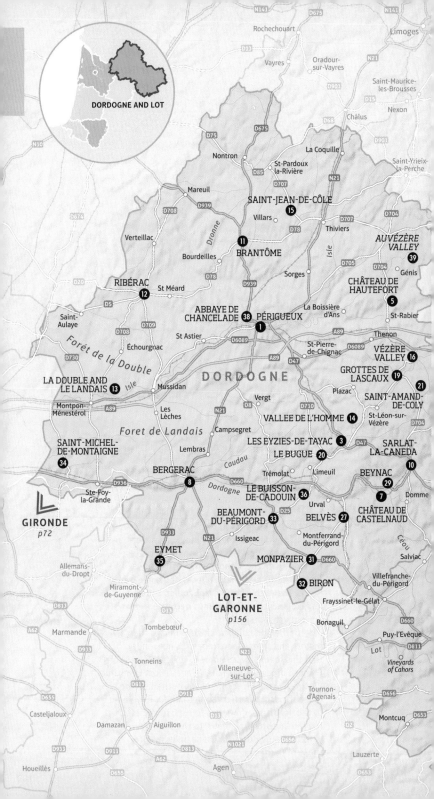

DORDOGNE AND LOT

Must Sees

1. Périgueux
2. Gardens of the Manoir d'Eyrignac
3. Les Eyzies-de-Tayac
4. Rocamadour
5. Château de Hautefort
6. Figeac
7. Château de Castelnaud
8. Bergerac
9. Grotte du Pech-Merle
10. Sarlat-la-Canéda

Experience More

11. Brantôme
12. Ribérac
13. La Double and Le Landais
14. Vallée de l'Homme
15. Saint-Jean-de-Côle
16. Vézère Valley
17. Terrasson-Lavilledieu
18. Castelnau-Bretenoux
19. Grottes de Lascaux
20. Le Bugue
21. Saint-Amand-de-Coly
22. Gouffre de Padirac
23. Martel
24. Souillac
25. Saint-Céré
26. Assier
27. Belvès
28. Saint-Cirq-Lapopie
29. Beynac
30. Gourdon
31. Monpazier
32. Biron
33. Beaumont-du-Périgord
34. Saint-Michel-de-Montaigne
35. Eymet
36. Le Buisson-de-Cadouin
37. Cahors
38. Abbaye de Chancelade
39. Auvézère Valley

↑ Ancient centre of Périgueux, built around the cathedral, on the banks of the River Isle

❶

PÉRIGUEUX

⬛E2 ➡🏛🚌 ℹ 9 bis place du Coderc; 05 53 53 10 63

At the turn of every street you move in time in Périgueux. You will see a Byzantine cathedral, a Gaelic temple, an amphitheatre, a marketplace once used for public executions, and museums that tell of the Romans. Shops and medieval houses line narrow boulevards and streets, and a Renaissance park is at its center.

① Vesunna

🏛 Parc de Vésone ☎ 05 53 53 00 92 🕐 Jul & Aug: daily; Sep-Dec & mid-Jan-Jun: Tue-Sun

This museum is named after the ancient city that occupied the site of modern Périgueux. Exhibits on show give an insight into daily life in Gallo-Roman times. Nearby is the Tour de Vésone. At 24 m (80 ft) high with an internal diameter of 17 m (56 ft), it gives an idea of the size of the temple, long gone, of which it formed part. The Jardin des Arènes has the remains of an amphitheatre.

② Château Barrière

🏛 Rue de Turenne 🕐 Daily

This 12th-century fortress served the aristocratic families of the Périgord. The oldest parts – a Gallo-Roman wall and keep – can be seen at the rear. The elegant five-tiered tower dates from the Renaissance.

③ Cathédrale Saint-Front

🏛 Place de la Clautre 🕐 Daily

The Byzantine-Romanesque elements of Saint-Front were added by Paul Abadie, later architect of the Sacré-Cœur in Paris. He added the five domes and installed 17 small steeples. The interior has a magnificent 17th-century Baroque altarpiece and Stations of the Cross by Jacques-Émile Lafon.

④ Église Saint-Étienne-de-la-Cité

🏛 Place de la Cité 🕐 Daily

Périgueux's first cathedral, a Romanesque, single-nave church, was built in the 11th century and remodelled in the 17th, when it also lost its cathedral status. It still has two of its four original domes.

⑤ Tour Mataguerre

🏛 Place Francheville ☎ 05 53 53 10 63 🕐 Jul & Aug: 10:30am-1pm & 2-5:30pm daily

Of the 28 towers that once surrounded Le Puy-Saint-Front, only this one still stands.

The tourist office next door organizes tours of this vestige of the fortifications that once encircled the city. A climb to the top is rewarded with breathtaking views.

⑥

Musée d'Art et d'Archéologie du Périgord

🏠 22 cours Tourny
🕐 Times vary, check website 🌐 perigueux-maap.fr

This fascinating prehistoric collection includes the world's most complete Neanderthal skeleton, as well as glass, mosaics and earthenware from ancient Vessuna.

---

⑦

Musée Militaire

🏠 32 rue des Farges 📞 05 53 53 47 36 🕐 Mon–Sat

Fascinating exhibits here include a series of drawings made in the trenches during World War I by Gilbert-Privat (1892–1965), winner of the Prix de Rome. Medals, insignia and other wartime memorabilia, help serve as a reminder of the sacrifice of those who fought.

TRUFFLES

The Périgordian truffle, *Tuber melanosporum*, is a highly prized delicacy for gourmets. An ingredient of many local specialities, this subterranean fungus is now scarce. In 1870, Sorges' limestone plateau alone produced 6 tonnes of truffles a year, which is equal to the yield obtained today from the whole of the Dordogne.

⑧

Écomusée de la Truffe

🏠 Sorges 📞 05 53 05 90 11
🕐 Tue–Sun (Summer: daily)

Northeast of Périgueux, Sorges is the Périgord's truffle capital. The Écomusée de la Truffe has displays showing how truffles grow, the methods of finding them and details of some spectacularly large examples.

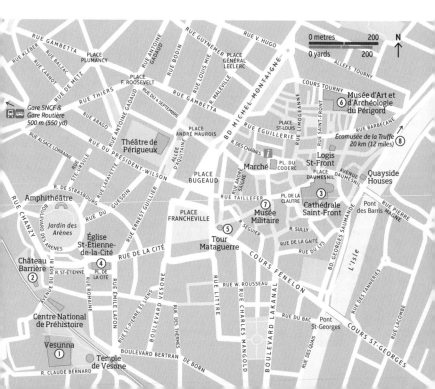

A SHORT WALK
PERIGUEUX

Distance 3 km (2 miles)   **Time** 30 minutes
Nearest station Gare de Périgueux

The ancient centre of Périgueux is one of the largest urban conservation areas in France. A programme of restoration, which began in 1970, has brought to life the narrow streets that run from the boulevards of the upper town down to the banks of the Isle river, and from the Mataguerre to the Plantier districts. Around the cathedral is the city's pleasant, pedestrianized, medieval area. On market days place de la Mairie, place du Coderc and place de la Clautre buzz with activity. Place Saint-Louis, not far from rue Limogeanne, and the alleys leading off place de la Vertu, make for a pleasant stroll.

Rue Limogeanne, *the city's main pedestrian thoroughfare, with shops and Renaissance houses.*

PLACE SAINT LOUIS

START

*The finest building on **place Saint-Louis** is Maison du Pâtissier, or Maison Tenant. This 14th-century townhouse is an important example of Renaissance building in the town.*

RUE ÉGUILLERIE

FINISH

RUE LAMMA

*The townhouse at 1 rue de la Sagesse is the magnificent **Hôtel La Joubertie**.*

RUE MALESHERBE

RUE DE LA SAGESSE

RUE LIMOGEANNE

RUE DE LA MISERICO

*Périgueux's colourful market stalls fill **place du Coderc**, near the Hôtel de Ville (town hall).*

RUE DES CHAINES

PLACE DU CODERC

RUE DE LA CLARTE

PLACE DE L'HÔTEL DE VILLE

RUE SALINI EEE

RUE DU SERMENT

RUE DENFERT ROCHE

Hôtel de Ville

PLACE DE LA CLAUTRE

Hôtel Estignard *is a townhouse built in the reign of François I (1515–47).*

Jardin du Thouin

←
Rue Limogeanne, a pedestrian shopping street lined with beautiful houses

Locator Map
For more detail see p113

↑ Canoeing past the Cathédrale
Saint-Front on the Isle river

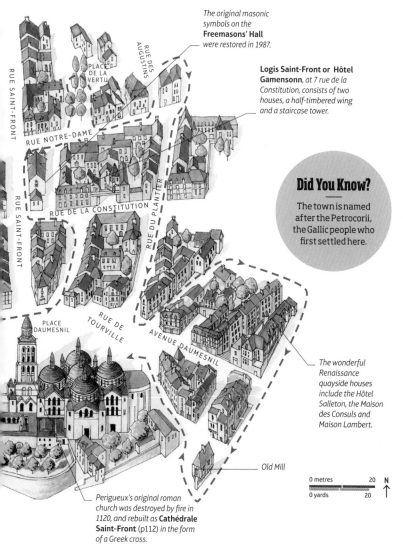

The original masonic
symbols on the
Freemasons' Hall
were restored in 1987.

**Logis Saint-Front or Hôtel
Gamensonn**, *at 7 rue de la
Constitution, consists of two
houses, a half-timbered wing
and a staircase tower.*

RUE SAINT-FRONT

PLACE
DE LA
VERTU

RUE DES AUGUSTINS

RUE NOTRE-DAME

RUE SAINT-FRONT

RUE DE LA CONSTITUTION

RUE DU PLANTIER

Did You Know?

The town is named
after the Petrocorii,
the Gallic people who
first settled here.

PLACE
DAUMESNIL

RUE DE
TOURVILLE

AVENUE DAUMESNIL

The wonderful
Renaissance
quayside houses
include the Hôtel
Salleton, the Maison
des Consuls and
Maison Lambert.

Old Mill

Perigueux's original roman
church was destroyed by fire in
1120, and rebuilt as **Cathédrale
Saint-Front** (p112) *in the form
of a Greek cross.*

| 0 metres | 20 |
| 0 yards | 20 |

N ↑

2 🜲 🜶 🍴

GARDENS OF THE MANOIR D'EYRIGNAC

ⒶF2 **🏠**Salignac **🚌**Souillac, Sarlat **🕐**Times vary, check website **Ⓦ**eyrignac.com

Enter Les Jardins du Manoir d'Eyrignac and explore seven unique gardens surrounding a 17th-century estate, family-owned for over 500 years. The grounds, complete with hand-clipped topiaries, vegetable patches and roses, create a paradise within Dordogne.

First laid out in the 18th century, the gardens of this manor house form a cool oasis of greenery amid the dry, rocky limestone of the Périgord Noir region in southwest Dordogne. Watered by seven springs, they were made over in the Romantic style in the 19th century, but within 100 years had fallen into such neglect that it took the owners – Gilles Sermadiras and later his son – nearly 40 years to restore them to their full glory. They finally opened to the public in 1987. Today, the gardens are a mix of the formal French and wild-looking Italian styles, with rolling lawns and a mass of mature trees and shrubs. The French garden, a masterpiece of symmetry and order, with topiary and carefully arranged parterres, stands in stark contrast to the more irregular "jigsaw" of the Italian garden. There are also many surprises to delight the visitor, such as secret nooks and unexpected vistas.

Did You Know?

Bring a picnic to join in the "White Picnic" family parties on Monday nights in July and August.

The "enchanted terrace" offers a fine view of the manor house and French gardens

Restaurant Côté Jardin

This long, grassy, hornbeam-lined avenue is a geometric masterpiece in a palette of harmonious greens.

Chinese pagoda

The layout of the Gardens of the Manoir d'Eyrignac ↑

↑ Walking down the shaded avenues in one of the estate's seven gardens

↑ The elegant, manicured grounds of the French-syle Jardin Fruitier

The terrace, which is laid out with flower-filled parterres, is fronted by a sandy courtyard and a small pond.

Le Jardin Fruitier, with pretty apple and pear trees

The White Garden is planted only with white roses

The rose garden is complemented by five pools laid out in a geometric pattern.

The Springs Garden and Wild Flower Meadows

The Kitchen Garden and the Flower Garden

The Manor of Artaban

The English Arcade is covered in vegetation that casts patterns of light and shade

❸

LES EYZIES-DE-TAYAC

Ⓐ E2 **Ⓡ Ⓘ** 19 avenue de la Préhistoire; www.lascaux-dordogne.com

At the heart of the Vézère valley, with its prehistoric painted caves and rock-shelters, sits the village of Les Eyzies. Known as "the capital of prehistory", it stretches out along the foot of ochre-coloured cliffs that bear traces of some of the earliest human settlements.

①

Abri du Cap Blanc

Ⓐ Marquay **Ⓒ 05 53 06 86 00** **Ⓞ Sun–Fri**

More than 15,000 years ago, prehistoric people carved images on the wall of this rock-shelter. A small display sheds light on the art and life during the Magdalenian period.

②

Abri du Poisson

Ⓐ On the D47 **Ⓒ 06 47 56 57 01** **Ⓞ Mon–Fri**

This small rock-shelter in the valley of the Gorge d'Enfer is named after the relief of a fish that was discovered here. It is of a salmon, 1 m (3 ft) long, carved in about 25,000 BC.

③

Abri Pataud

Ⓐ 20 rue du Moyen Âge **Ⓒ 05 53 06 92 46** **Ⓞ Times vary, call ahead**

The walls of this engraved rock-shelter contain traces of around 40 encampments dating from between 35,000 to 20,000 BC. Below this is another rock-shelter, its ceiling decorated with a splendid relief of an oryx made around 17,000 BC.

④

Musée National de la Préhistoire

Ⓐ 1 rue du Musée **Ⓒ 05 53 06 45 45** **Ⓞ Jul & Aug: daily; Sep–Jun: Wed–Mon**

Exhibits in the museum cover most of what is known about early man, and would make an ideal preliminary to any visit to the nearby painted caves.

⑤

Le Moustier, La Micoque and La Ferrassie

Ⓒ 06 47 56 57 01 **Ⓞ Mon–Fri; by appointment (call ahead)**

The rock-shelter at Le Moustier, where a Neanderthal skeleton was discovered, gave its name

> 💬 **INSIDER TIP**
> ### What to Wear when Caving
> Touring dark and dank caves can be quite chilly, so be prepared with layered clothing, good sturdy shoes, and a sense of adventure as you head deep into the belly of the mountains.

Tucked beneath the rocks, the charming village of Les Eyzies-de-Tayac

to the Mousterian culture (80,000–30,000 BC). The oldest site in the Dordogne, La Micoque was inhabited from 300,000 BC. The rock-shelter of La Ferrassie contained Neanderthal burials.

⑥ Abri de Laugerie Haute

🏠 On the D47 📞 06 47 56 57 01 🕐 Mon-Fri; by appointment (call ahead)

This huge rock-shelter was inhabited from 22,000 to 12,000 BC. It was abandoned when the ceiling fell in. Flint and bone tools, as well as a large number of harpoons, were discovered here.

⑦ Grotte des Combarelles

🏠 On the D47 📞 05 53 06 97 72 🕐 Sun-Fri

Used during the Magdalenian period (around 15,000 BC), this cave has engravings and drawings of horses, reindeer,

mammoths, woolly rhinoceros and anthropomorphic figures.

⑧ Grotte de Font-de-Gaume

📞 05 53 06 86 00 🕐 Sun-Fri

These caves walls are covered with coloured paintings dating from the Magdalenian period, and drawings and engravings of around 200 animals.

⑨ Grotte du Grand Roc

🏠 1-4 avenue des Grottes 📞 05 53 06 92 70 🕐 Mid-Jan-Dec: daily

Lit to reveal its wonders, this cave contains fantastic mineral formations, including stalagmites, stalactites and an assortment of rather weird shapes.

⑩ Abri de Laugerie Basse

🏠 On the D47 🕐 Times vary, check website 🌐 abris-laugerie-basse.fr

This rock-shelter, from the Magdalenian period, contains displays on the life of Cro-

Must See

EAT

Moulin de la Beune
Dine on local trout and porcini mushrooms at this converted water-mill by the river.

🏠 2 Rue du Moulin Bas
🌐 moulindelabeune.com

€€€

Magnon people. The earliest female figure to be discovered in France, known as the Venus Impudique (Shameless Venus), was found here in 1864.

⑪ Grotte de Bernifal

🏠 La Petite Beune 📞 06 74 96 30 43 🕐 Jun-Sep: daily, by appointment (call ahead)

This small cave is reached by walking up through an atmospheric woodland. By torchlight, representations of mammoths and human figures, and signs and symbols, dating from the Magdalenian period, can be seen.

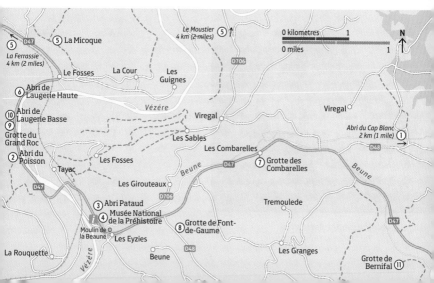

④

ROCAMADOUR

⚑ F3 🅟 𝒊 L'Hospitalet, Cour du Prieuré; www.vallee-dordogne.com

Here history, legend, nature and religion converge. An important stop along the pilgrimage path to Santiago de Compostela, the famous town is a stunning cliff-hanging backdrop for old stone houses, Gothic churches, and religious relics.

Sitting on a rocky plateau high above the Alzou valley, Rocamadour looks as if it is carved straight out of the limestone rock face. The town became one of the most famous centres of pilgrimage in France because of the 12th-century statue of the Black Virgin and Child in the Chapelle Notre-Dame that was believed to have miraculous powers. An account dating from 1172 describes the 126 miracles granted by the Madonna, who is still honoured on 8 September each year during the Semaine Mariale (Marian Week).

> 💬 **INSIDER TIP**
> **Going Up**
>
> There is a lift dug into the rock face, which ascends (for a fee) from the base of the town to the sanctuaries and chapels that form the Cité Religieuse, though it does not go to the château at the top.

The château stands on the site of a fort that protected the sanctuary from the west.

Chapelle Saint-Michel is decorated with beautiful 12th-century frescoes

The Tomb of St Amadour once held the body of the hermit from whom the town took its name.

Pilgrims would climb this broad flight of steps on their knees as a penance.

↑ The spectacular town of Rocamadour clinging to a cliff

St Amadour's body was found under the floor in front of the chapel. On the altar is the statue of the miraculous Black Virgin and Child.

Pilgrims encounter the 14 stations of the Cross on their way up the hillside to the château.

Ramparts

Cross of Jerusalem

↑ A busy pedestrianized street in popular Rocamadour

The Basilique Saint-Sauveur backs on to the bare rock face.

Chapelle Sainte-Anne, has a fine 17th-century gilded altarpiece.

The Chapelle Saint-Jean-Baptiste faces the fine Gothic portal of the Basilica Saint-Sauveur.

Chapelle of Saint-Blaise

← Rocamadour's shrines and chapels climbing the cliff above the village

5 ✍ Ⓜ

CHÂTEAU DE HAUTEFORT

🅰 F2 📍 Le Bourg d'Hautefort ⏰ Times vary, check website
🌐 chateau-hautefort.com

Hautefort Castle towers over the village below with a peacefulness that belies its tormented past. Rising more than once from the ashes, the castle has been the possession of French and English noblemen, a stronghold of the church and home to the Hautefort family.

Originally the site of a medieval fortress, the imposing residence that replaced it was built for the Marquis de Hautefort, who envisaged a classic building in the style of a Loire Valley château. Work began in 1630 and was completed in 1670. The castle was used as a prison during the French Revolution (p54), and despite being recovered by the Damas family, the estate was later sold and fell into disrepair.

The next owners, Baron and Baroness de Bastard, began restoring the main building in the 1920s, but this was brought to an abrupt end by a fire in August 1968, and the castle was left in ruins. Photographs showing the devastation of the fire are on view in the 14th-century Tour de Bretagne, the only surviving medieval part of the castle. Further phases of restoration were completed in 1995 and 2005.

Did You Know?

Guided tours on Wednesday nights in July and August include costumed actors and entertainers.

The large drawing room is hung with Brussels tapestries. Monumental wooden chimneypieces fill each end of the room.

The master bedroom is decorated with wood carvings and filled with antique furniture.

→ Château de Hautefort, surrounding an impressive courtyard

The roof structure of the Tour de Bretagne dates from 1678.

1 One of the rooms of the château, refurnished and redecorated after the 1968 fire.

2 The fabulous formal French garden was intended to marry the castle architecture with the natural beauty of the surrounding countryside.

3 The magnificent Château de Hautefort.

The Grand Staircase curves back on itself to lead to the upper floor.

The chapel ceiling, a trompe l'oeil coffered dome, looks down on a simple clay floor.

The terrace was rearranged in the 1930s. Box and yew have been clipped into domes.

The formal gardens are best seen from above, particularly from the main courtyard, which also commands a view of the village on its southern side.

6

FIGEAC

🅰G3 🅰𝒊 Hôtel de la Monnaie, place Vival; www.tourisme-figeac.com

"A flight of doves forming a cross in the sky over Saint-Sauveur," is the legend of the ancient abbey of Figeac and a reason the "Town of Art and History" is one of the "Great Sites of Midi-Pyrénées" to visit.

The town of Figeac, which sits clustered around its 9th century abbey, grew and prospered as the result of trade. By the Middle Ages, its growing wealth enabled many inhabitants to build fine houses here. Fortified in the 14th century, the town still has a medieval appearance, reflecting its past importance.

A place that refuses to alter its medieval past, Figeac conceals stories of kings, pilgrims and religious armies within its narrow streets, timber-framed houses and stately mansions. With this rich architectural heritage, Figeac offers a complete panorama of local urban architecture from the 12th century to the present day. Discover here, too, the history of mining, coin-making, and the secret code of hieroglyphics.

①
Hôtel de la Monnaie

🏠 Place Vival 📞 05 65 34 06 25 🕐 Jul & Aug: daily; Sep-Jun: Mon-Sat

Although the Ortabadial quarter was partly demolished, this 13th-century townhouse survived. A fine example of a grand Renaissance residence, it has an arcaded ground floor and gemelled windows. It now houses the tourist office and a small local history museum.

②
Place Champollion

This is one of Figeac's main squares. Maison du Griffon, at No. 4, dates from the Middle Ages and has carved Romanesque decoration. The 14th-

century Gothic house at No. 5 has a stone solelho (open attic).

③
Abbaye Saint-Sauveur

🏠 6 rue Ferrer 📞 05 65 34 11 63 🕐 Sat & Sun

This church is one of the surviving elements of the abbey around which the town grew. The medieval chapter room is now the Chapelle Notre-Dame-de-la-Pitié. It is decorated with 17th-century painted panels.

④
Place des Écritures

This unusual area was laid out by Joseph Kosuth (1945–), a

> **💬 INSIDER TIP**
> **Medieval Gems**
>
> Other buildings in Figeac worth checking out include: Hôtel Galiot de Genouillac, with a spiral staircase; 14th-century Palais Balène, arranged around a courtyard; and Hôtel d'Auglanat, with a turret and 14th-century decorated doorway.

←

Restaurant tables set out before medieval buildings on place Champollion

pioneer of conceptual art. Part of his permanent installation here features an enlarged replica of the Rosetta Stone.

---

⑤
Hôtel de Colomb

🏠 5 rue de Colomb
📞 05 65 50 05 40 🕐 10 Jul-15 Sep: daily; Apr-9 Jul & 16 Sep-3 Nov: Tue-Sun pm

With a restrained façade and a highly decorated staircase, this townhouse is typical of the 17th-century. It has been the town hall since 1877, and houses the Espace Patrimoine, an exhibition on Figeac's history and heritage.

→

Video lounge at Musée Champollion: Les Écritures du Monde

⑥ ⚙
Musée Champollion: Les Écritures du Monde

🏠 Place Champollion
📞 05 65 50 31 08 🕐 Jul & Aug: daily; Sep-Jun: Tue-Sun (Nov-Mar: pm only)

The museum is in the house where Jean-François Champollion (1790–1832), the great Egyptologist, was born. Dating from the 13th and 14th centuries, the collection focuses on different sorts of writings including Egyptian hieroglyphics.

EAT

Commanderie des Templiers

Take refreshment in the 13th-century courtyard of this former hostel for the Knights Templar.

🏠 41 rue Gambetta
🌐 commanderie-des-templiers.com

€€€

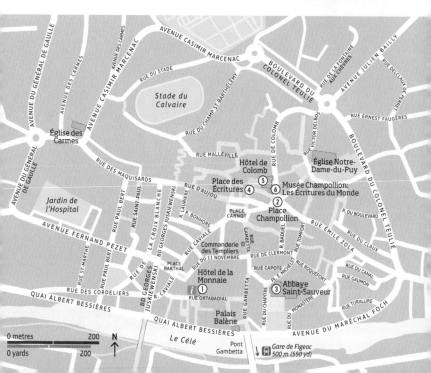

0 metres 200
0 yards 200

N ↑

Château de Castelnaud, sitting above the hillside village of Castelnaud ↑

7 ⚔ Ⓜ

CHÂTEAU DE CASTELNAUD

🅰F3 🏠Castelnaud-la-Chapelle ⏰Daily; times vary, check website
🅦castelnaud.com

Castelnaud Castle could easily take up a whole chapter in a book on French history. The prized possession of French and English kings, the castle saw battles that decided the fate of nations. Today, visitors delight over the building's authenticity, its war museum and its quaint hilltop village.

Castelnaud has been an enduring presence in this region despite centuries of turmoil. Destroyed by fire during an attack in the 13th century, besieged in 1442 by those seeking revenge after the Hundred Years' War *(p54)* and abandoned during the French Revolution.

After such a turbulent life, the castle gradually fell into ruin until the estate was bought in 1966 and classed as a historic monument. Visitors can now come to see impressive displays of medieval armour and weapons that evoke the war-torn history of the castle.

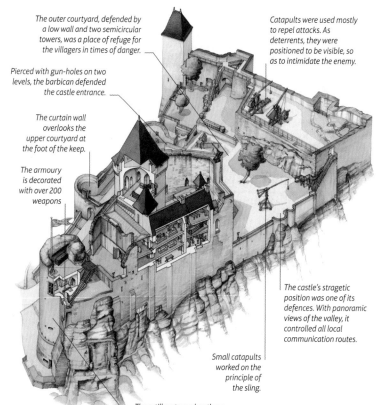

The outer courtyard, defended by a low wall and two semicircular towers, was a place of refuge for the villagers in times of danger.

Catapults were used mostly to repel attacks. As deterrents, they were positioned to be visible, so as to intimidate the enemy.

Pierced with gun-holes on two levels, the barbican defended the castle entrance.

The curtain wall overlooks the upper courtyard at the foot of the keep.

The armoury is decorated with over 200 weapons

The castle's strategic position was one of its defences. With panoramic views of the valley, it controlled all local communication routes.

Small catapults worked on the principle of the sling.

The artillery tower has three floors with different types of cannons and two organ guns (mounted on wheels.)

↑ The heavily fortified cliff top Château de Castelnaud

8

BERGERAC

🅰E3 ⊠🚉 ℹ️ 97 rue Neuve-d'Argenson; www.pays-bergerac-tourisme.com

Bergerac blends the charm of the Dordogne and its half-timbered houses, squares, churches and stone bridges with the best of a busy city. Museums throughout the town tell of the area's involvement with tobacco and wine. At the centre of the old town, flowered-filled place Pélissière is surrounded by shops and outdoor cafés.

①
Vieille Ville

The old, half-timbered houses of master-boatmen line place de la Mirpe, where there is a statue of Cyrano de Bergerac, Edmond Rostand's long-nosed hero. Rue Saint-Clar is lined with corbelled houses, with cob, brick and half-timbered walls. Place Pélissière, in a restored area of the town, is named after the skinners whose work-shops once stood there. With the Église Saint-Jacques and Fontaine Font-Ronde, once a public washhouse, it forms a pretty enclave. Place Pélissière is the setting for another statue of Cyrano de Bergerac, which was erected in 2005. Rue Saint-James has interesting houses, including an 18th-century townhouse with a shop on the ground floor and bosses on its façade, a 16th-century house with mullioned windows, and 17th- and 18th-century half-timbered houses. Rue des Fontaines has two medieval houses.

②
Église Saint-Jacques

🅰 Place Pélissière

This 12th-century chapel on the pilgrim route to Compostela was enlarged in the 13th century, when it became the medieval town's church, with a single-wall belfry. It was later remodelled, the nave being rebuilt in the 18th century. The Neo-Gothic organ, built by Aristide Cavaillé-Coll in 1870, is listed as a historic monument.

③ 🔄
Musée Costi

🅰 Via the inner courtyard of place de la Petite-Mission
📞 0553630413 🕐 Jul & Aug: Tue-Sun; Sep-Jun: Wed

This museum fills two cellars of the Presbytère Saint-Jacques. It contains works donated by Costi, a sculptor who studied

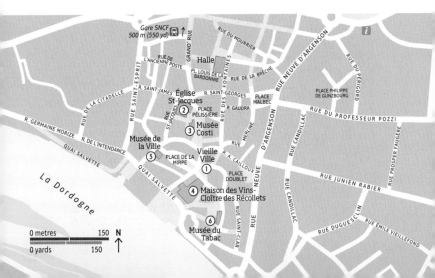

↑ A *gabare*, a traditional barge, taking a tour on the Dordogne river, Bergerac

under Antoine Bourdelle. They consist of 52 bronzes and seven plaster casts, dated 1926–73.

④
Maison des Vins-Cloître des Récollets

🏠 1 rue des Récollets 📞 05 53 63 57 55 🕐 Jul & Aug: daily; Sep-Jun: Tue-Sat

Cloître des Récollets was built in 1630 on the site of the former gardens of the Château de Bergerac. The 16th- and 18th-century galleries look on to the courtyard. It now houses the Maison des Vins de Bergerac, which offers wine tastings.

⑤
Musée de la Ville

🏠 5 rue des Conférences 📞 05 53 63 04 13 🕐 Jun-Sep: Tue-Fri, Sat & Sun; Oct-Mar: Wed & Fri, Sat

This museum is devoted to the history of river shipping

and the local wine trade. Displays include artifacts, models, documents, photographs and archive materials that have been donated by wine-producing and boat-owning families in the area.

⑥
Musée du Tabac

🏠 Maison Peyrarède, place du Feu 📞 05 53 63 04 13 🕐 Apr-Sep: Tue-Fri, Sat & Sun; Oct-Mar: Wed & Fri, Sat

Created in 1950 by the Direction des Musées de France, this museum occupies Maison Peyrarède, a townhouse built in 1604 and restored in 1982. The museum traces the history of tobacco over 3,000 years. Its collections illustrate the earliest use of the plant, its spread throughout the world, the ways that it was smoked, and its impact on society and the economy. Various smoking implements, with details of their manufacture, are shown. The

importance of tobacco-growing in the Dordogne valley is also highlighted at the museum.

BERGERAC WINES

Bergerac wines were highly thought of in England during the Hundred Years' War, and in Holland when the town was a Protestant stronghold, but their renown goes back to the 13th century. Today there are 124 sq km (48 sq miles) of vineyards in the area, with 13 *appellations*, for red, rosé and white wines. For details on wine routes, contact the Interprofession des Vins de Bergerac et de Duras (IVBD): www.vins-bergeracduras.fr. You can also pick up the Wines of Bergerac map from the tourist office or the Maison des Vins-Cloître des Récollets.

GROTTE DU PECH-MERLE

🅰F3 🅾Peche-Merle 🅾Times vary, check website; maximum of 700 visitors per day, book at least 3-4 days in advance 🆆pechmerle.com

Pech-Merle is one of the few original, ornate Palaeolithic caves open to the public. A fence protects paintings and engravings, yet visitors have the extraordinary opportunity to view hundreds of painted or engraved motifs of animals, humans, and signs in their original prehistoric environment.

To visit this cave is literally to tread in the footsteps of early *Homo sapiens*. About 50 million years ago, a subterranean gallery was carved out over time by an underground river. The space, full of extraordinary natural rock formations, consists of several halls and chambers that contain hundreds of paintings, drawings and engravings showing animals, human figures and abstract symbols. Unique to Pech-Merle is the way in which these prehistoric images have been combined with the geological features of the cave. Because it was blocked up by a rockfall around 10,000 years ago, at the end of the ice age, the cave remained well-preserved and fully intact until its discovery in 1922.

Roots of an oak tree

Cave entrance

Modern stairway

Displays of the fossilized bones of bears, hyenas, horses, bison and deer discovered in the cave

The cavern known as the Chapel of the Mammoths contains depictions of 11 mammoths, 5 bisons, 4 horses and 4 aurochs (cattle) and clusters of red spots.

FRIEZE OF THE DAPPLED HORSES

In this large frieze, the artist has used the unevenness of the cave wall to give a three-dimensional effect to their paintings. The main subjects are two horses, a red fish and the negative prints of six human hands. Incredibly, this magnificent work of art is 25,000 years old.

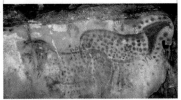

Bear hollow

Ossuary closed to the public

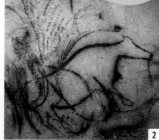

1 Visitors preparing to enter the caves.

2 Prehistoric paintings of a mammoth and an auroch, which used to live in this region.

3 The Amédée Lemozi Regional Prehistory Museum explores the story of the caves.

In the Hall of the Discs, the calcite from the lime stone has crystallized in concentric circles.

Fossilized human footprints

In the Bear Gallery, with a ceiling 11 m (36 ft) high, the calcite has formed strange translucent discs and drapes.

Beads and top symbol

Painting of wounded man

Handprints, believed by some archeologists to be those of women, are a rare motif in cave art. To spray the paint onto the wall, the artist is thought to have spat it out of his or her mouth.

Red deer painting

The Frieze of the Bison-Women appears on the underside of an overhanging rock in the cavern with the Ceiling of the Hieroglyphs. It shows a mammoth and stylized female shapes drawn in red.

↑ The layout of the Grotte du Pech-Merle, showing the various chambers

Did You Know?

Ten other caves with prehistoric art have been discovered in the vicinity of Pech-Merle.

10

SARLAT-LA-CANÉDA

🅰 F3 🚇ℹ 3 rue Tourny; www.sarlat-tourisme.com

Sarlat-la-Canéda, simply known as Sarlat, is a picture-book medieval town. With its cobblestone streets, sandstone buildings, elegant city squares, and market days that are particularly colourful and bustling, it is no wonder that tourists flock here.

In summer, when it is closed to traffic, the heart of Sarlat's old town, with its architectural jewels, is a pleasure to explore on foot. On place de la Liberté is the Hôtel de Maleville (or Hôtel de Vienne), a townhouse in a combination of French and Italian Renaissance styles. Passage Henri-de-Ségogne, in the restored quarter of the town, is lined with 13th-, 15th- and 16th-century half-timbered corbelled houses with tiled roofs.

①

Cathédrale Saint-Sacerdos

🅰 Place du Peyrou 📞 05 53 59 03 16

Sarlat's cathedral was rebuilt in the 16th and 17th centuries on the site of an early Roman-esque abbey church. The interior is arranged around a nave with four ribbed-vaulted sections. A stroll in the vicinity of the cathedral takes in the Cour des Fontaines and the Chapelle des Pénitents Bleus, the remains of the old cloister, and the Jardin des Enfeus, a former cemetery with burial niches carved into the wall. The purpose of the 12th-century Lanterne des Morts (Lantern of the Dead) is still unclear.

②

Western Sarlat

Half-timbered houses line rue des Armes, and can be seen from the ramparts. The

↑ Pretty restaurants on a charming cobbled street in Sarlat-la-Canéda

Chapelle des Pénitents Blancs is the remains of a 17th-century convent. Further on is the former Abbaye Sainte-Claire, also from the 17th century.

To the southeast of Sarlat is **Château de Fénelon**, where philosopher François de Salignac de la Mothe Fénelon (1651–1715) was born.

Château de Fénelon

♿ Ⓢ 🏠 Sainte-Mondane
📞 05 53 29 81 45 🕐 Apr–Oct: Sun, Mon, Wed–Fri (Jul & Aug: Sun–Fri)

---

③

Eastern Sarlat

The former Présidial, in rue Landry, was the seat of the law courts in the 17th century, and is now a restaurant. The façade has a low arch with a loggia, containing a lantern,

←

Mannequin representing François Fénelon sitting at his desk, Château de Fenélon

---

above. On either side of the town hall are old gabled houses. On rue Fénelon, opposite the alley leading to the Hôtel de Gérard, is a doorway framed by four columns decorated with fleurs-de-lis. It was once the town hall entrance.

---

④

Place de la Liberté

This picturesque square sits at the heart of Sarlat. The late medieval Manoir de Gisson, with tiled roof, is the hub of Sarlat's summer drama festival. Gargoyles stare down from on the bell tower of the Église Sainte-Marie, now a covered market.

---

⑤

Rue des Consuls

This street is lined with many fine townhouses. Among

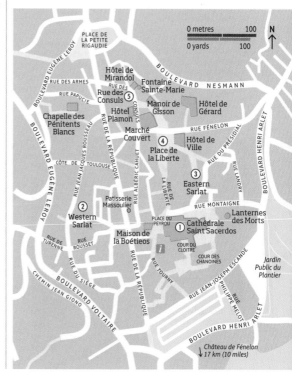

them are the Hôtel Plamon, dating from the Middle Ages and modified in the 17th century, and Hôtel de Mirandol, near the Fontaine Sainte-Marie. Beyond the arch is the Hôtel Tapinois de Bétou with its wooden staircase dating from the *Ancien Régime* era.

Must See

SHOP

Patisserie Massoulier

Indulge in one of this patisserie's gorgeous slices of cake, whimsical chocolate creations or fluffy pastries.

🏠 33 rue de la République
📞 33 6 86 51 02 00

A SHORT WALK
SARLAT-LA-CANÉDA

Distance 1 km (0.5 miles) **Time** 10 minutes
Nearest station Gare de Sarlat

Nestling at the foot of a cluster of *pechs* (small hills), Sarlat-la-Canéda (often called simply Sarlat) has undergone extensive restoration, returning its narrow streets and courtyards to their original splendour. A number of houses here consist of a medieval ground floor with Renaissance floors above. This centre of trade on the road to Santiago de Compostela *(p226)* grew rapidly in the mid- and late Middle Ages, when its splendid Renaissance houses were built. Rue de la République, laid out in the 19th century and nicknamed "La Traverse", runs between the picturesque medieval district and the town's other ancient streets. Although Sarlat's restored quarter is an architectural jewel, the town's seasonal truffle markets *(p31)* also attract foodies from near and far.

Did You Know?

Sarlat has been used as a location for many films, including Ridley Scott's *The Duellists*.

Place aux Oies
(Goose Square) was once the venue of Sarlat's live-fowl market. This is commemorated by bronze statues of geese by Lalanne. Sarlat is still well known for its foie gras.

START

FINISH

RUE PEYRAL

RUE DE LA CHARITÉ

COTE DE TOULOUSE

RUE JEAN-JACQUES ROUSSEAU

RUE DE LA RÉPUBLIC

RUE DE LA BOÉTIE

RUE DU SIÈGE

← Place aux Oies, a medieval area that was once used for busy markets

→

Lanterne des Morts (Lantern of the Dead) in the grounds of the Bishop's Palace

Locator Map
For more detail see p133

Rue des Consuls *is a street lined with fine 15th- to 17th-century houses.*

The hub of Sarlat, **place de la Liberté** *square is lined with picturesque 16th- and 18th-century houses. The Église Sainte-Marie, in the background, was restored by the architect Jean Nouvel, and is now a covered market.*

The beautiful Renaissance **Maison de La Boétie** *was the birthplace of philosopher Étienne de La Boétie. The ornately decorated upper storeys have mullioned windows, and the building is crowned by an elegant tiled roof.*

The **Lanterne des Morts** *tower was constructed in the Middle Ages to commemorate a visit to Sarlat by St Bernard, a prominent abbot.*

Begun in 1504 and completed in the 17th century, **Cathédrale Saint-Sacerdos** *lacks stylistic unity, resulting in an eclectic mix of designs. A notable feature of the interior is the overhanging organ loft of 1770.*

Chapelle des Pénitents Bleus *is the only surviving element of an earlier Romanesque abbey church.*

Bishop's Palace *has fine Gothic and Renaissance windows and an upper gallery. It now houses the tourist office, which puts on excellent exhibitions in the summer.*

RUE FÉNELON

R. VICTOR HUGO

PLACE DE LA LIBERTÉ

RUE DE PRÉSIDIAL

RUE DE LA LIBERTÉ

RUE D'ALBUSSE

RUE MONTAIGNE

PL. DU PEYROU

RUE TOURNY

0 metres 50
0 yards 50

N

EXPERIENCE MORE

⑪

Brantôme

🅐 E1 🛈 Église Notre Dame; 05 53 05 80 63

The pretty town of Brantôme sits on an island, encircled by a loop of the river Dronne. Its buildings cluster around the 9th-century Benedictine abbey. The bell tower, dating from the 11th century, is one of the oldest in France. A 16th-century bridge links the abbey to its gardens.

Brantôme makes an excellent base from which to explore other sights in the area. Around 10 km (6 miles) to the southwest stands the 13th-century **Château de Bourdeilles**, with an octagonal keep and fine Renaissance buildings. The nearby **Château de Puyguilhem** is a picture perfect castle with equally impressive interiors. The **Grotte de Villars**, 15 km (9 miles) northeast of Brantôme, is a network of caves with 13 km (8 miles) of galleries, filled with fascinating rock formations and prehistoric paintings.

Château de Bourdeilles

♿ ⓢ 🅲 05 53 03 73 36
🕒 May–Oct: daily

Château de Puyguilhem

♿ ⓢ 🅰 Villars 🅲 05 53 54 82 18 🕒 Apr–Sep: daily; Oct–Mar: Wed–Sun

Grotte de Villars

♿ ⓢ 🕒 Apr–Sep: daily
🅦 grotte-villars.com

---

⑫

Ribérac

🅐 D2 🛈 Place du Général-de-Gaulle; 05 53 90 03 10

Riberac's medieval abbey church, has 17th-century art and a dome above the choir. Dotted around Ribérac are many more Romanesque domed churches, including the fortified church at Sioracde-Ribérac; the church at Grand-Brassac with its splendid carved doorway, and the church at Saint-Privat-des-Prés, with an ornate circular arch.

Some 25 km (15 miles) northwest of Ribérac are the **Tourbières de Vendoire**, peat bogs where visitors can see extraordinary water-filled plant fossils.

Tourbières de Vendoire

♿ 🅲 05 53 90 79 56
🕒 Easter–Jun & Sep: Thu–Sun; Jul & Aug: Wed–Mon

---

⑬

La Double and Le Landais

🅐 D2 🅰 Between Montpon and Ribérac, via the D708

The stunning, wild, marshy countryside here is covered with areas of dense forest,

← The attractive town of Brantôme set on a tranquil stretch of the Dordogne

dotted with ponds and clearings. At the **Ferme du Parcot**, visitors can see local houses made with cob-filled wooden frames. Saint-Aulaye is a village known for its church, Cognac museum (open Jul & Aug) and riverside beach along the Dronne.

Ferme du Parcot

⊗ 🏠 On the Saint-Astier road, Échourgnac 📞 05 53 81 99 28 🕑 May, Jun & Sep: Sat & Sun; Jul & Aug: Tue–Sun

↑ Replica of part of the Lascaux cave at Le Parc du Thot, showing prehistoric animals such as aurochs

⑭ Vallée de l'Homme

🅰 E2 🏠 On the D706, between Montignac and Les Eyzies

This section of the Vézère valley, also known as the Vallée de l'Homme ("Valley of Mankind"), contains a large number of prehistoric sites.

The animal park at **Le Parc du Thot** contains species descended from the wild creatures that inhabited the region in the Upper Palaeolithic period, and whose likenesses can be seen on the walls of the prehistoric caves at Lascaux (*p140*). Among them are reindeer, aurochs (long-horn African cattle) and Przewalski's horses. There are also models of extinct species, such as mammoths and woolly rhinos. The museum features the re-creation of a prehistoric cave, showing methods used for painting and engraving the walls.

HIDDEN GEM
Laugeral

In 1977, a hillside overlooking the Vezere Vézère was chosen by a group of Tibetan Buddhists as the site of a new community. Anyone is welcome to visit, as long as they come in a spirit of peace.

Offering reconstructions of daily life in prehistoric times, as well as workshops, the family-oriented **Préhisto Parc** takes visitors on a journey through time.

The rock-shelter at **Village de La Madeleine** gave its name to the Magdalenian society of hunter-gatherers that lived in the area from around 18,000–10,000 BC. Excavations at this site brought to light a large array of artifacts, including a fragment of engraved mammoth ivory. A child's grave, decorated with shells and red ochre, was also discovered here.

Roque-Saint-Christophe, a sheer rockface above the Vézère, is 80 m (260 ft) high and 1 km (0.6 mile) long. It has been inhabited since prehistoric times. The troglodytic fort and town carved in the rock here dates from the 10th century and could hold over 1,000 people.

A 15th-century carved cross stands at the entrance to the village of **Sergeac**, which was the Knights Templar's main base in the Périgord. Near the commander's residence, a house dating from the 14th–15th centuries, is a fortified church roofed with traditional Périgordian tiles.

Not far from Sergeac is the small valley of Castel-Merle, with rock-shelters that were inhabited from

the Palaeolithic period to the Iron Age. Between Thonac and Sergac is the splendid Château de Blecayre.

The exhibiton at **Grottes du Roc de Cazelle**, one of the many rock-shelters in this area, tells the story of the human habitation of these caves from Upper Palaeolithic times to 1966. The tour includes the reconstruction of scenes from the daily life of the early hunter-gatherers. Other displays show how houses here were cut out of the living rock.

Le Parc du Thot

⊗ ⊗ 🏠 Thonac 📞 05 53 50 70 44 🕑 Feb–Dec: daily

Préhisto Parc

⊗ 🏠 Tursac 📞 05 53 50 73 19 🕑 Apr–mid-Nov: daily

Village de la Madeleine

⊗ 🏠 Tursac 📞 05 53 46 36 88 🕑 Apr–Oct: daily; Nov–Mar: Sat, Sun & hols

Roque-Saint-Christophe

⊗ ⊗ 🏠 Peyzac-Le Moustier 🕑 Daily 🖥 roque-st-christophe.com

Sergeac

🛈 place Bertran-de-Born, Montignac; 05 53 51 82 60

Grottes du Roc de Cazelle

⊗ ⊗ 🏠 Beyond Les Eyzies, on the D47 to Sarlat 📞 05 53 59 46 09 🕑 Daily

15

Saint-Jean-de-Côle

🅰E1 🛈Rue du Château;
05 53 55 12 50

One of France's prettiest villages, Saint-Jean-de-Côle sits on the banks of the river Côle. Its focal point is a late 11th-century priory, torched by the English during the Hundred Years' War and looted by Protestants in 1569, during the Wars of Religion. It was rebuilt in the 17th century. The 12th-century Byzantine-Romanesque church has an unusual plan: it forms a semicircle around the apse. Wooden carvings in the choir date from the 18th century.

The medieval bridge and the rue du Fond-du-Bourg, lined with 14th-century half-timbered houses, add to the village's picturesque appeal. The handsome 12th-century Château de la Marthonie, on place Saint-Jean, was rebuilt in the 15th century and enlarged in the 17th.

The **Château de Jumilhac**, 26 km (16 miles) northeast of Saint-Jean-de-Côle, is a 13th-century castle. A magnificent roof set with pepperpot towers and sky-lights was added in 1600. The out-buildings and ramparts were demolished in the 17th century to make room for luxurious reception areas, including a drawing room

based on that at Versailles and a magnificent Louis-XIII-style staircase.

Château de Jumilhac

⊗⊗ 🚗Jumilhac 📞05 53 52 42 97 🕐Apr, May & Oct-mid-Nov: daily; Jun-Sep: daily; mid-Nov-Mar: Sat & Sun

16

Vézère Valley

🅰E/F2 🚊🚌 🛈19 avenue de la Préhistoire, Les Eyzies; 05 53 06 97 05

The Vézère valley is dotted with small, picturesque towns. Condat-sur-Vézère, once a Templar town, stands at the confluence of the Vézère and the Coly. It has a Romanesque church and a castle with a square tower. The town of Fanlac, clustered round its church and bell tower, was the setting for *Jacquou le Croquant*, the 2007 film of the novel by Eugène Le Roy. The backdrop to the story was the Forêt Barade and **Château de l'Herm**, nearby. Set in woodland, these atmospheric ruins include a polygonal tower with a Gothic doorway that leads to a spiral staircase.

↑ A picturesque back street in the village of Saint-Jean-de-Côle

The town of Rouffignac was almost totally destroyed during World War II, although the church was thankfully spared. Nearby is the **Grotte de Rouffignac**, inhabited around 10,000 BC and open to visitors since the 16th century. A little train takes visitors down 8 km (5 miles) of tunnels, which are covered with paintings and engravings, including 158 depictions of mammoths.

At Plazac, the 800-year-old keep was converted into a Romanesque church with a square belfry and an adjoining cemetery. The village of Saint-Geniès is filled with attractive ochre sandstone houses. The village also has a medieval church and a 17th-century château. The Gothic chapel at Le Cheylard, just outside the village, is decorated with biblical scenes completed during the Middle Ages. The château at Salignac, once a walled fortress, is now an elegant residence with a tiled roof. The 400-year-old Manoir de Lacypierre at Saint-Crépin is definitely worth a detour.

Crossing the Beune, the road leads from Tamniès to Marquay, a village with a fortified Romanesque church. Further on is the **Château de Commarque**, in a valley that has been settled since prehistoric times. The castle, partly in ruins, has a 4th-century church. The walk to the keep offers a fine view of the Château de Laussel. *Bories*, Périgordian dry-stone circular huts, can be seen around Sireuil. A group of these at Bénivès, the **Cabanes du Breuil**, form part of an open-air museum.

The **Château de Puymartin** is almost completely hidden by trees. It was built during the Middle Ages, and rebuilt in the 15th and restored around 1890. It contains period furniture, tapestries, ceiling frescoes and paintings.

Château de l'Herm
⊘ ⊘ 🅐 Via the D31, Rouffignac-St-Cernin-de Reilhac 📞 05 53 05 46 61 🕐 Apr–Sep: daily (by appointment)

Grotte de Rouffignac
⊘ ⊘ 🅐 Via the D82, Le Cluzeau, Villars 📞 05 53 05 41 71 🕐 Apr–mid-Nov: daily

Château de Commarque
⊘ ⊘ 🅐 Via the D48, Sireuil 📞 05 53 59 00 25 🕐 Apr–mid-Nov: daily

Cabanes du Breuil
🅐 Via the D47, Saint-André-d'Allas 📞 06 80 72 38 59 🕐 Apr–mid-Nov: daily; mid-Nov–Mar: by appointment

Château de Puymartin
⊘ ⊘ 🅐 Via the D47, Marquay, midway between Sarlat and Les Eyzies 📞 05 53 59 29 97 🕐 Apr–Sep: daily; Oct–mid-Nov: daily

---

⑰
Terrasson-Lavilledieu
🅰F2 🔲🚍 🛈 Rue Jean-Rouby; 05 53 50 37 56

At the head of the Vézère valley, which leads down into the Périgord, the town of Terrasson-Lavilledieu grew up around a Merovingian abbey. The Pont Vieux, the town's old stone bridge, dates back to the 12th century; it was damaged during the Hundred Years' War and largely rebuilt in the late 15th century, as were the church and the monastery. Terrasson was a strategic town during the Wars of Religion (1562–98) and opposed the French Revolution (1789–99).

The **Jardins de l'Imaginaire**, overlook the old town. These vast gardens include a rose garden, a sacred wood, a water garden, a belvedere and scattered springs, all designed around historical and mythological themes.

Jardins de l'Imaginaire
⊘ ⊘ 🛈 Place de Genouillac; 05 53 50 86 82 🕐 Apr–Jun & Sep: Wed–Sun; Jul & Aug: daily

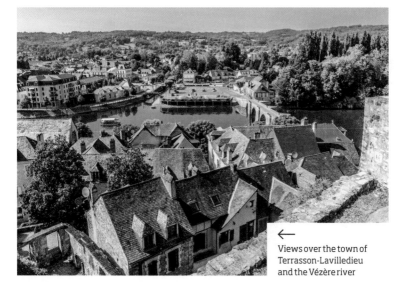

← Views over the town of Terrasson-Lavilledieu and the Vézère river

18 Castelnau-Bretenoux

G2 **On the D43** **05 65 10 98 00** **Daily** **Oct–Mar: Tue**

With a square keep and seigneurial quarters, this château is a resolutely defensive building and one of the area's best examples of military architecture. It was founded in the 12th century by the barons of Castelnau, and clear traces of its military past can still be seen in its elegant outline. Remodelled in the 16th and 17th centuries, then abandoned in the 18th and sacked in the French Revolution, the castle was restored in the late 19th century with funds provided by Jean Mouliérat, the famous tenor, who sang at Paris's Opéra Comique. He built up a fine collection of paintings and furniture, which are now on display in the château's rooms. There are some wonderful views from the château's ramparts; the distant towers of Turenne (p142) are visible on a clear day.

19 Grottes de Lascaux

F2 **Avenue de Lascaux, Montignac** **lascaux.fr**

The cave that became known as the "Sistine Chapel of prehistory" was discovered on 12 September 1940 by a young man out walking his dog. Its paintings, which date from around 18,000 BC, provide a glimpse of that remote age. It is now known that the cave was never inhabited, and the precise meaning of the images on its walls remains unclear. The prehistoric artists who created them used the relief of the cave walls to help breathe a sense of life into their depictions of bulls, deer, horses and ibexes that cover every surface from floor to ceiling.

The cave rapidly became a major attraction, but was closed in 1963 to prevent the deterioration of the paintings.

Lascaux II, a remarkable feat of scientific accuracy and artistic skill, opened in 1983. Executed by an artist using the same techniques and materials as her distant ancestors, the paintings are an accurate reconstruction of the originals, around 70 per cent of which have been replicated on the walls of two main cavities – the Diverticule Axial (Central Passage) and the Salle des Taureaux (Hall of Bulls).

Lascaux IV is part of the Centre International de l'Art Pariétal Montignac-Lascaux, designed by Duncan Lewis Architects in partnership with Snohetta and SRA Architectes. Visitors walk along a landscaped path to a tunnel that leads into the replica of the original cave and paintings. Inside the main building, the Cave Art Theatre tracks the history of the work and shows videos of painted caves around the world.

Montignac itself is also worth a visit. A bustling town, it contains a number of fine 14th–16th-century houses.

Lascaux II and Lascaux IV
Times vary, check website **Jan–early Feb**

20 Le Bugue

E2 **22 place de l'Hôtel de Ville; 05 53 07 20 48**

An important tourist centre, this sizeable town offers a

Lascaux IV and a detail of one of the replica paintings (inset)

→ The beautifully simple interior of Saint-Amand-de-Coly's abbey church

variety of attractions, from the **Aquarium du Périgord Noir** to the **Parc le Bournat**, where scenes of rural life in the Périgord region in times gone by are recreated in a large open-air museum.

This is also the gateway to several more prehistoric cave systems. The **Grotte de Bara-Bahau** cave has a large gallery of unusual rock formations. This leads to a cavity with engravings of bears, horses and bison, as well as hands, a phallus and other symbols. The cathedral-like domed interior of the **Gouffre de Proumeyssac** cave contains mineral formations in a huge variety of shapes. There is also a fascinating display on geological formations. By prior arrangement, visitors can descend into the chasm in a cradle suspended on cables, as the first people to explore this cave would have done.

Elsewhere in the local area, at the confluence of the Vézère and the Dordogne, is the village of Limeuil. It has a pleasant riverside beach and many craftsmen's workshops. Narrow streets lead up to the grounds of the château and a botanical garden. Thomas à Becket once visited the Chapelle Saint-Martin here.

At Le Buisson de Cadouin, 110 km (76 miles) south of Le Bugue, are the **Grottes de Maxange**, a cave system with some extraordinary rock formations.

Aquarium du Périgord Noir

🏛 99 allée Paul-Jean Souriau 🕐 Times vary, check website 🌐 laquarium perigordnoir.com

Parc Le Bournat

🏛 191 allée Paul-Jean Souriau 🕐 Apr–Sep: daily 🌐 parclebournat.fr

Grotte de Bara-Bahau

🏛 Le Bugue 🕐 Apr–early Nov: Tue–Sun; Jul & Aug: daily 🌐 bara-bahau.fr

Gouffre de Proumeyssac

🏛 4 km (2.5 miles) from Le Bugue 🕐 Times vary, check website 🕐 Jan 🌐 gouffre-proumeyssac.com

Grottes de Maxange

🏛 Le Buisson de Cadouin 🕐 Easter–early Nov 🌐 lesgrottesdemaxange.com

21

Saint-Amand-de-Coly

📍 F2 🚗 Off the D704 or D62 ℹ Maison du Patrimoine (summer); 05 53 51 82 60

Originally part of a Romanesque abbey founded in the 7th century, the massive, fortified church here, with a nave 48 m (158 ft) long, still has defensive elements. Built on the plan of a Latin cross, it is enclosed by 300 m (985 ft) of walls. Its 30-m- (98-ft-) high belfry-keep is crowned by a garrison. The nave is lit by a stained-glass window set above the three-arched doorway. The floor of the beautifully empty interior slopes gently down towards the choir.

Concerts of classical music, forming part of the Festival du Périgord Noir, are held here and in the churches of Saint-Léon-sur-Vézère and Auriac. These beautiful Romanesque churches provide both a magical setting and fine acoustics.

💬 INSIDER TIP
Vézère Fishing

There is excellent fishing to be had on the Vézère river. Salmon, sea trout, shad, lamprey and pike and other fish are plentiful. You can pick up a "fishing card" at the tourist office in Le Bugue or Les Eyzies.

GREAT VIEW
Chemin de Fer Touristique du Haut Quercy

Steam and diesel trains chug along a scenic stretch of old railway track from Martel to Saint Denis (www.train duhautquercy.info).

see the remains of the old ramparts, the medieval century Palais de la Raymondie and the 18th-century covered market. Vendors set up here twice a week, and a truffle market is also held in winter.

Some 7 km (4 miles) south of Martel on the N140 is the pre-Romanesque church at Creysse. It is unusual in having two identical apses against the straight wall of its east end. The nave follows the rocky spur's convex shape. The church's interior is not open to the public.

From 1681 to 1695, the controversial archbishop François Fénelon was prior of the fortified monastery at Carennac, 16 km (10 miles) southeast of Martel via the D803, then the D43. All that remains of the monastery are the dean's residence, now a local tourist office, the church, with an arresting depiction of the Last Judgment in the tympanum, and the cloister and chapter room. The village, opposite the Île de la Calypso, an island in the river, is dotted with interesting old houses.

With its lofty setting, the village of Loubressac, 20 km (12 miles) southeast of Martel, offers a wide view of the Cère, Bave and Dordogne valleys. From here the Château de Castelnau, Saint-Céré and the towers of Saint-Laurent can be seen. Inside the ramparts,

↑ The dramatic entrance to the Gouffre de Padirac, a series of underground caverns and lakes

22

Gouffre de Padirac

🅰 G3 🚗🅰 Le Gouffre, Padirac ⏰ Times vary, check website 🌐 gouffre-de-padirac.com

Viewed from above, the huge opening in the earth that forms the entrance to this series of underground caverns seems almost to be attempting to swallow up the sky. Discovered in 1889, the tunnels inside this geological curiosity were formed at least 1 million years ago, although the gaping hole in the ground that has made them accessible was probably created just 10,000 years ago. Reaching down to about 100 m (230 ft), the caves have a steady temperature of around 13 °C (55 °F). Tours consists of a short walk and a boat ride.

Some 10 m (33 ft) beneath the ground, under the 94 m (300 ft) Great Dome is a spectacular group of giant stalagmites. Beyond this lies a lake, fed solely by water filtering through the rock, that sits "suspended" some 27 m (89 ft) above the level of an underground river.

23

Martel

🅰 F2 🚉 Saint-Denis-lès-Martel 🅸 Palais de la Raymondie, place des Consuls; www.vallee-dordogne.com

Once the seat of the Vicomte de Turenne, Martel has seven towers, including the bell tower of its fortified Gothic church, which is pierced with arrow slits. Visitors can also

→ The impressive abbey church of Souillac

narrow streets wind between the ochre-coloured houses.

Autoire, a village 30 km (19 miles) southeast of Martel, is best approached from the crest of the limestone plateau above a waterfall that crashes down for a sheer 40 m (130 ft). Flanked by majestic cliffs, here the rustic architecture of Quercy rubs shoulders with grand manor houses.

24

Souillac

A F2 **R i** Boulevard Louis-Jean-Malvy; www.vallee-dordogne.com

The town of Souillac lies between the Dordogne and the Borrèze. It grew up around a Benedictine monastery that was founded around 655 and became an abbey in the 16th century. Souillac later became a centre of trade, with goods arriving by barge until the arrival of the railway.

The **Abbaye Sainte-Marie**, the town's abbey church, was erected in the Middle Ages. It is built in a splendidly pure Byzantine-Romanesque style inspired by the church of Haghia Sophia in Istanbul. Two notable features of the church are the doorway, which was reversed in the 17th century so as to face inwards, and the medieval carvings.

The tourist office occupies a deconsecrated church, the Église Saint-Martin, which has a damaged belfry and Gothic vaulting. Art exhibitions are also held here. Parts of the town worth exploring include rue des Oules, rue des Craquelin and place Roucou.

With 3,000 exhibits, the **Musée de l'Automate** (Automaton Museum) in the abbey gardens, is the largest in Europe. The 19th- and 20th-century collections come mostly from the Roullet-Decamps workshops, which began making automata in 1865. The exhibits, including a woman powdering her face, a jazz band and a snake charmer, are very expressive, their movements controlled by finely tuned mechanisms.

Nearby are the **Grottes de Lacave**, caves that were discovered in 1902. Riding on a small train, then taking a lift, visitors travel along 1.5 km (1 mile) of galleries and through a dozen caverns. The sheer variety of weird shapes formed by its stalactites and stalagmites, including some that suggest fantastic animals, makes this the most impressive of all such caves in France.

↑ Autoire's waterfall near Martel cascading down the limestone cliffs

Abbaye Sainte-Marie

A Place de l'Abbaye **C** 05 65 32 71 00 **⊙** 8am–7pm daily

Musée de l'Automate

⊘ ⊛ **A** Place de l'Abbaye **⊙** Apr–Oct: Tue–Sun (Jul & Aug: daily) **w** musee-automate.fr

Grottes de Lacave

⊘ ⊛ **A** 10 km (5 miles) southeast of Souillac **⊙** Early Feb–Dec: daily **w** vert-marine.com/grottes-de-lacave-46

㉕ Saint-Céré

🅰 G3 🛈 13 avenue François de Maynard; www.vallee-dordogne.com

Saint-Céré grew thanks to the traffic of pilgrims visiting the tomb of St Spérie, which stands here. In the Middle Ages, craftsmen settled and markets were established. The town suffered as a result of epidemics and wars, but it regained some of its splendour in the 17th century.

Remains of past prosperity can be seen in many beautiful historic buildings, carefully preserved to give an old world charm to the town, as in many places throughout Dordogne. Place du Mercadial, on rue du Mazel, with the Renaissance-era Hôtel d'Auzier and Maison Queyssac, and in impasse Lagarouste, with its half-timbered corbelled houses. Hôtel d'Ambert, in rue Saint-Cyr, has turrets and a Renaissance doorway. Rue Paramelle leads to Maison Longueval and Hôtel de Puymule, in the Flamboyant Gothic style. The church contains an 18th-century marble altarpiece and has a Carolingian crypt. On a hill above the town are the Tours de Saint-Laurent, a keep dating back to the Middle Ages – and now all that remains of the castle. In 1945, they were acquired by Jean Lurçat (1882–1966), the painter and tapestry maker, and are now a museum-workshop, the **Atelier-Musée Jean-Lurçat**.

The **Château de Montal**, 3 km (2 miles) from Saint-

↑ Traditional half-timbered houses bordering place du Mercadial, one of the main squares in Saint-Céré

Céré, was stripped of its finest architectural elements in the 19th century. However, thanks to the work of entrepreneur and arts patron Maurice Fenaille (1855–1937), the castle's original tapestries and furniture have been restored to their original setting. The medieval circular towers frame a beautiful Renaissance courtyard with a double staircase. A 17th-century Aubusson tapestry hangs in the guardroom. The upper floor rooms have ceilings with exposed beams.

Atelier-Musée Jean-Lurçat

⊛ 🕑 Apr–Sep: Tue–Sun 🖳 musees.lot.fr

Château de Montal

⊛⊛ 🕖 Saint-Jean-Lespinasse 🕑 Apr–Sep: daily; Oct–Mar: Wed–Sun 🖳 chateau-montal.fr

---

㉖ Assier

🅰 G3 🛈 Hôtel de La Monnaie, place Vival, Figeac; www.tourisme-figeac.com

This small town is best known for the remains of the **Château d'Assier**, which show that this was a Renaissance palace on a par with the finest châteaux of the Loire. It was built by Jacques Galiot de Genouillac (1465–1546), an

artillery commander under Louis XII and François I. Of the building completed in 1535, only the entrance wing, with a spectacular portico doorway, survives. The decoration consisted of mythological and classical scenes, Renaissance figures and military emblems. The carved staircase is the finest feature of the interior.

Assier's church is unique in France for its dome over the burial chapel, which has triple groined vaulting that forms an elaborate star pattern.

Near the village are two dolmens known as the Table de Roux and Bois des Bœufs. There are 11 of these burial chambers, dating from around 1,500 BC, in the vicinity.

Château d'Assier

⊛⊛ 🕿 05 65 40 40 99 🕑 May–Aug: Wed–Sun; Sep–Apr: by appointment 🕑 Public hols

---

㉗ Belvès

🅰 E3 🕑🛈 1 rue des Filhols; www.perigordnoir-valleedordogne.com

Set on a hilltop, this village was a fort in the 11th century. Its medieval heart centres on the castle and place d'Armes, where there is a 500-year-old covered market. Nearby is the 13th-century Hôtel Bontemps,

Did You Know?

From late July to early August, the Festival Lyrique in Saint-Céré holds free opera performances.

with a Renaissance façade. The town has seven towers, some of them bell towers. These include one from the late-Middle Ages, the 11th-century keep (known as Tour de l'Auditeur) and the Tour des Frères. Église Notre-Dame, with its Flamboyant Gothic doorway, is all that remains of Belvès's abbey. The troglodytic dwellings cut into the village's medieval fortifications were in use from the 13th century right up to the era of the *Ancien Régime*.

To the northwest, on the edge of Forêt de la Bessède, lies the attractive village of Urval. It has a 13th-century communal oven, a rare vestige of medieval village life. Close by is a fortified Romanesque church from the Middle Ages.

28

Saint-Cirq-Lapopie

Ⓐ F4 ℹ️ **Place du Sombral; 05 65 31 31 31**

Its exceptionally picturesque location and ensemble of attractive buildings make Saint-Cirq-Lapopie one of

Saint-Cirq-Lapopie stunningly perched above the Lot river ↓

the jewels of the Lot valley. Rising in tiers up the limestone cliff-face, it sits some 100 m (300 ft) above the river. Along its narrow streets are small courtyards and attractive stone and wooden houses. In the lower village, a 13th-century gate, Porte de la Pélissaria (or Porte de Rocamadour), opens onto Grand'Rue, where the medieval village begins.

Places of note include place du Carol, with a belvedere-dovecote, where the painter Henri Martin (1860–1943) lived; the 13th-century Maison Vinot; the 14th-century Maison Médiévale Daura; Maison Breton, once owned by the Surrealist writer André Breton (1896–1966); Maison Bessac, with double corbelling; place du Sombral with the 15th-century Maison Larroque and Maison Rignault, which houses the Musée Rignault; and Maison de la Fourdonne, which contains the Mairie. Near the ruined castle, stands a late 16th-century fortified church.

The economy of the village, which had 1,500 inhabitants during the Middle Ages, was based on manufacturing, with craftsmen's workshops under the arcades along rue de la Pélissaria and Peyrolerie. Today, the work of *robinetaïres*,

specialist wood-turners who make taps for the Cahors wine barrels, is a craft peculiar to Saint-Cirq-Lapopie.

From Bouziès, 5 km (3 miles) from Saint-Cirq, visitors can take a boat ride on the Lot with **Les Croisières de Saint-Cirq-Lapopie**.

Cajarc, 20 km (12 miles) east of Saint-Cirq-Lapopie, is a fine medieval village clustered around Maison de l'Hébrardie, a 13th-century former castle.

Les Croisières de Saint-Cirq-Lapopie

🆆 croisieres-saint-cirq-lapopie.com

↑ Picture-perfect Beynac, magnificently set atop a rocky bluff overlooking the Dordogne river

29 Beynac

⒜F3 ⒤La Balme; www.sarlat-tourisme.com

The village of Beynac, which clings dramatically to a steep cliff-face, has attracted a clutch of artists and writers, including Camille Pissarro (1830–1903), Henry Miller (1891–1980) and the poet Paul Éluard (1895–1952), who spent the last years of his life here. The village is still filled with the artists' studios. The narrow street from the lower village up to the castle passes several ancient houses and offers expansive views.

Perched on a rock 150 m (490 ft) above the river, the **Château de Beynac** is visible from afar. The seat of one of the Périgord's four baronies, it occupies a strategic position, like its rival, Castelnaud. The castle repeatedly came under attack during the Hundred Years' War and again during the Wars of Religion. Restoration began in 1961.

Entry to the castle is via a double moat and through lines of ramparts. The 13th-century keep is flanked by the main building, dating from the same period but remodelled in the 16th

century, and another building dating from the 14th and 17th centuries. The great hall, with vaulted ceiling, has a Renaissance chimneypiece. The castle was bought in 1962 by Lucien Grosso, who painstakingly restored the building to evoke life as it was lived here in the past. The exquisite 12th-century chapel, now a parish church, is roofed with

---

△ GREAT VIEW
Cazenac

Adjoining Beynac is the delightful hamlet of Cazenac. A walk along the road, running down to the left of it, offers a stunning panorama of the valley below, with the Château de Beynac in the distance.

---

traditional Perigordian tiles. The **Parc Archéologique** at the foot of the castle features the reconstruction of a Bronze Age settlement, creating a vivid impression of the food, clothing, houses and farms of that time. There are also workshops giving visitors an insight into life in the Neolithic period and the Iron Age.

Château de Beynac

⊛ ⊛ ☎ 05 53 29 50 40
◷ Feb–Dec: daily

Parc Archéologique

⊛ ⊛ ☎ 05 53 29 51 28
◷ Jul–mid-Sep: Mon–Fri

---

30 Gourdon

⒜F3 ⒝⒤20 boulevard des Martyrs; www.tourisme-gourdon.com

The attractive town of Gourdon, which comes to life on market days (Thursday and Saturday), is the capital of the unspoilt and rural region of Bouriane. In the 16th century it grew rich from its weaving industry. The medieval heart of the town has a 13th-century fortified gate and some fine houses, including the Maison du Sénéchal, Maison Cavaignac and Maison d'Anglars. Two particularly picturesque streets are rue du Majou,

→ Beautiful old village square in the *bastide* town of Monpazier

which was filled with drapers' shops in the Middle Ages, and rue Zig-Zag. The Église Saint-Pierre, a Gothic church with asymmetrical towers, has some splendid 16th-century stained-glass windows and Baroque wood-carvings. The town is dotted with other religious buildings. Among them are the Église des Cordeliers, built in the 13th century and altered in the 19th, Chapelle Notre-Dame-des-Neiges, Église Saint Siméon and Chapelle du Majou. The medieval castle was destroyed in the 18th century, but the esplanade that fronted it remains and offers good views of the Bouriane river.

The **Grottes de Cougnac** at Payrignac, 3 km (2 miles) from Gourdon on the D17, are full of stalactites and stalagmites, and other interesting rock formations, which look magical when lit up. The Cro-Magnon people who used the cave 25,000 to 14,000 years ago decorated some walls with paintings of moufflon (wild sheep), human figures and symbols.

Grottes de Cougnac
♦ ♦ 🅞 Early Apr–Sep: daily; Oct–Nov: Mon–Sat
🅦 grottesdecougnac.com

🔟 **31**

Monpazier

🄰E3 🛈 Place des Cornières; www.monpazier.fr

Set on a hill overlooking the river Dropt, Monpazier is a classic *bastide* town. With a grid of streets and alleyways within its ramparts, it is also one of the most attractive in southwest France. Founded in 1284 by Edward I, king of England, Monpazier has remained almost unchanged for 800 years, although only three of its original six fortified gates still stand. It has been used as a medieval location for several films. Its picturesque central square, the place des Cornières, is lined with arcades that are filled with shops. The square also has a 16th-century covered market, which still contains some antique grain measures. On Thursday mornings the square hosts a market, and in December truffles are sold here. Monpazier is the birthplace of the writer and explorer Jean Galmot (1879–1928).

Around 19 km (12 miles) southeast of Monpazier lies Villefranche-du-Périgord, another *bastide* town, established in 1261 at the meeting point of Périgord, Quercy and Agenais. From May to October, it hosts a famous *cèpes* (boletus) market. This takes place on the town square in the covered market area, which still has antique grain measures. Attractive arcaded houses stand opposite this market. The oak forests nearby are a pleasant place to take a walk.

A further 8 km (5 miles) along the D57 lies Besse, a village with some handsome ochre-coloured houses and a splendid fortified church. The single-walled bell tower has an 11th-century doorway, with three archivolts that are covered with carvings of mythological animals.

32

Biron

⚠ E3 **ⓘ Place des Cornières, Montpazier; 05 53 22 68 59**

Once the seat of one of Périgord's four baronies, the massive **Château de Biron** dominates the surrounding countryside and straddles the border between the Périgord and the Agenais. With a 12th-century keep, Renaissance living quarters, a Gothic chapel and a small 14th-century manor house, decorated with 16th-century frescoes, it embodies a stunning medley of architectural styles spanning the 12th to the 18th centuries.

Having given asylum to Cathars in 1211, the castle was besieged by Simon de Montfort, and it changed allegiance countless times during the Hundred Years' War, suffering attack and damage as a result. It was largely rebuilt during the Renaissance and now towers over the attractive village of Biron, which has some fine houses around its covered market.

Château de Biron

🔄 🚭 **⬛ Le Bourg, Vergt-de-Biron** **⬛ Times vary, check website** **ⓦ chateau-biron.fr**

33

Beaumont-du-Périgord

⚠ E3 **ⓘ 16 place Jean Moulin; 05 53 22 39 12**

Since its foundation in 1272, Beaumont, a *bastide* town built by the English, has undergone much alteration. Of the 16 gates that once formed part of its fortifications, only one, the Porte de Luzier, remains, forming the present entrance into the town. The central square was remodelled in the 18th century and the covered market no longer exists. There are some fine medieval houses, particularly in rue Romieu and rue Vidal. The town's architectural jewel is its impressive fortified church, the Église Saint-Laurent-et-Saint-Front. One of the finest in southwest France, this huge, austere church is in a military Gothic style, with four belfry-like towers, linked by a wall-walk. The church was built from 1280 to 1330 and formed part of the town's defences. The doorway is decorated by a frieze filled with grimacing figures. The medieval

📷 PICTURE PERFECT
Château de Bannes

Near Beaumont-du-Perigord stands the turreted Château de Bannes sitting atop a grassy outcrop. Although it's closed to the public, it makes for a striking photograph.

village of Saint-Avit-Sénieur, 5 km (3 miles) east of the town of Beaumont, is visible from afar thanks to its church. This Romanesque structure was fortified in the 14th century, and a wall-walk connects its two towers.

Some 10 km (6 miles) east of Beaumont lies the village of Montferrand-du-Périgord. It has a splendid 16th-century covered market and the ruins of a castle with a 12th-century keep. A short walk up the hill from the village is the little church of St-Christophe, set on its own and surrounded by a cemetery. The interior contains surprisingly well-preserved medieval frescoes.

The **Château de Lanquais**, 13 km (8 miles) northwest of Beaumont, has a 15th-century circular tower and polygonal staircase tower, as well as residential quarters dating from the 16th and 17th centuries. It is also a *chambres d'hôte*, with elegant rooms.

Château de Lanquais

🚫🚫 🕐 Apr–Jun & Sep: Wed-Mon; Jul & Aug: daily
ⓦ chateaudelanquais.fr

34

Saint-Michel-de-Montaigne

🅰 D2 🅘 Place Clemenceau, Montpon-Ménestérol; 05 53 82 23 77

This village is best known for its associations with Michel de Montaigne, the Renaissance philosopher and writer. Of the impressive château where Montaigne lived, only the 16th-century **tower**, where he had his library and where he wrote his famous *Essais*, is original, while the rest has been rebuilt. The beams of his study, on the top floor, are inscribed with 57 Greek and Latin sentences and maxims, that represent the Epicurean, Stoic and sceptic ideas that influenced Montaigne. The views from the terrace stretch out over the Lidoire valley.

The town's Romanesque church has a doorway with columns and four intricately moulded arches. The interior features carved 17th-century furniture and the Stations of the Cross by the artist Gilbert Privat (1892–1969).

About 5 km (3 miles) from Saint-Michel-de-Montaigne on the D936 is the village of Montcaret. The Romanesque church here has capitals that may have been taken from an earlier Gallo-Roman building. Nearby are the remains of a large Gallo-Roman villa, discovered in 1827. It has fine mosaic flooring, an inner

←

The fine Gothic-Renaissance chapel in the grassy courtyard of the Château de Biron

↑ The Gothic cloisters of Abbaye de Cadouin at Le Buisson-de-Cadouin

courtyard lined with columns, a 60-sq-m (645-sq-ft) main room with a pool with mosaics of aquatic subjects and baths with a sophisticated heating system. The quality of workmanship suggests that this was a place of luxury. Archaeological evidence suggests that the site has been inhabited since antiquity.

Tower

🚫🚫 🕐 Feb–Jun & Sep–Dec: Wed-Sun; Jul & Aug: daily
ⓦ chateau-montaigne.com

35

Eymet

🅰 D3 🅘 45 place Gambetta; 05 53 23 74 95

This *bastide* town, built in the Dropt valley in 1270, retains its original square layout. Gargoyles look down from the keep, and the medieval houses have turrets with mullioned windows. A 17th-century fountain sits in the main square.

Some 20 km (12 miles) northeast of Eymet is the picture-perfect village of Issigeac, which dates back to Roman times. It has a spiral layout and has 13th-century ramparts. It is best known for its wonderful Sunday morning food market. The Gothic church, with a bell tower over its entrance, stands on the site of a priory. The former bishop's palace, its two pavilions set with turrets, is now the tourist office, and the former tithe barn houses

a shop. The main street is lined with fine houses, one of which has 14th-century carved beams.

36

Le Buisson-de-Cadouin

🅰 E3 🚉🅘 Place André Boissière, Le Buisson; 05 53 22 06 09

The village grew up round the 12th-century Cistercian **Abbaye de Cadouin** (a World Heritage Site), on the pilgrim route to Compostela. Until 1932, what was believed to be the Holy Shroud was kept here, and the village grew wealthy from the pilgrims who flocked to this sacred relic. Behind the abbey's imposing buttressed façade is the cloister, built in the 15th and 16th centuries in a mixture of Flamboyant Gothic and Renaissance styles. The carved finials and images, of both biblical and secular subjects, are a masterpiece of stone carving.

From the belvedere, at Trémolat, 13 km (8 miles) northwest of Le Buisson-de-Cadouin, there are stunning views of the Cingle de Trémolat (the great loop in the Dordogne) and of the fertile plain. The fortified church, with its keeplike bell tower, is arrestingly austere.

Abbaye de Cadouin

🚫🚫 🕐 Place de l'Abbaye
📞 05 53 63 36 28 🕐 Mid-Feb-Dec: Tue-Sun (Apr-Oct: daily)

37

Cahors

🅐 F4 **ℹ️** Place François-
Mitterrand; www.
tourisme-cahors.fr

Evidence of Cahors' ancient
past can be seen in the ruins
of the Gallo-Roman baths,
now known as the Arc de
Diane, which date back to
the 1st century BC. In the
13th century, trade brought
prosperity, leading to the
creation of the town's elegant
mercantile sector (now rue
du Château-du-Roi). The
fortifications date from the
14th century and include
the ramparts, set with 11
towers and two gatehouses.
In the 19th century, Cahors
began to spread out from this
medieval core. This was when
boulevard Gambetta, with
the town hall, theatre and
law courts, was built, and the
quayside, walks and gardens
were laid out.

Cahors' Vieille Ville (Old
Town) is characterized by
decorated courtyards, half-
timbered houses with brick
overhangs and houses with
carved façades. Typical of
the Renaissance is a form
of decoration consisting of
branches, roses and suns;
particularly fine examples
can be seen on the doors and
chimney-pieces. Later, in the
16th century, many windows
were decorated in the Italian
style, and in the 17th century
many townhouses with ornate
doorways were built.The most
picturesque areas of the
Vieille Ville are rue du Dr-
Bergounioux, rue de Lastié,
rue Saint-Urcisse, place Saint-
James, rue de la Chantrerie,
the Daurade quarter and the
cathedral quarter.

Cahors' most iconic sight,
the Port Valentré, was built
in the 14th century and never
attacked. This impressive
fortified bridge has six Gothic
spans with chamfered piers.
It was restored in 1879 by
French architect Paul Gout
and is the best preserved
medieval bridge in Europe.
Cahors' other main sight
is its cathedral, **Cathédrale
Saint-Étienne**. A stopping-
place on the pilgrim route
to Compostela (p226), the
building underwent several
phases of construction from
the 11th to the 17th centuries,
and was restored in the 19th
century. The result is a

> **Did You Know?**
> ──
> Almost all of Lot's
> harvest of black
> truffles comes from the
> countryside around
> Lalbenque.

A DEVILISH TALE

Pont Valentré took almost 50 years to build. According to
a legend that grew up around it, the architect asked the
Devil to help him complete this feat of civil engineering,
in return for his soul. To escape the agreement, he tried to
dupe the Devil, who took his revenge: each night the last
stone to be laid in the central tower would mysteriously
fall, to be replaced the next day. In 1879, while restoring
the bridge,the architect immortalized this tale by
setting a carving of the Devil on the central tower.

beautiful, harmonious mix of styles, ranging from a Romanesque doorway, to a Flamboyant Gothic cloister.

The old **La Chantrerie** building was once a wash-house, but now houses a museum about local produce, including truffles and wine.

Cahors makes a great base from which to explore other towns in the surrounding countryside. The village of Lalbenque, 17 km (11 miles) southeast of Cahors, is renowned for its truffle market, which takes place on Tuesday from December to mid-March, and for its festivities celebrating this "black diamond". Some 32 km (20 miles) to the southwest of Cahors is Montcuq. The pretty streets here are lined with timbered houses and its 17th-century tower is the last surviving remnant of the ancient Cathar stronghold.

Cathédrale Saint-Étienne

🏠 17 place Jean Jacques Chapou 🕐 Daily

←

The graceful medieval Pont Valentré bridge, which has become a symbol of Cahors

La Chantrerie

🏠 35 rue de la Chantrerie
📞 05 65 35 74 55 🕐 Wed & Sat-Sun

38 Ⓜ

Abbaye de Chancelade

🅰 E2 🏠 Place de l'Abbaye, Chancelade 🕐 Daily (access to the exterior only)
🌐 abbaye-chancelade.com

Set in the Beauronne valley, the Augustinian Abbaye de Chancelade was founded in the 12th century and became an important centre of intellectual life. Having survived the Hundred Years' War and the Wars of Religion, it once again became influential in the 17th century. It is well preserved, with a washhouse, stables, workshops and a mill.

39

Auvézère Valley

🅰 E/F1, E/F2 ℹ Place du Marquis, Hautefort; www.vezere-perigord.fr

Throughout this valley there are several interesting sights. The Chapelle d'Auberoche

← Carved choir stalls and ancient frescoes inside the Abbaye de Chancelade

---

🗻 GREAT VIEW
Mont St Cyr

Overlooking Cahors is the Mont St Cyr, well worth climbing for spectacular views of the town. Cross Pont Louis-Philippe and climb up behind the statue of the Virgin. It takes about 30 minutes.

---

perches high on a cliff, offering dramatic views. Upriver, the Blâme cascades dramatically into the Auvézère at La Boissière d'Ans. Commanding views of the Loue and Auvézère valleys can also be had from the Colline de Saint-Raphaël. Two massive columns, in front of the church here, are the remains of a Benedictine priory. Génis is also set high up, on a granite plateau, looking down on the gorges of the river Dalon.

Upstream is an old mill, the Moulin du Pervendoux, beyond which are rapids and the Cascade du Saut-Ruban. A path (GR 646) leads down to this waterfall from the Église de Saint-Mesmin.

At Le Puy-des-Âges, set on a quartz-rich spur, is the little chapel of Notre-Dame-de-Partout. The hilltop château close to Savignac-Lédrier looks down on a 17th-century forge, while at Payzac is the former Vaux papermill.

A DRIVING TOUR
VINEYARDS OF CAHORS

Length 70 km (45 miles) **Starting point** Montcabrier
Stopping-off points Parnac, where you can sample local wine at Cave Coopérative du Vignoble de Cahors in summer

The vineyards around Cahors *(p150)* are among the oldest in Europe. Since the Middle Ages, Cahors wine has been noted for its excellent ageing properties, which stem from the high-quality vine-growing soil on the limestone plateau of the Causse. Vineyards stretch out for 60 km (35 miles) on either side of the Lot river, mainly in the valley below the city. While an exploration of the region offers many opportunities for wine tasting, the countryside itself provides a visual feast.

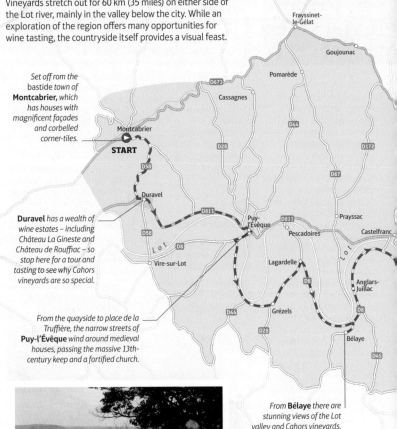

Set off from the bastide town of **Montcabrier,** *which has houses with magnificent façades and corbelled corner-tiles.*

START

Duravel has a wealth of wine estates – including Château La Gineste and Château de Rouffiac – so stop here for a tour and tasting to see why Cahors vineyards are so special.

From the quayside to place de la Truffière, the narrow streets of **Puy-l'Évêque** *wind around medieval houses, passing the massive 13th-century keep and a fortified church.*

From **Bélaye** *there are stunning views of the Lot valley and Cahors vineyards. In the village are the remains of a bishop's castle and a church from the Middle Ages.*

Frayssinet-le-Gélat

Goujounac

Pomarède

Cassagnes

Montcabrier

Duravel

Puy-l'Évêque

Pescadoires

Prayssac

Castelfranc

Vire-sur-Lot

Lagardelle

Anglars-Juillac

Grézels

Bélaye

← Looking out at the Lot valley scenery from the village of Bélaye

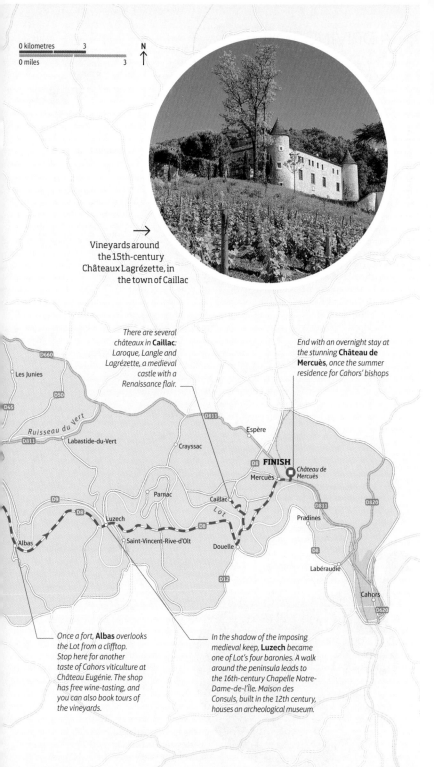

0 kilometres 3
0 miles 3

N

→ Vineyards around the 15th-century Châteaux Lagrézette, in the town of Caillac

There are several châteaux in **Caillac**: *Laroque, Langle and Lagrézette, a medieval castle with a Renaissance flair.*

End with an overnight stay at the stunning **Château de Mercuès**, *once the summer residence for Cahors' bishops*

Les Junies

D660

D50

D45

D811

Ruisseau du Vert

D811

Labastide-du-Vert

Crayssac

D811

Espère

D8 **FINISH**

Mercuès

Château de Mercuès

D9

D8

Parnac

Luzech

Saint-Vincent-Rive-d'Olt

Caillac

Lot

D8

Douelle

D811

D820

Pradines

D8

D12

Labéraudie

Cahors

D620

Albas

Once a fort, **Albas** *overlooks the Lot from a clifftop. Stop here for another taste of Cahors viticulture at Château Eugénie. The shop has free wine-tasting, and you can also book tours of the vineyards.*

In the shadow of the imposing medieval keep, **Luzech** *became one of Lot's four baronies. A walk around the peninsula leads to the 16th-century Chapelle Notre-Dame-de-l'Île. Maison des Consuls, built in the 12th century, houses an archeological museum.*

A DRIVING TOUR
DORDOGNE VALLEY

Length 35 km (20 miles) **Starting point** Cingle de Montfort
Stopping-off points From the esplanade at Domme, the loop in the river at Montfort is a stunning sight

Probably no river in France crosses so varied a landscape and such different geological formations as the Dordogne. Starting in deep granite gorges in the Massif Central, the Dordogne is almost 3 km (2 miles) wide by the time it joins the Garonne. This drive takes in some of the Dordogne's classic countryside scenery, as well as fine châteaux that line this stretch of the river. You can even stop to admire them from the river – either in a rented canoe or on a *gabare* (local rivercraft) tour.

Locator Map

DORDOGNE AND LOT
■ *Dordogne Valley*

Following the Dordogne beyond the pretty village of Envaux, the narrow road sweeps across the plain, bringing the imposing **Château de Beynac** (p146) *into view.*

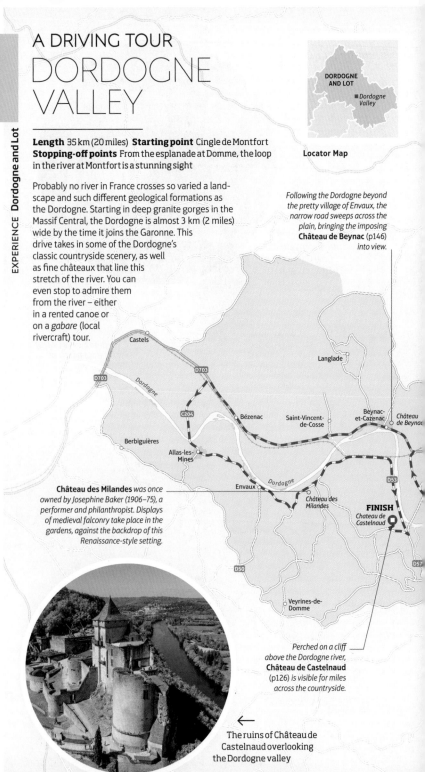

Castels

Langlade

D703

D703

Dordogne

C204

Bézenac

Saint-Vincent-de-Cosse

Beynac-et-Cazenac

Château de Beynac

Berbiguières

Allas-les-Mines

Dordogne

D53

Envaux

Château des Milandes *was once owned by Josephine Baker (1906–75), a performer and philanthropist. Displays of medieval falconry take place in the gardens, against the backdrop of this Renaissance-style setting.*

Château des Milandes

FINISH
Chateau de Castelnaud

D50

D57

Veyrines-de-Domme

Perched on a cliff above the Dordogne river, **Château de Castelnaud** (p126) *is visible for miles across the countryside.*

← The ruins of Château de Castelnaud overlooking the Dordogne valley

← Paddingling along the Cingle de Montfort riverbend towards the cliff-top château in the town of Montfort

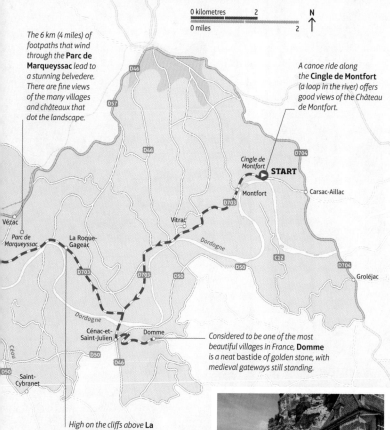

0 kilometres 2
0 miles 2

N ↑

*The 6 km (4 miles) of footpaths that wind through the **Parc de Marqueyssac** lead to a stunning belvedere. There are fine views of the many villages and châteaux that dot the landscape.*

*A canoe ride along the **Cingle de Montfort** (a loop in the river) offers good views of the Château de Montfort.*

Cingle de Montfort
START

Carsac-Aillac

Montfort

Vézac

Parc de Marqueyssac

La Roque-Gageac

Vitrac

Dordogne

Groléjac

Cénac-et-Saint-Julien

Domme

*Considered to be one of the most beautiful villages in France, **Domme** is a neat bastide of golden stone, with medieval gateways still standing.*

Saint-Cybranet

*High on the cliffs above **La Roque-Gageac** stands a troglodytic fort. The steep walk up to it is rewarded by a view of the valley.*

→ Picturesque brick houses in La Roque-Gageac

LOT-ET-GARONNE

Lot-et-Garonne lies between territories once held by the kings of France and the kings of England, and was the object of bitter dispute until it was finally won by France in 1472. In the 13th and 14th centuries, more than 40 *bastide* towns were built here on the orders of various French and English lords. With their central arcaded squares and streets laid out to a grid pattern, such towns were built not only as a response to a rapidly growing population, but also to the conflict between France and England that raged over southwest France until well into the 15th century.

With its fertile, rolling hills and valleys, and pine forests that encroach across from the Landes, the Lot-et-Garonne is a region rich in pleasant, rural countryside. Miles of navigable waterways are provided by the Lot, the Garonne and the Baïse rivers, and the canal that runs alongside the Garonne. Today, as a prime producer of fruit and vegetables, Lot-et-Garonne serves as the orchard of Europe. Its fine wines compare favourably with those of neighbouring Bordeaux and are an important element in the bounty of gastronomic specialities to be enjoyed in this corner of France.

LOT-ET-GARONNE

Must Sees

❶ Château de Bonaguil
❷ Agen

Experience More

❸ Gavaudun
❹ Monsempron
❺ Villeréal
❻ Sauveterre-la-Lémance
❼ Puymirol
❽ Saint-Avit
❾ Penne-d'Agenais
❿ Tournon-d'Agenais
⓫ Pujols
⓬ Laroque-Timbaut
⓭ Villeneuve-sur-Lot
⓮ Prayssas
⓯ Casseneuil
⓰ Sainte-Livrade-sur-Lot
⓱ Monclar-d'Agenais
⓲ Clairac
⓳ Granges-sur-Lot
⓴ Duras
㉑ Castillonnès
㉒ Monflanquin
㉓ Lauzun
㉔ Marmande
㉕ Casteljaloux
㉖ Pays de Serres
㉗ Mézin
㉘ Aiguillon
㉙ Poudenas
㉚ Le Mas-d'Agenais
㉛ Laplume
㉜ Beauville
㉝ Saint-Maurin
㉞ Nérac
㉟ Vianne
㊱ Barbaste
㊲ Moirax
㊳ Aubiac
㊴ Layrac
㊵ Estillac

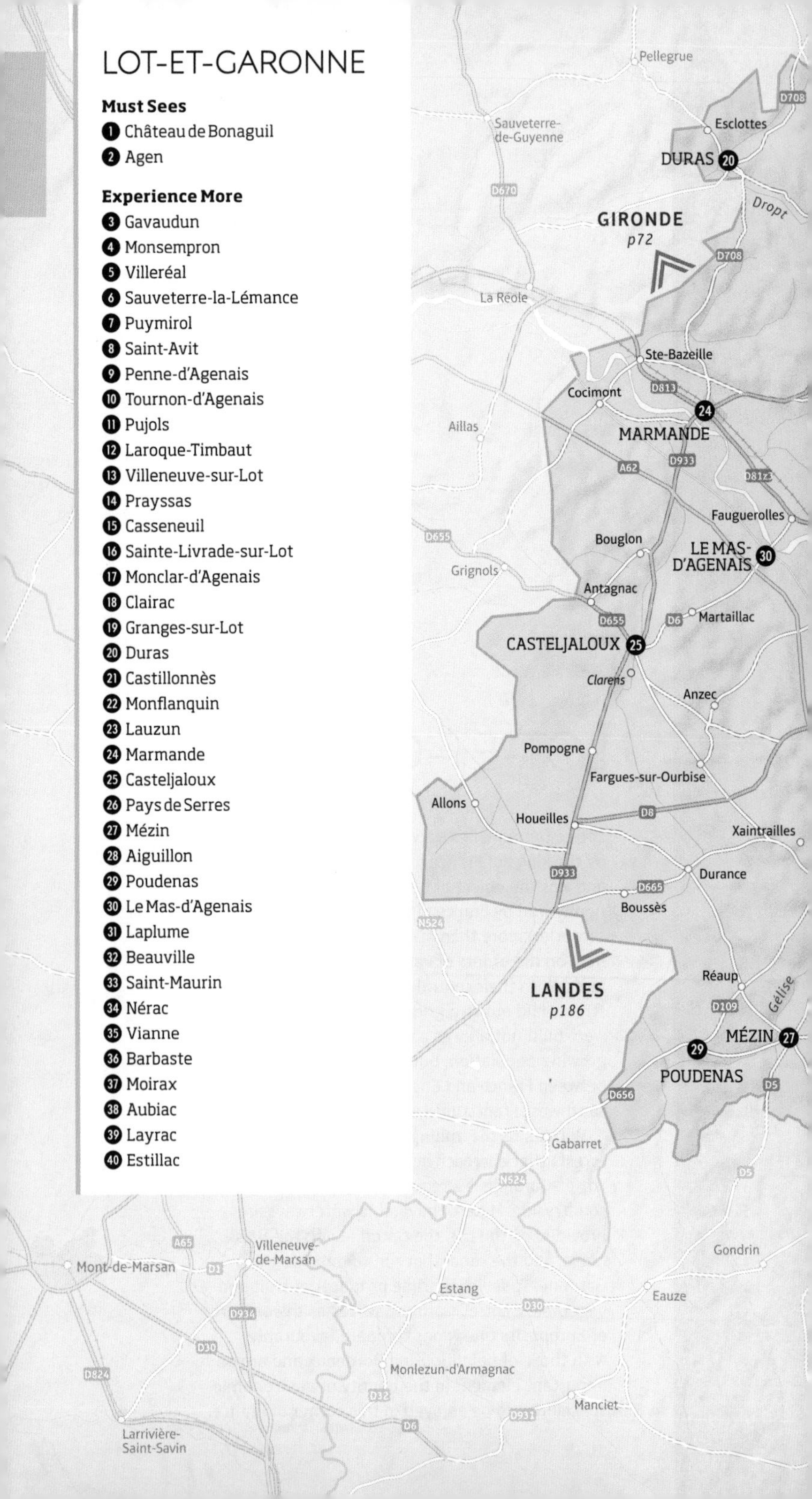

Bouniagues

Beaumont-du-Périgord

Saint-Avit-Sénieur

Belvès

Loubès-Bernac

Bouillac

Issigeac

La Sauvetat-du-Dropt

Fonroque

CASTILLONNÈS

Rives

Drop

Allemans-du-Dropt

Miramont-de-Guyenne

23

LAUZUN

21

Montaut

5

VILLERÉAL

SAUVETERRE-LA-LÉMANCE

6

Seyches

Monbahus

Cancon

Lède

SAINT-AVIT

8

Puymician

Tombeboeuf

MONFLANQUIN

22

Lacaussade

3

GAVAUDUN

CHÂTEAU DE BONAGUIL

1

Fumel

MONSEMPRON

4

Brugnac

MONCLAR-D'AGENAIS

17

CASSENEUIL

15

VILLENEUVE-SUR-LOT

13

Trentels

TOURNON-D'AGENAIS

L O T - E T - G A R O N N E

Tonneins

SAINTE-LIVRADE-SUR-LOT

16

Castelmoron-sur-Lot

Port-de-Penne

10

CLAIRAC

18

19

PUJOLS

11

PENNE-D'AGENAIS

9

Dausse

Pech-de-Berre

GRANGES-SUR-LOT

Temple-sur-Lot

Grotte de Lastournelle

Hautefage-la-Tour

Montaigu-de-Quercy

AIGUILLON

28

14

PRAYSSAS

PAYS DE SERRES

26

12

LAROQUE-TIMBAUT

32

BEAUVILLE

Damazan

Bazens

Port Ste-Marie

Colayrac-St-Cirq

SAINT-MAURIN

VIANNE

35

Sérignac-sur-Garonne

2

AGEN

PUYMIROL

7

33

Lavardac

BARBASTE

36

ESTILLAC

40

MOIRAX

Clermont-Soubiran

NÉRAC

34

AUBIAC

38

37

39

LAYRAC

Valence

Moissac

Baïse

LAPLUME

31

Gers

Caudecoste

Francescas

Astaffort

Estressol

Lannes

Moncrabeau

Condom

Lectoure

Mouchan

Valence-sur-Baïse

LOT-ET-GARONNE

0 kilometres 15

0 miles 15

N

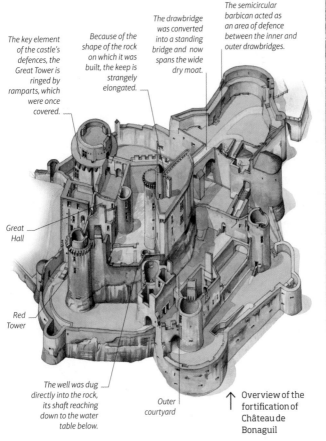

CHÂTEAU DE BONAGUIL

⊞ E3 🏠 Saint-Front-sur-Lémance 🕐 Times vary, check website 🌐 chateau-bonaguil.com

Bonaguil Castle is a monument to the Middle Ages and its defences. Its imposing fortifications were ahead of their time and remain intact on the well-preserved fortress, now renovated as a residence.

The colossal Château de Bonaguil stands majestically on a rocky spur, its ramparts and turrets fleetingly visible from behind lush greenery. Founded in the 13th century, it was eventually abandoned during the French Revolution (p54) before being sold to Fumel's municipal authorities. It is an impressive example of the transition between medieval military architecture and an early Renaissance noble residence.

The key element of the castle's defences, the Great Tower is ringed by ramparts, which were once covered.

Because of the shape of the rock on which it was built, the keep is strangely elongated.

The drawbridge was converted into a standing bridge and now spans the wide dry moat.

The semicircular barbican acted as an area of defence between the inner and outer drawbridges.

Great Hall

Red Tower

The well was dug directly into the rock, its shaft reaching down to the water table below.

Outer courtyard

↑ Overview of the fortification of Château de Bonaguil

800
—
The number of steps up to the top of the lookout post, from which there are stunning views.

↑ View from the ramparts and a family exploring inside the castle *(inset)*

AGEN

⚫E4 ✈🚗🚌 ℹ 38 rue Garonne; www.destination-agen.com

Once a busy river port, Agen has many historic buildings that are still a part of the modern cityscape. Religious buildings of the Middle Ages that graced the old town sit alongside revitalized shopping boulevards and plazas. Old ramparts are now roadways, and the magnificent episcopal palace is the region's *préfecture*.

The largest town in the Garonne valley, Agen still has many fine buildings dating from its prosperous period as a manufacturing and trading centre. In the heart of town are narrow streets with half-timbered, medieval houses, grand townhouses and arcaded squares. There are also early Neo-Classical buildings. Between esplanade du Gravier and the canal running parallel with the river, are pleasant green areas.

①
Vieille Ville

This part of town is crammed with many interesting features. These diverse buildings include the medieval Chapelle Notre-Dame-du-Bourg, on rue des Droits-de-l'Homme. Faced with red brick, the church has a single-walled pointed belfry that looks down onto an attractive small square. Also here is one of France's earliest reinforced concrete buildings, the 1906 Théâtre Ducourneau, in place du Docteur-Esquirol. The Neo-Classical theatre is renowned for its accoustics.

Rue Beauville, a well-restored, narrow thoroughfare, is lined with beautiful late medieval half-timbered houses with an overhanging upper storey. The Église Notre-Dame-des-Jacobins, which was once the chapel of a Dominican monastery built here in 1249, is now used for exhibitions.

Arcaded galleries line the nearby place des Laitiers. Ruelle des Juifs, a narrow alleyway, was, until the end of the 14th century, a street of bankers' and merchants.

Rue des Cornières, on the other side of boulevard de la République, was a major thoroughfare for trade in the Middle Ages. It is now lined with attractive restored houses, set above rows of arcades in a variety of styles.

Other houses worth seeing are the beautiful 14th-century Maison du Sénéchal in rue du Puits-du-Saumon, and the 18th-century Hôtel Amblard, at 1 rue Floirac.

② Ⓜ
Cathédrale Saint-Caprais

🏠 Place du Maréchal-Foch
📞 05 53 66 37 27 🕐 Daily

Originally built in the 12th century, the cathedral has

Boat cruising the canal
↓ at Agen; Boulevard de
la République *(inset)*

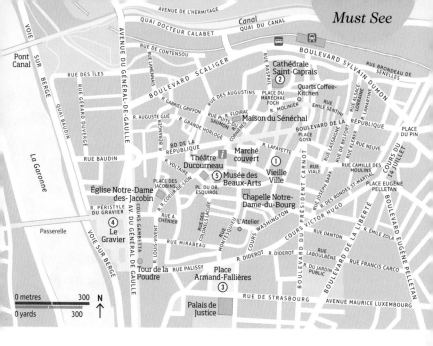

been remodelled several times. It has a magnificent Romanesque apse and its walls are covered with richly coloured frescoes.

---

③ Place Armand-Fallières

The bishop's palace here, now used as the offices of the local council, was built in 1775 and added to later. A grand staircase, flanked by allegorical statues, fronts the Neo-Classical lawcourts.

---

④ Le Gravier

During the reign of Louis XIII, (from 1610 to 1643)this area near the river bank hosted regional fairs. The esplanade is now a popular place for strolling. On avenue Gambetta is Hôtel Hutot-de-Latour, an 18th- century, pink brick building that was the tax-collector's house. To its right is the Tour de la Poudre, once part of the medieval ramparts.

⑤ Musée des Beaux-Arts

ℹ Place du Docteur-Esquirol ☎ 05 53 69 47 23
🕐 Wed-Mon (excluding public hols)

Founded in 1876, this museum, one of the finest in southwest France, , whose collections gives an excellent insight into the cultures of the Lot and Garonne valleys. The collections cover almost every period from prehistory to the 20th century.

The works are displayed in four beautiful old town-houses. On show here is the Vénus du Mas, a Roman statue from Le Mas-d'Agenais, as well as Flemish, Dutch, French and Italian paintings of the 16th and 17th centuries and an important collection of Spanish paintings, including five works by Goya. Paintings by Courbet, Corot and Sisley cover the 19th century, and canvases by Roger Bissière and sculptures by Claude and François-Xavier Lalanne represent the modern era.

EAT

Quarts Coffee-Kitchen
This modern eatery serves up fabulous and healthy breakfast bowls, smoothies and sandwiches.

🏠 63 rue Molinier
☎ 05 53 96 63 74
🕐 Sun-Mon

€€€

L'Atelier
A lively restaurant in a carpenter's workshop, serving tasty dishes based on local produce, such as Rocamadour cheese and lentil salad.

🏠 14 rue Jeu de Paume
☎ 05 53 87 89 22
🕐 Sat breakfast and lunch; Sun

€€€

A SHORT WALK

AGEN

Distance 1 km (0.5 miles) **Time** 15 minutes
Nearest station Agen

The French capital of rugby and of prunes,
Agen was originally a Gallo-Roman town
known as Aginnum. It grew rapidly during
the late Roman Empire, but suffered as a
result of invasions in the 5th and 6th centuries.
Control of the town passed between France
and England during the Hundred Years' War
(p54). Agen later became a major manufacturing
and trading base, exploiting its position on the
Garonne river to export its produce. Today,
it is an important administrative centre and
university town, so a stroll through the heart
of town will reveal both modern hotspots as
well as remnants of Agen's storied past.

↑ Outside dining at the quaint
place des Laitiers on the
boulevard de la République

Hôtel Amblard

Maison du
Sénéchal
(14th-century)

At **place des Laitiers** *is a statue of a
pilgrim on the road to Santiago de
Compostela (p226). It was made by
Jean-Luc Toutain in 1998.*

*Renowned for its acoustics, the
Neo-Classical* **Théâtre Ducourneau**
opened in 1908.

This well-restored thoroughfare of
rue Beauville *is one of the most
picturesque in Agen. Both sides are
lined with half-timbered houses with
an overhanging upper storey.*

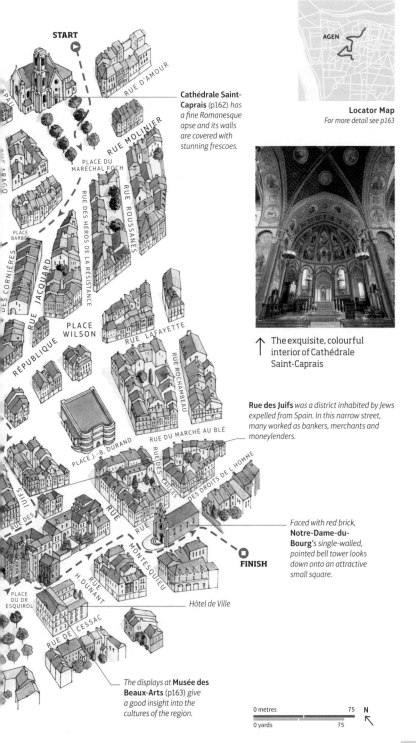

START

RUE D'AMOUR

RUE MOLINIER

PLACE DU MARÉCHAL FOCH

RUE ROUSSANES

RUE DES HÉROS DE LA RÉSISTANCE

PLACE BARBÈS

DES CORNIÈRES

RUE JACQUARD

PLACE WILSON

RÉPUBLIQUE

RUE LAFAYETTE

RUE ROCHAMBEAU

PLACE J.-B. DURAND

RUE DU MARCHÉ AU BLÉ

RUE DES CALTES

RUE DES DROITS DE L'HOMME

RUE DES JUIFS

RUE

RUE MONTESQUIEU

RUE H. DUNANT

PLACE DU DR ESQUIROL

RUE DE CESSAC

FINISH

Cathédrale Saint-Caprais (p162) *has a fine Romanesque apse and its walls are covered with stunning frescoes.*

Rue des Juifs *was a district inhabited by Jews expelled from Spain. In this narrow street, many worked as bankers, merchants and moneylenders.*

Faced with red brick, **Notre-Dame-du-Bourg**'s *single-walled, pointed bell tower looks down onto an attractive small square.*

Hôtel de Ville

The displays at **Musée des Beaux-Arts** (p163) *give a good insight into the cultures of the region.*

AGEN

Locator Map
For more detail see p163

↑ The exquisite, colourful interior of Cathédrale Saint-Caprais

0 metres   75
0 yards   75

N

EXPERIENCE MORE

③

Gavaudun

▲E3 **ⓘ Place des Arcades, Monflanquin; 05 53 36 40 19**

Perched on a rocky hill, the village of Gavaudun stands proud of the wooded valleys around it. The ruins of the 11th–13th-century **Château, de Gavaudun** particularly the keep with its limestone entrance, are very impressive. This stunning setting is regularly used for carnivals and musical events.

Château de Gavaudun

Ⓒ Ⓒ ▲ Le Bourg - Mairie Ⓒ Apr-Nov: Fri-Tue (Jul & Aug: daily) ⓦ chateaude gavaudun.com

④

Monsempron

▲E3 **ⓘ Place Georges-Escande, Fumel; 05 53 71 13 70**

Here the imposing outline of the Benedictine priory of Saint-Géraud-de-Monsempron

overlooks the confluence of Lot and the Lémance. This fortified village has a beautifully proportioned Romanesque church. Although it was remodelled in the 16th century, it retains some earlier elements, including a barrel-vaulted nave with carved capitals, a dome supported on stone columns above the central crossing and a minimalist doorway. The semicircular recesses of the apses overlap one another.

⑤

Villeréal

▲E3 **ⓘ Place de la Halle; www.coeurdebastides.com**

Founded in 1265, the *bastide* town of Villeréal is laid out to a regular plan. The main square, at the centre of the town, is lined with arcades with corbelled houses above. The large, late 14th-century covered market has an upper storey, with half-timbered cob walls, which housed the town hall and courts. The fortified

> ### Did You Know?
>
> Château de Fumel, near Monsempron, has gardens with superb views over the Lot.

medieval church, which once served as a place of refuge, has two turrets that are connected by a wall-walk. Up to the later years of the *Ancien Régime*, access was still by drawbridge.

There is a cluster of interesting Romanesque churches in the villages sprinkling the countryside around Villeréal. The 12th-century church at Bournel, 7 km (4 miles) to the south, is dedicated to St Madeleine, whose statue can be seen above the arched main doorway. The medieval church at Rives, 2 km (1.5 miles) north, has an unusual triangular bell tower, with two arches and a round apse. The church at Montaut, 8 km (5 miles) to the southwest, was very important in the Middle Ages, being the seat of the archpriest with around 91 parishes. It has a five-arched bell tower, hung with two bells, astride two towers.

⑥
Sauveterre-la-Lémance

🅐 E3 👤 Rue Notre Dame, Villefranche-du-Périgord; www.perigordnoir-valleedordogne.com

This village, dominated by the privately owned Château des Rois-Ducs, gave its name to the Sauveterrian, a major period of the Mesolithic age. The small **Musée de la Préhistoire** displays objects found when excavations began in 1920 on a site known as Le Martinet.

At Saint-Front-sur-Lémance, 4 km (3 miles) southwest, there is an interesting 11th–14th-century fortified church.

Musée de la Préhistoire

♦ ⊘ 🅐 Le Bourg 📞 05 53 40 73 03 🕐 Times vary; call ahead

⑦
Puymirol

🅐 E4 👤 La Mairie, 49 rue Royale; 05 53 95 32 10

Founded in 1246, Puymirol was the first *bastide* town to be built in the Agenais – an ancient region of France that is now part of Lot-et-Garonne. It was well known for its fairs during the Middle Ages.

From the heights of the rocky spur on which it perches, the town looks down into the scenic Séoune valley. Puymirol is surrounded by ramparts with a wall-walk, and entry is via a gate known as Porte Comtale. The main street is rue Royale, and the

←

Inside the towering medieval Église Notre-Dame in Villeréal

↑ Horseriding in the little hamlet of Saint-Avit, best known for its Musée Bernard-Palissy

main square, which is lined with arcades, still has its ancient well. The church, rebuilt in the 17th century, has a 13th-century doorway with a wide carved archway.

Some 8 km (5 miles) to the southeast is the hilltop village of Clermont-Soubiran, with stunning views of the rolling landscape and woodland all around. The Château de la Bastide houses a small museum, Musée du Vin et de la Tonnellerie, which has exhibits on local wine.

⑧
Saint-Avit

🅐 E3 👤 Rue Notre Dame, Villefranche-du-Périgord; www.perigordnoir-valleedordogne.com

This attractive hamlet on a hillside in the Lède valley has just one street. The 13th-century Romanesque church is decorated with frescoes. Saint-Avit is the birthplace of Bernard Palissy, the famous potter, born in around 1510. He was known for his large plates, dishes, ewers and other vessels encrusted with "rustic figulines" in high relief, featuring reptiles, fish, shells and plants, modelled from life and realistically painted. He was patronized by the queen, Catherine de' Medici, but later imprisoned in the Bastille prison for his Protestant faith. He died in prison aged 80. The **Musée Bernard-Palissy** is devoted to his life and work, and also displays contemporary ceramics.

Musée Bernard-Palissy

⊘ 🅐 Saint-Avit 🕐 May–Jun: Sun; Jul–Sep: Wed–Mon 🌐 museepalissy.net

↑ The Basilique Notre-Dame de Peyragude, Penne-d'Agenais

⑨ Penne-d'Agenais

🅐 E4 🚉 🅘 Rue du 14-Juille; www.tourisme-fumel.com

The history of Penne-d'Agenais is as tumultuous as that of the whole Aquitaine region. By turns a mighty base for Richard the Lionheart (1189–99), a possession of the counts of Toulouse and of Simon de Montfort's Crusaders, this town was held alternately by the French and the English during the Hundred Years' War (1337–1453), then passed from the Protestants to the Catholics during the Wars of Religion (1562–98). Filled with picturesque restored houses

> **💬 INSIDER TIP**
> **Penne d'Art**
>
> In the summer months, a contemporary art festival – the Penne d'Art – is held in Penne-d'Agenais. During the event, dozens of local artists display their artwork in various locations around town.

set on narrow paved streets that run down the hillside, it is crowned by the silvered dome of a great neo-Byzantine basilica, which was built from 1897 to 1947.

The remains of the medieval town include part of the 12th-century walls, as well as fine houses with Gothic doorways, and the square keep of the castle, which was dismantled in the reign of Henri IV (1589–1610). Some houses on the main square have windows with intricate Gothic tracery. A small, restored gateway, the Porte de Ricard, is framed by buttresses. The defence tower on rue des Fossés once formed part of the ramparts. Place du Mercadiel and place Paul-Froment are lined with old arcaded merchants' houses. Beneath the town hall is the former "royal" prison.

⑩ Tournon-d'Agenais

🅐 E4 🅘 Place de l'Hôtel de Ville; www.tourisme-fumel.com

Set on a rocky promontory in the Boudouyssou valley,

this *bastide* town was built in about 1270, and soon after came under English control.

Houses built into the ramparts look down from the high clifftop. Constructed from a mix of uncut boulders and dressed stone, some, like those in rue du Bousquet, also have half-timbered walls. The medieval Maison de l'Abescat in rue de l'École housed the bishops of Agen during the Middle Ages. The bell tower in the square was built in 1637 and is crowned by a wooden steeple with a fine lunar clock that was added in 1843. Above place de la Mairie is a municipal garden, laid out on the site of a church destroyed in the 16th century during the Wars of Religion.

⑪ Pujols

🅐 E4 🅘 Place Saint-Nicolas; 05 53 36 78 69

Officially listed as one of France's prettiest villages, this heavily fortified town was dismantled several times in the course of its history.

Porte de Ville, the fortified gate, is the only entrance to this walled town. The gate also serves as the bell tower

of the Église Saint-Nicolas, which dates back to the late Middle Ages. The main street is lined with half-timbered and corbelled houses, many of which are over 500 years old. The Église Sainte-Foy, decorated inside with 16th-century frescoes, hosts temporary exhibitions.

A few minutes' drive south, the **Grotte de Lastournelle** and **Grottes de Fontirou** are caves that feature interesting natural rock formations inside.

Grotte de Lastournelle

◈◈ 🏠1851 route des Grottes de Lastournelles, Sainte-Colombe-de-Villeneuve 🕒Apr–Sep: daily 🌐grotte-de-lastournelle.fr

Grottes de Fontirou

◈◈ 🏠Off the N21, Castella ☎0553 40 15 29 🕒Mid-Jun–mid-Sep: daily

---

⑫ Laroque-Timbaut

🅐E4 ℹ️Place de l'Hôtel de Ville; 05 53 95 71 36

Laroque-Timbaut was founded on a rocky outcrop. The 13th-century covered market has a wooden roof supported on Tuscan columns.

Walking down the pretty rue du Lô, visitors can see the foundations of a medieval castle and its old outbuildings. Just outside the village is a memorial to its famous sons, who include the cyclist Paul Dangla (1878–1904) and Louis Brocq (1856–1928), famous for his pioneering work in the treatment of skin disorders.

In the valley is a chapel dedicated to St German, where pilgrims gather on the last Sunday of May each year.

Hautefage-la-Tour, 5 km (3 miles) to the north, has an unusual hexagonal tower, built in the 15th century. The church, completed several decades later, has a fine wooden roof. About 8 km (5 miles) northwest of Laroque-Timbaut is the fortified medieval village of Frespech. The **Musée du Foie Gras** in nearby Souleilles traces the 4,500-year-old history of the local speciality of *foie gras*.

Musée du Foie Gras

◈◈ 🏠Lieu Dit Souleilles 🕒Daily 🕒Jan & Feb: Sun 🌐souleilles-foiegras.com

↓ Attractive half-timbered houses in the pretty village of Pujols

Did You Know?

In summer, an evening market is held on Friday at place Lafayette in Villeneuve-sur-Lot.

⑬ Villeneuve-sur-Lot

🅐E4 🚆🚌 ℹ️Allée Federico Garcia Lorca; www.tourisme-villeneuvois.com

Straddling the Lot river, Villeneuve was founded by Alphonse de Poitiers in 1264. It is the largest *bastide* town of the Lot-et-Garonne.

The town's symbol is its bridge, Pont Vieux, which was built across the Lot in 1287 and restored about 400 years later. On the north bank of the river stands the Chapelle du Bout-du-Pont, built in the 17th century and dedicated to sailors and boat-men. Two majestic gates – Porte de Paris and Porte de Pujols – once formed part of the town's medieval ramparts. Markets are still held on place Lafayette, a square lined with arcades, and concerts held there animate the town centre.

The Église Sainte-Catherine was built in the 19th century on the site of an earlier building that had been demolished. Following Byzantine-Romanesque style, it has stained-glass windows and wooden statues that date back to the *Ancien Régime* era.

In the Quartier d'Eysses, to the north of Villeneuve, is an archaeological site with a 1st-century Gallo-Roman villa. Amphorae and various other objects discovered here are displayed at the site's small **Musée Archéologique**.

Musée Archéologique

◈ 🏠Place Saint-Sernin-d'Eysses ☎07 88 16 83 50 🕒Jul & Aug: daily

14

Prayssas

AE4 **ℹ**Place de l'Hôtel-de-Ville; 05 53 95 00 15

Surrounded by low hills covered with fruit trees and Chasselas vines, this attractive *bastide* town was built on an oval plan in the 13th century.

The fortified village of Clermont-Dessous, located 7 km (4 miles) to the southwest, is dominated by its castle. There is also a beautiful 11th-century Romanesque church situated here.

15

Casseneuil

AE4 **🚍ℹ**Allée Federico Garcia Lorca, Villeneuve-sur-Lot; 05 53 36 17 30

For centuries, this town, set on a peninsula, depended on river transport and river trade for its wealth. In 1214, it held out against the English under Simon de Montfort. Overhanging houses line the riverbank. **Église Saint-Pierre** contains some fine 13th- and 15th-century frescoes.

Église Saint-Pierre
🏠21 place Saint-Pierre
📞05 53 36 17 30 (tourist office) **⏰**By appointment

16

Sainte-Livrade-sur-Lot

AE4 **🚍ℹ**Allée Federico Garcia Lorca, Villeneuve-sur-Lot; 05 53 36 17 30

The church in this *bastide* town was built in the 12th to 14th centuries. It has an attractive stone-built Romanesque tiered apse and contains a white-marble effigy of a 14th-century bishop. Another interesting feature of Sainte-Livrade is the Tour du Roy, a tower that formed part of a castle built here by Richard the Lionheart.

17

Monclar-d'Agenais

AE4 **ℹ**Place Saint-Nicolas, Pujols; 05 53 36 78 69

Perched on a narrow spit of land, the *bastide* town of Monclar was founded by Alphonse of Poitiers in 1256. From its elevated site the town offers magnificent views of the Tolzac valley. One side of the town's main square is lined with arcades. The

PICTURE PERFECT
Jardin des Nénuphars

Visitors can see nearly 300 varieties of water lily in the beautiful water garden, the Jardin des Nénuphars "Latour-Marliac" *(www.latour-marliac.com)*, near Monclar-d'Agenais.

covered market abuts the Église Saint-Clar, which has a 16th-century porch.

Castelmoron-sur-Lot, 8 km (5 miles) to the southwest, has a pleasant man-made lake, beside which stands a Moorish town hall. The church at Fongrave, 7 km (4 miles) south, has a fine wooden sculpted altarpiece.

18

Clairac

AD4 **ℹ**Place de la Halle; www.valdegaronne.com

Once a Protestant town, Clairac was besieged by Louis XIII in 1621 and its fortifications were razed.

↑ Displays of vintage plum tins at the Ferme et Musée du Pruneau near Granges-sur-Lot

However, several 15th-century half-timbered houses survive. The town's Benedictine abbey was founded in the Early Middle Ages century and by the 13th century it had become the most influential abbey in the Agenais. It is now closed to the public as it is privately owned. The handsome timbered Maison Montesquieu is where the writer of the same name is believed to have written his famous political satire, the *Persian Letters* (1721).

The town of Tonneins on the banks of the Garonne, was once the capital of ancient Gaul. This was a former tobacco manufacturing town, as is evident from the beautiful exterior of the Manufacture Royale des Tabacs (Royal Tobacco Factory) here, built in 1726.

Just 9 km (6 miles) south-east of Clairac, in a wooded valley, is the village of Lacépède. At the edge of the village is **Lac du Salabert**, a reservoir and nature reserve. The Maison de la Nature here has information on the local flora and fauna. There are lakeside observation posts for watching the local wildlife, as well as a botanical trail.

Lac du Salabert
🏠 Maison de la Nature;
🕐 Mon–Fri 🌐 sentier-lac-du-salabert.com

19

Granges-sur-Lot

🅰 E4 ℹ Place de la Halle, Clairac; www.valdegaronne.com

Founded in 1291 on the banks of the Lot, this *bastide* town was largely destroyed during the Hundred Years' War (1337–1453), during which Britain and France fought over Aquitaine.

The **Ferme et Musée du Pruneau**, 2 km (1 mile) away in the town of Le Gabach, is devoted to the history of the local prune industry. It has displays of 19th–20th-century ovens, drying cupboards and other equipment, as well as old documents. The museum is set in an orchard with more than 3,000 plum trees.

At the **Chaudron Magique** farm at Brugnac, 11 km (7 miles) north, visitors can buy mohair from the angora goats kept there.

Ferme et Musée du Pruneau
◎ ◎ 🏠 Le Gabach 📞 05 53 84 00 69 🕐 Mon–Sat, Sun

Chaudron Magique
◎ 🏠 1219 route de Brugnac 🕐 Times vary, check website 🌐 chaudronmagique.fr

←

The pretty town of Casseneuil, set on a peninsula in the Lot

⊕ Duras

🅐D3 **ⓘ** 14 boulevard Jean-Brisseau; www. paysdeduras.com

Built on the plan of a *bastide*, this ancient fortified town looks down from a high promontory above the river Dropt. The **Château de Duras** was built in about 1137 and later remodelled several times. By the late Middle Ages, it was a fortress set with eight towers; by the 17th century, it had developed into a grand residential château. During the French Revolution (*p54*), it was almost reduced to a ruin. The state acquired it in 1969.

The castle is open to visitors, who can walk through almost 35 of its great rooms. These include the Salle des Maréchaux (Marshals' Hall) and a barrel-vaulted ballroom dating from 1740. The tower offers a panoramic view of the Pays de Duras. The museum of local history, in the basement, documents life in Duras, focusing on such aspects of the area as vine-growing, local crafts and other folk traditions.

Château de Duras

🅰️ 🕙 🏠 Place du Château ⏰ Feb–Dec: daily 🌐 chateau-de-duras.com

---

㉑ Castillonnès

🅔E3 **ⓘ** 71 Grand'Rue; www.castillonnes tourisme.com

Founded in about 1259, the *bastide* town of Castillonnès perches on a rocky spur. During the Hundred Years' War (*p54*), the town passed between the French and the English seven times, but was finally taken by the French in 1451. Two gates are all that remain of the original medieval ramparts.

On place des Cornières, the main square, is an unusual 20th-century covered market. On the other side of the main square is the former Maison du Gouverneur, graced with a Renaissance courtyard. The building is now the town hall.

The church, which was extensively rebuilt after the Wars of Religion, has a 17th-century Baroque altarpiece and stained glass by the master-craftsman Louis Franchéo.

About 22 km (14 miles) to the west of Castillonnès is Miramont-de-Guyenne. Founded in 1278 by Edward I, this *bastide* town was built on a site that was once used as a lookout post for the Knights Templar. A stroll around Miramont leads to the central square, with its reconstructed covered market and elegant arcades. The town also has a thriving shoe industry, which started in the 1800s with the creation of a unique, sheep-skin clog.

㉒ Monflanquin

🅔E3 **ⓘ** Place des Arcades; www.coeurdebastides. com

This attractive, exceptionally well-preserved *bastide* town, officially listed as one of France's prettiest villages, is laid out to an oval plan. It clings to the hillside rising sharply from the Lède valley. Built around 1240, with a grid pattern of streets, the *bastide* developed in 1252 under the leadership of Alphonse de Poitiers, but its defences were

Did You Know?

Monflanquin's market has taken place every Thursday morning in the place des Arcades since 1256.

↤ The arcaded houses of Monflanquin, a perfectly preserved *bastide* town

dismantled on the orders of Cardinal Richelieu. The streets intersect at place des Arcades, at the top end of the town. The main square is lined with handsome arcaded houses, including the Maison du Prince Noir (House of the Black Prince), with Gothic rib-vaulting and moulded panels. The church, the beautiful **Église Saint-André**, has a single-wall bell tower, whose façade dates from 1927, and a relief-decorated medieval doorway.

Rue de l'Union, rue des Arcades and rue Sainte-Marie are lined with some fine stone houses, sporting arcades on the ground floor and old half-timbered façades above.

Overlooking the town on a rocky spur above stands the Château de Roquefère, a fortified castle that is open to the public only on European Heritage Days (dates vary each year).

The **Musée des Bastides** shows how *bastide* towns were constructed, from the Middle Ages onwards, and how they served their purpose.

Église Saint-André
🕒 Daily

Musée des Bastides
🎟️🎟️ 🏠 Maison du Tourisme, place des Arcades 📞 05 53 36 40 19 🕒 Apr–Jun & Sep: Tue–Sat; Jul & Aug: daily

---

23
Lauzun

🅰️E3 ℹ️ 5 rue Pissebaque; 05 53 94 13 09

The eventful life of the Duc de Lauzun, marshal of France and a courtier of Louis XIV, is conjured up in the rooms of the **Château de Lauzun**, which was built in the 13th century and remodelled around a hundred years later. The listed Renaissance wing has two monumental chimney-pieces with carvings and marble capitals, and the vast *salle des gardes* ("guard room") still has its original 16th-century terracotta-tiled floor. The Gothic church, Église Saint-Etienne, in the village, opposite a house with caryatids, contains a Renaissance-era pulpit and altarpiece.

Château de Lauzun
🎟️ 📞 05 53 94 18 89 🕒 Jul & Aug: daily

EAT & DRINK

Lot-et-Garonne has a rich food culture that revolves around its local farm produce and fine wines. Seek out one of these options to enjoy the best of the region's gastronomic traditions in a beautiful setting.

La Bastide des Oliviers
🅰️E3 🏠 1 Tour de Ville, Monflanquin 🌐 la bastidedesoliviers.fr

€€€

Vins et Flots
🅰️D3 🏠 16 place du 11 Novembre, Duras 📞 05 53 94 13 66

€€€

Hostellerie des Ducs
🅰️D3 🏠 Boulevard Jean-Brisseau, Duras 🌐 hostellerieducs-duras.com

€€€

↑ The distinctive towers of the 13th-century Château de Lauzun rising up over the historic town of Lauzun

The Lot-et-Garonne countryside around Monflanquin village

㉔

Marmande

🅐D3 🚌 🚍 ℹ️11 rue
Toupinerie; www.valde
garonne.com

The Marmande area has been a major producer of tomatoes for several hundred years, and now also grows strawberries. Rival factions fought over the town during the Hundred Years' War, but in 1580 it was finally won by France. The **Église Notre-Dame**, founded in 1275, has a listed organ built by Cavaillé-Coll in 1859. The church's Chapelle Saint-Benoît contains a 17th-century altarpiece with two carved scenes at the centre. Access to the cloister is through gardens.

Rue Labat is lined with half-timbered houses and the old ramparts are decorated with a modern mosaic, depicting

Did You Know?

The statue in front of Marmande's town hall is dedicated to the "Pomme d'Amour", or tomato.

major episodes throughout the town's 800-year history.

Around 8 km (5 miles) northwest stands the **Musée Archéologique André-Larroderie** at the Gallo-Roman site of Sainte-Bazeille. It contains artifacts from the Iron Age to the time of Louis XIV, found at various digs in the Marmande area.

Église Notre-Dame
🕐 🚪Rue de la République
📅Daily

Musée Archéologique André-Larroderie
♿ 🚪Place René-Sanson 📞06 85 23 60 52
📅Jul & Aug: Wed–Mon; Sep–Jun: Sun

㉕

Casteljaloux

🅐D4 ℹ️Maison du Roy;
www.tourisme-coteauxet
landesdegascogne.fr

On the edge of the Landes forests, this spa town is closely associated with the Albret dynasty. Some 40 half-timbered corbelled houses, built

in the 15th and 16th centuries, date from the period when the town was the capital of Gascony and a base for Henri IV's hunting expeditions.

The Maison du Roy (King's House) is a fine 16th-century residence associated with Louis XIII and Louis XIV. Tour Maquebœuf is one of the few surviving vestiges of the town's medieval fortifications.

At Clarens, 2 km (1 miles) south of Casteljaloux, is a vast lake surrounded by pine trees and fringed by sandy beaches. The lake is a popular local leisure spot where people come to enjoy a range of water sports, as well as treetop rope courses, which include a zipwire over the lake. Nearby, the town of Bouglon has a viewpoint that offers fine views of the Forêt des Landes and Garonne river valley. The Église Saint-Savin, 1 km (0.5 mile) south of Villefranche-du-Queyran, is a jewel of Romanesque architecture. Dating from the 11th–12th centuries, it has a beautiful 12-arched choir and 20 magnificently carved capitals.

→ The gardens and cloisters of Marmande's church

26

Pays de Serres

D/E4 **Place de l'Hôtel-de-Ville, Prayssas; 05 53 95 00 15**

The steep valleys and plateaus of the Pays de Serres form a geologically distinct area of land, bordered by the river Lot to the north and the Garonne to the south. Narrow bands of limestone, known as *serres* ("long crests") run right across this landscape, which is dotted with villages and old *bastide* towns that perch on the outcrops of rock. There are also many picturesque man-made structures, such as dovecotes, farmhouses and a number of Romanesque churches and chapels.

27

Mézin

D4 **Place Armand-Fallières; 05 53 65 77 46**

The town of Mézin grew up around its medieval

monastery, of which nothing now remains, and its church. The main square is lined with picturesque arcades. In the narrow, winding streets all around there are half-timbered houses and a number of fine stone-built residences. The Gothic-arched Porte de Ville, a gateway also known as Porte Anglaise, is a vestige of the town's 13th-century ramparts.

On the square stands the restored medieval **Église Saint-Jean-Baptiste**. Despite the rather functional, slightly leaning, six columns that flank the nave, the church has an elegant interior. The climb up the bell tower's 90 steps is no longer permitted because it is too dangerous. The wrought-iron cross to the left of the main doorway into the church dates from 1815. It bears the instruments of the Passion, which are surmounted by the

INSIDER TIP
Tourist Train

In the summer months a tourist train runs between Nérac and Mézin along a decommissioned stretch of railway (*www.chemin-de-fer-touristique-du-pays-de-l-albret.blog4ever.com*).

cock that crowed when Peter denied Jesus. There are several gardens in the town; it is particularly pleasant to walk around the ramparts, in the rue Neuve quarter and also along the rue des Jardins.

The **Musée du Liège et du Bouchon** is devoted to the cork-making industry, for which the town was famous in the 19th and early 20th centuries. Exhibitions focus on the daily lives of workers, as well as more unusual modern uses of cork – for example in aircraft.

There are dozens of interesting Romanesque churches in the area. The fortified ancient churches at Villeneuve-de-Mézin, Lannes and Saint-Pé-Saint-Simon are especially fine and worth seeking out for lovers of architecture and history.

East of Mézin, the village of Moncrabeau is known as the "liars' capital". The local Liars' Academy, founded in 1748, hosts the International Festival of Lies on the first Sunday in August. French- and Gascon-speaking contestants compete by telling convincing lies in an effort to be crowned King of Liars.

Église Saint-Jean-Baptiste

Place Armand-Fallières
Daily

Musée du Liège et du Bouchon

Rue du Puits Saint-Côme 05 53 65 68 16
Apr-May & Oct-Nov: Tue-Fri & Sun; Jun-Sep: daily

←

Picturesque Poudenas, set on the river Gélise and overlooked by its château

---

a seigneurial residence. It is fronted by arcaded galleries.

30

Le Mas-d'Agenais

🅐D4 **ℹ**11 rue Toupinerie, Marmande; www.valdegaronne.com

This ancient village spreads out along the canal that runs parallel to the Garonne. Evidence of Roman occupation has been discovered here, including a marble statue known as the *Vénus du Mas*, now in the Musée des Beaux-Arts in Agen *(p163)*. The Collégiale Saint-Vincent, a fine 11th–12th-century abbey church, has 17th-century choir stalls and finely carved capitals. It also contains a very small painting of *Christ on the Cross* (1631) by Rembrandt, one of a series of seven paintings depicting the Stations of the Cross; the other six are in Munich. The 17th-century corn market in the square has a fine wooden roof. The washhouse nearby is also worth a detour.

28

Aiguillon

🅐D4 🚗🚌 **ℹ**30 rue Triers; 05 53 88 95 85

The small town of Aiguillon, at the confluence of the Lot and the Garonne, has been inhabited since Gallo-Roman times, and was a focus of conflict during the Hundred Years' War. The Château des Ducs was built by the Duc d'Aiguillon between 1775 and 1781. This luxurious residence was pillaged during the French Revolution, and in 1966 it was converted into a secondary school.

The **Musée Raoul-Dastrac**, in a deconsecrated church, contains a fine collection of the artist's Post-Impressionist paintings and stages regular temporary exhibitions.

Pech-de-Berre, 4 km (2.5 miles) north of Aiguillon, offers expansive views of the Lot and Garonne valleys. Damazan, 7 km (4 miles) to the west on the Canal de Garonne, is a *bastide* town with fine half-timbered houses and a covered market with the town hall on its upper floor. Around 8 km (5 miles) south-west of Aiguillon, houseboats can be seen on the canal at Buzet-sur-Baïse, which is noted for its vineyards. At Saint-Pierre-de-Buzet, 7 km (4 miles) southwest, is an attractive 12th-century fortified church.

Musée Raoul-Dastrac
⚙🕙 🅗Rue de la République 📞05 53 84 41 44 🕙Call ahead to check

---

29

Poudenas

🅐D5 **ℹ**7 avenue Mondenard, Nérac; www.albret-tourisme.com

This medieval village was once a staging post, where Henri IV was a frequent visitor. With old stone buildings covered in ivy, historic architecture and a quiet, rural atmosphere, Poudenas is a fine stop for those who want to experience the quintessential French countryside.

It even has its own castle: the Château de Poudenas, built above the village by the lords of Poudenas, who were vassals of King Edward I of England. It is now a stunning luxury hotel. In the 1500s the castle, set in wooded parkland, was converted into

---

31

Laplume

🅐E4 **ℹ**64 Grande Rue; 05 53 95 16 67

Once the capital of the small Brulhois area to the south-west of Agen, the village of Laplume looks out across the landscape from its vantage point, high on a rocky out-crop of limestone. Parts of the medieval village survive,

→

The town hall on the central place de la Mairie in the old *bastide* town of Beauville

HIDDEN GEM
Lac de Lamontjoie

West of Agen, Lac de Lamontjoie is a peaceful spot for fishing (in particular carp) and birdwatching. Camping here is possible and in summer there's a lakeside restaurant.

including sections of the ramparts and two gates. The 16th-century Église Saint-Barthélemy was restored in the 17th and 18th centuries.

Just outside Laplume is the Lavoir de Labat, a curious five-sided washhouse that dates from the 17th or 18th century. Around 10 km (16 miles) north of Laplume, the village of Sainte-Colombe-de-Bruilhois is worth visiting for its historic centre and its Gothic-Romanesque church.

32
Beauville

A D3 **i** Place de la Mairie; 05 53 47 63 06

Sheltering behind a row of trees, the old *bastide* town of Beauville clings to the hillside, commanding an impressive view of the surrounding landscape. The attractive arcaded main square is lined with half-timbered houses. The Château de Beauville was built in the Middle Ages, with further alterations made several hundred years later. The 16th-century church has a bell tower at the entrance.

33
Saint-Maurin

A E4 **i** 38 rue Garonne, Agen; www.destination-agen.fr

This peaceful village, set in a lush valley, developed around an 11th-century Benedictine abbey, dedicated to Saint Maurin; unusually, it's the only village in France of that name. The abbey was partly destroyed during the Crusades, then further damage was inflicted by the English in the 14th century. Now all that remains is part of the church and the abbot's house. Built on the plan of a Latin cross, this church has a semicircular choir with six exquisitely carved capitals, including a depiction of the martyrdom of St Maurin (he was decapitated). The nave once covered what is now part of the village square. Other vestiges of the abbey lie between newer buildings.

The abbot's house contains a **museum**. Designed by the village's inhabitants and with exhibits contributed by them, it documents daily life in the area in the early 20th century. There is also a model of the abbey as it was at the height of its splendour.

On the square in front of the abbot's house are an attractive covered market hall, restored in 1625, a well and several pretty half-timbered houses.

The Église Saint-Martin-d'Anglars, above the village, was founded in the 13th century and rebuilt in the 16th. The furnishings inside it include a carved wooden altar from the Renaissance era and an 18th-century statue of St Joseph.

Abbey Museum

Ⓐ Ⓐ **A** Palais Abbatial **C** 05 53 95 31 25 (Mairie, Beauville) ◑ Jul & Aug: Wed–Mon

← The charming streets of Nérac and the interior of the Église Saint-Nicolas *(inset)*

34 Nérac

D4 ⛳ ℹ 7 avenue Mondenard; www.albret-tourisme.com

The Baïse, now a navigable river, runs through the centre of Nérac, with the castle and the new town on one bank, and the district of Petit Nérac on the other. In the 14th century, Nérac – capital of the Albret region – was a favourite base of the Albret family. They had settled in the region in the around two hundred years earlier and married into the Navarrese and the French royal family. Nérac was an important Protestant stronghold and, in 1621, its fortifications were dismantled on the orders of Louis XIII. The castle, built above the Baïse in the 14th to 16th centuries, reflects the importance of the Albret family at the height of their power. The castle once consisted of four wings set with circular towers. It was abandoned after the 16th century, and only the north wing now remains. It has an elegant corbelled gallery of twisted columns, built between 1470 and 1522. Since 1934 the wing has housed the **Château-Musée Henri IV**, with exhibits on the Albret family and life at court in Nérac.

The 18th-century **Église Saint-Nicolas**, with a Neo-Classical façade, is known for its stained-glass windows, which show monumental figures of the prophets, and for its frescoes.

The Maison des Conférences, a 16th-century townhouse on rue des Conférences, has its original tiered galleries and a façade decorated with Renaissance motifs. It is named for the meetings *(conférences)* that Catherine de' Medici and Henry of Navarre held here from 1578, to bring about a reconciliation between Catholics and Protestants. Petit Nérac is full of pretty half-timbered houses. It lies along the Baïse, near the lock (dating from 1835). The district's main feature is the 19th-century Église Notre-Dame. The Maison de Sully, at the other end of the Vieux-Pont, rebuilt in the early modern era, was home to the young Duc de Sully in 1580. He later became first minister to Henri IV.

The Parc Royal de la Garenne, now a public park, stretches for 2 km (1 mile) along the river bank. It has several fountains, including

Did You Know?

Nérac is generally recognised as the place where the recipe for foie gras was invented.

the Fontaine du Dauphin, which was built in 1601 to mark the birth of Louis XIII, and the Fontaine de Fleurette, named after a young girl who drowned herself after being seduced and abandoned by the Prince of Navarre.

Chateau-Musée Henri IV
♿🚫 🏠 Impasse Henri IV
📞 05 53 65 21 11 🕐 Jun–Sep: daily; Oct–May: call ahead to make a reservation

Église Saint-Nicolas
🏠 Place Saint-Nicolas
🕐 Daily

Vianne

🅰 D4 🛈 Place des Marronniers; 05 53 65 27 75

This *bastide* town was set up in 1284 on the banks of the Baïse. Its focal point is a 12th-century church. The nave, capitals and choir are Romanesque, while the doorway, decoration of the apse and bell tower fortifications are in Gothic.

The glassmaker's workshop here has closed down, but the tradition is kept alive by local glass-blowers and engravers. Nearby, the town of Xaintrailles has a medieval keep. You can see how honey is made at the **Musée de l'Abeille** (Bee Museum) here. To the north is the 13th-century *bastide* town of Francescas. Here in a beautiful old building is the surprising and quirky **Musée de la Boîte Ancienne en Fer Blanc** (Tin Can Museum).

Musée de l'Abeille
🚫🕐 🏠 Jeandouillard
🕐 Times vary, check website
🌐 museedelabeille.
wordpress.com

Musée de la Boîte Ancienne en Fer Blanc
🏠 Place du Centre, Au Bourg
📞 05 53 65 42 78 🕐 9am–12:30pm Mon–Sat

💬 INSIDER TIP
River trips

Enjoy a leisurely trip from Nérac down the river Baïse aboard an old-fashioned *gabare*, a wooden boat once used to transport merchandise. *(www.croisieresduprincehenry.com).*

Barbaste

🅰 D4 🛈 Rue du Moulin des Tours; 05 53 65 09 37

Built in the Middle Ages and set with four towers, the **Moulin des Tours de Barbaste** is a fortified mill that looks out over the Gélise river, onto a 10-span Romanesque bridge. In the late 19th century, the building was converted into a cork factory. It was damaged by fire in 1906 and again in 1937.

The *bastide* town of Lavardac, 2 km (1 mile) to the northeast, was founded in 1256. The harbour, on the Baïse, is a stopping place for pleasure boats. The medieval tower is all that remains of a medieval castle.

The tiny village of Durance lies 11 km (7 miles) west. This *bastide* village is surrounded by pine forest. All that remains of the fortifications is the south gate, next to the ruins of a castle.

Moulin des Tours de Barbaste
🚫 🏠 Rue du Moulin des Tours 📞 05 53 65 27 75 🕐 Call for times 🚫 Oct–mid-Apr

← Barbaste's ancient Romanesque bridge spanning the Gélise river

37

Moirax

⚠E4 **ℹ️12 Grand Rue; 05 53 67 01 99**

The ancient village of Moirax, which clusters around its majestic Romanesque church, looks out onto the flatlands of the Agenais.

In the early Middle Ages, the local baron, Guillaume de Moirax, donated land to the Cluniac order and a monastery was built here. Suffering at the hands of various warring factions, the monastery experienced turbulent times during the Middle Ages. Towards the end of the 17th century, a major programme of rebuilding work was started, but this was brought to an abrupt halt by the outbreak of the French Revolution in 1789.

The **Église Notre-Dame**, which was once part of the monastery, is an exquisite example of Romanesque architecture, and has been superbly restored. An arcaded bell tower now rises above the projecting central section of the façade. This is crowned by a limpet-shaped roof. A double tier of arches lines the buttressed aisles. The arches of the porch are decorated with beading and carved foliated scrolls, and rest on four slender columns. The Gothic arch above frames a semicircular window. Over the choir is a dome decorated with shingles and crowned by a lantern. The arched windows of the apse and side apses are decorated with further beading. The church is laid out to the plan of a basilica, having a nave that is flanked by aisles, a feature which is quite rare in the southwest of France. The only lighting for the nave comes from the window in the west wall.

The strictly symmetrical transept is divided into three equal sections. Each arm of the transept, which is lit by a set of double windows, has steps that lead up to a raised platform or stand. The dome that sits above the central crossing point has been rebuilt in a star shape.

The choir is lit by arched windows framed by slender columns. Four supporting arches rise up from its square base to the octagonal dome above. Five arched windows illuminate the vaulted apse. More than 100 ornate capitals decorate the various columns found in this church. As well as abstract geometric and plant motifs, the lion motif features on many of them, while birds, rams and all manner of fantastic monsters also appear. Thirteen of the capitals are carved with biblical scenes, including depictions of Adam and Eve in the Garden of Eden, Saint Michael killing the dragon and Daniel in the lions' den. The aisles are decorated with 17th-century woodcarvings, showing various scenes taken from the Old Testament.

Église Notre-Dame

⊘ 🏠10 Grand Rue 📞05 53 67 01 99 ⏰Daily

38

Aubiac

⚠E4 **ℹ️64 Grande Rue, Laplume; 05 56 25 29 29**

Nestling in lush greenery, the beautiful fortified Romanesque Église Sainte-Marie towers over the village. The church was built between the 9th and the 12th centuries on the site of a Merovingian building. Appearing as a square, severely plain fortress from the outside, the church has a contrastingly ornate interior, with rounded arches in the apse and barrel vaulting above the doorway. The dome over the square choir is decorated with 16th-century frescoes depicting the four Evangelists. The medieval castle next to the church belonged to a branch of the Galard family. It was rebuilt during the *Ancien Régime* era.

An important archaeological find from Aubiac is a Celtic bronze head of a horse, now in the Musée des Beaux-Arts in Agen (*p163*).

←
Field beside Église de Notre-Dame in Moirax, a Romanesque church

→ One of the magnificently decorated rooms in the Château de Monluc

39 Layrac

⒜E4 ⒤8 place du 11 novembre 1918; 05 53 66 51 53

Layrac commands stunning views over the Gers and Garonne valleys. The medieval Église Saint-Martin is crowned by an 18th-century dome, and it has a particularly fine apse. The capitals on the church's façade are carved with monsters and demons. The church contains a marble altarpiece and on the floor are traces of mosaic from the Middle Ages, depicting Samson overcoming the lion. The bell tower is all that remains of the older church, which was destroyed in 1792. On place de Salens are a fountain and a washhouse, built against the remains of the ramparts.

Astaffort, a small town in the Brulhois area, is the birthplace of the singer Francis Cabrel. It has some half-timbered houses and the remains of ramparts. The Romanesque Église Saint-Félix was remodelled in the 17th century.

Caudecoste, on a hilltop, 8 km (5 miles) southeast of Layrac, was built in 1273. It is one of the few *bastide* towns to have been founded by a religious order. Half-timbered houses on wooden pillars cluster round its small arcaded square. The church, on the edge of the town, is also worth a visit.

40 Estillac

⒜E3 ⒤05 53 67 80 36 (Mairie)

A stronghold in the Middle Ages, Estillac was once owned by Blaise de Monluc (c 1500–77), the writer and Maréchal de France (marshal of France) who led the Catholic armies in the 16th-century Wars of Religion. He also distinguished himself in the Franco-Italian wars, and is noted for his *Commentaires*, a treatise on soldiery. A white marble effigy of the former Maréchal lies in the grounds of his old home, **Château de Monluc**, in the nearby town of Saint-Puy. Visitors can enjoy guided tours here, but the focus is more on the estate's wine production (and free tastings) than the château's former inhabitant.

Sérignac-sur-Garonne, northwest of Estillac, was once a leading *bastide* town. As it is located on the canal, it is a very popular spot for visitors on boating holidays. It has some half-timbered houses and medieval church with a Romanesque porch and a spiral belfry, rebuilt in 1922, a replica of the 16th-century original.

Château de Monluc
Ⓧ ☐Saint-Puy ⒪Times vary, check website ⓦmonluc.fr

EAT

Auberge Le Prieuré
Contemporary French dishes are served in a charming old village house at this Michelin-starred restaurant with a relaxed and friendly atmosphere.

⒜E4 ☐Le Bourg, Moirax ⓦauberge leprieure.fr

€€€

A DRIVING TOUR
PAYS DU DROPT

Length 55 km (35 miles) **Starting point** Sainte-Colombe-de-Duras **Stopping-off points** Dine at Hostellerie des Ducs, a former convent that serves fine wines and traditional dishes

Occupying the northwestern corner of the *département* of Lot-et-Garonne, the Pays du Dropt is bisected by the Dropt river. It's a wonderful palce for a relaxed drive – a region of gentle valleys covered with vines and plum trees, dotted with small, white, stone Romanesque churches. The vineyards of the Côtes de Duras occupy some 20 sq km (8 sq miles), many of them part of small family estates. The Côtes de Duras area was granted its own *appellation* in 1937.

Locator Map

The church in the attractive village of **Saint-Sernin-de-Duras** is picturesquely covered in Virginia creeper. The building was restored in the 15th and 19th centuries.

The village of **Esclottes** is named for its clottes (boundary stones) that marked the borders of the dioceses of Agen and Bazas.

This route will take you on a loop from **Sainte-Colombe-de-Duras**. The choir of its small Romanesque church has carved capitals, and a fresco shows scenes from the life of St Colomba.

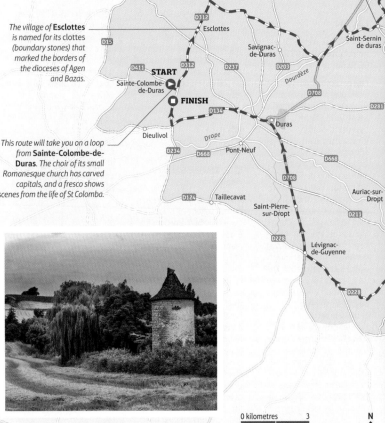

↑ An old *pigeonnier* (dovecote) in the fields around Esclottes

0 kilometres   3

0 miles   3

N ↑

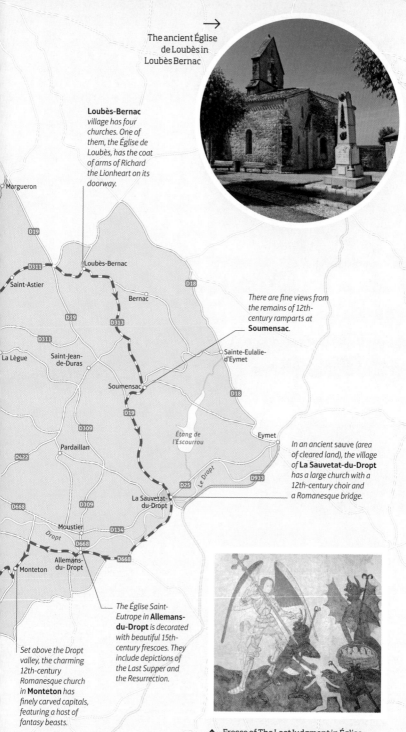

The ancient Église de Loubès in Loubès Bernac →

Loubès-Bernac village has four churches. One of them, the Église de Loubès, has the coat of arms of Richard the Lionheart on its doorway.

There are fine views from the remains of 12th-century ramparts at **Soumensac**.

In an ancient sauve (area of cleared land), the village of **La Sauvetat-du-Dropt** has a large church with a 12th-century choir and a Romanesque bridge.

The Église Saint-Eutrope in **Allemans-du-Dropt** is decorated with beautiful 15th-century frescoes. They include depictions of the Last Supper and the Resurrection.

Set above the Dropt valley, the charming 12th-century Romanesque church in **Monteton** has finely carved capitals, featuring a host of fantasy beasts.

↑ Fresco of The Last Judgment in Église Saint-Eutrope, Allemans-du-Drop

LANDES

Settlement of Landes goes back to prehistoric times, but the region's most visible historic legacy is that of the Hundred Years' War (1337–1453), during which many *bastide* towns were built up in strategic locations across the countryside. In this difficult, marshy terrain, life was hard. To keep watch over their sheep, local shepherds used to walk on stilts to make crossing the muddy ground easier. During the Second Empire (1852–1870), the landscape changed, as marshland was drained and extensive pine forests were planted for their resin and timber. Also at this time, the coming of the railways and better roads greatly improved communication between the towns and cities. However, the creation of the Parc Naturel Régional des Landes de Gascogne, in 1970, has helped to preserve Landes' traditional way of life.

Today, thousands of visitors flock to the Landes region every year, drawn by the beauty of its forests and the long, sandy beaches stretching along its Atlantic coastline, a paradise for surfers. but it is also well worth exploring the picturesque hinterland, with its colourful festivals and many gastronomic treats.

LANDES

Must See

1 Parc Naturel Régional des Landes de Gascogne

Experience More

2 Hossegor
3 Mimizan
4 Biscarrosse
5 Courant d'Huchet
6 Pays d'Orthe
7 Sorde-l'Abbaye
8 Capbreton
9 Pomarez
10 Montfort-en-Chalosse
11 Dax
12 Labastide-d'Armagnac
13 Soustons
14 Mont-de-Marsan
15 Saint-Sever
16 Aire-sur-l'Adour
17 Grenade-sur-l'Adour
18 Peyrehorade
19 Brassempouy

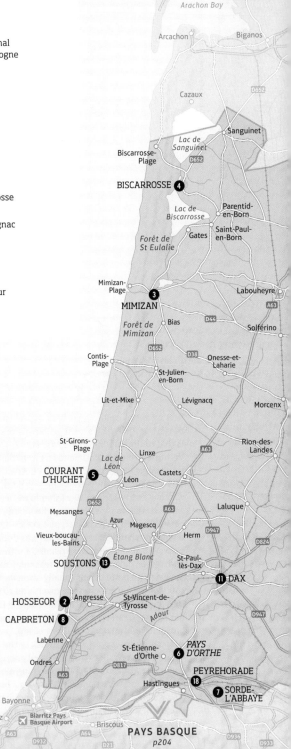

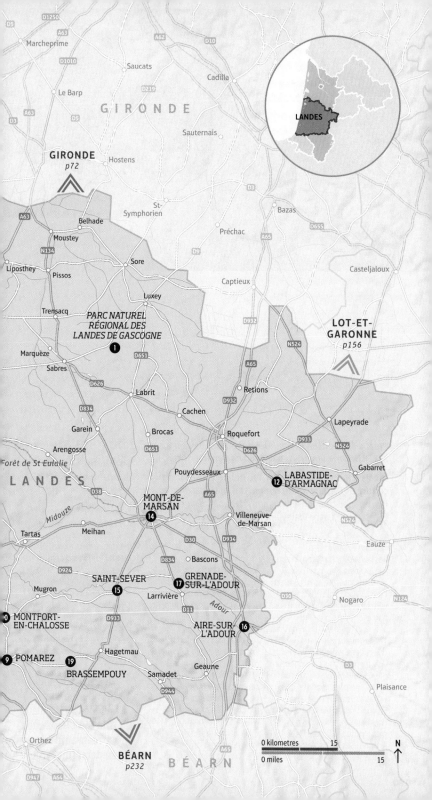

← Horse riding through the Parc Naturel Régional des Landes de Gascogne

❶

PARC NATUREL RÉGIONAL DES LANDES DE GASCOGNE

🅰B/C4 🅿️ℹ️ Maison de la Nature, 33 route de Bayonne, 33830 Belin-Beliet; www.parc-landesde-gascogne.fr

Created in 1970 to preserve and enhance the land and culture of the Gascogne region, this park has three landscapes that live in harmony: "Pignada" or pine forests, the Leyre Valley and the Arcachon Basin.

This paradise for nature lovers lies between the Gironde and the Landes. The extensive plateau, covering over 3,360 sq km (1,300 sq miles), is covered with forests of deciduous trees and evergreen pines, interspersed with large fields of maize. The farmland is irrigated by the river Leyre, which flows all the way through this conservation area. Besides these forested areas, the park contains many waterways and small lakes. From the unspoiled banks of the river Leyre, visitors can see picturesque villages, ancient farmhouses and splendid Romanesque churches.

①

Vallées des Leyre

The river Leyre, formed by the Grande Leyre and Petite Leyre, flows into the Arcachon Basin. As it is the source of 80 per cent of the basin's water, the river plays a key role in the important ecological balance of that watery expanse.

No roads run along its course, so the Leyre can only be explored by canoe or on foot. The forest, through which it flows for 100 km (60 miles), is surrounded by valleys and marshland with lots of wildlife.

②

Solférino

The charming village of Solférino was founded by Napoléon III in 1863. He and his wife, Eugénie, were very fond of southwest France and often travelled to the region's resorts towns, such as Biarritz *(p216)* and Cambo-les-Bains *(p221)*.

Napoléon wanted to create an ideal model of rural life. To populate the region and promote agriculture, the Emperor purchased 70 sq km (27 sq miles) of flatland on which he built 10 farmhouses,

> **The charming village of Solférino was founded by Napoléon III in 1863. He wanted to create an ideal model of rural life.**

28 family houses and 10 craftsmen's houses, as well as a church and a school.

③ Musée des Forges

🏠 Rue Tinarage, Brocas 📞 05 58 51 44 56 🕐 Mid-Jun–mid-Sep: Tue–Sun

In the 19th century, Brocas was an important ironworking centre. The museum, in a disused flour mill, shows the tools and techniques that were used in this industry, and also displays cast-iron objects such as firebacks. Next to the blast-furnace are workshops, a barn and ironworkers' houses.

④ Écomusée de Marquèze

🏠 Route de Solférino, Sabres 🕐 Apr–early Nov: daily 🌐 marqueze.fr

The Écomusée de Marquèze is an open-air museum with three locations: Luxey, devoted to resin-tapping; Moustey, which focuses on local religious traditions; and Marquèze, which illustrates daily life in past times.

To create the sense of going back in time, take a ride on a vintage steam train.

The Ecomusée, which opened in 1969, explores traditional rural and agricultural life in the Grande Lande, using the reconstruction of a small farming community from the late 19th century. Different types of buildings are represented, including a manor house, cottages and sheep barns. Specialist occupations, as well as other aspects of rural life, are demonstrated in an informative way.

⑤ Luxey

From the 1850s to the 1950s, the resin industry contributed to the economic prosperity of the Landes. A resin-processing workshop at Luxey still has its old buildings, dating from 1859, along with equipment used. Fires that ravaged the forests of the Landes severely affected the industry, and the **Musée de l'Estupe-Huc** documents the difficult task of fighting these forest fires.

La Maison d'Estupe-Huc
♿ 📞 05 58 04 70 70 🕐 By appointment (call ahead)

ROMANESQUE CHURCHES

Built during the early centuries of the second millennium, the churches of this area were important meeting places for the St Jacques de Compostela pilgrims. Certain sanctuaries were built by the pilgrims themselves, who were almost the only people to cross the marshy flatlands of Les Landes at this period.

⑥ Moustey

Moustey has two churches, which stand opposite one another. The late 15th-century parish church of St Martin, to the north, is in the late Gothic style. The Église Notre-Dame, which was connected to a hostel, served pilgrims on their journeys across southwest France (p226). It has an interesting 16th-century keystone. The village also has two rivers, which are good for kayaking in summer.

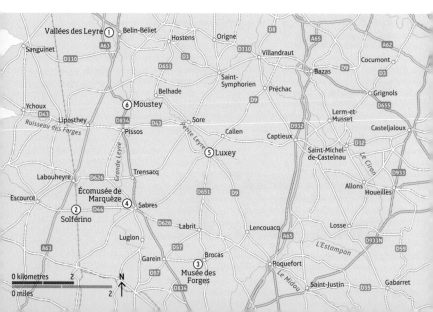

EXPERIENCE MORE

②

Hossegor

🅰A5 📧*i*166 avenue de la Gare; www.hossegor.fr

In the early 20th century, a number of writers – including Paul Margueritte and Rosny Jeune – fell under the spell of this picturesque village, surrounded by pine trees. Ever since, Hossegor has drawn a steady stream of visitors. In the 1930s, it became a coastal resort, and the **Sporting-Casino** was built, along with a traditional *fronton* where the ballgame *pelote basque* is still played. The elegant villas around the golf course and the sea lake evoke the resort's heyday in the 1920s and 1930s. Built in a Basque-Béarn style, they have Basque features, such as white roofs and façades, as well as typical features of Landes buildings, such as low-pitched roofs and half-timbering. Hossegor is now also an international surfing hotspot. The Quiksilver Pro festival that takes place in October attracts some of the best surfers in the world.

Sporting-Casino

🏠119 avenue Maurice Martin 🕐10:30am–3am Sun–Mon (to 4am Fri–Sat) 🌐casino-hossegor.com

---

③

Mimizan

🅰B4 📧*i*38 avenue Maurice-Martin; www.mimizan-tourisme.com

In summer, the town of Mimizan attracts large numbers of visitors who come to enjoy its 10 km (6 miles) of beaches, as well as its vast forests, with their 40 km (25 miles) of cycle tracks. The town has an abbey church whose 13th-century bell tower is listed by UNESCO. A small museum in the abbey grounds, the **Musée du Prieuré à Mimizan**, illustrates life here during the Middle Ages. It also explores local geography and history as well as the area's changing relationship with the surrounding forest. Excursions organised by the tourist office introduce visitors to forestry in the area, with tours of local woodland and forestry businesses.

At Saint-Julien-en-Born, south of Mimizan, the Courant de Contis river flows down to the Plage de Contis, a beach with a lighthouse. At Lit-et-Mixe, a bit further south, is the **Musée Landes d'Anton**, which documents local traditions.

Musée du Prieuré à Mimizan

⊘ 🏠Rue de l'Abbaye 📞0558090061 🕐By appointment, call ahead

Musée Landes d'Anton

🏠Lit-et-Mixte 📞0558427014 🕐Jun: Thu; Jul & Aug: Mon-Sat; Sep: Mon-Fri

---

④

Biscarrosse

🅰B4 📧*i*55 place Georges-Dufau; www.biscarrosse.com

Biscarrosse, with a beach that stretches for 15km (9 miles) –as far as the Adour river –marks the beginning of the Côte d'Argent (Silver Coast). Sited between the ocean and the forest, the town has two lakes, which offer a range of water sports.

Visitors with an interest in aviation will enjoy the **Musée Historique de l'Hydraviation**, devoted to seaplanes with many craft on display. The

↑ Hossinger beach, sharing the excellent surfing conditions found along the Côte d'Argent

Glorious sands at Moliets-et-Maa beach, at the mouth of the Courant d'Huchet

museum stands next to the Établissements Latécoère, which produced seaplanes from 1930 to the end of the 1950s. There's a fantastic seaplane airshow held biennially here in June (in even-numbered years).

The **Musée des Traditions et de l'Histoire de Biscarrosse** documents the town's history and the lives of resin collectors and shepherds on the Landes.

North of Biscarrosse is the Lac de Sanguinet. Its 56 sq km (2 sq miles) of clear, fresh waters are ideal for fishing and water sports. Sanguinet itself, on the site of a Gallo-Roman village, has an interesting archeological museum, **Le Musée du Lac Sanguinet**.

Musée Historique de l'Hydraviation

⊗ ⌂ 332 avenue Louis-Bréguet ℂ 05 58 78 00 65 ⊙ Feb, Jun & Sep–Dec: Tue-Sun; Jul & Aug: daily;

Musée des Traditions et de l'Histoire de Biscarrosse

⊗ ⌂ 216 avenue Louis-Bréguet ℂ 05 58 78 77 37 ⊙ May–Jun & Sep: Tue-Sat; Jul & Aug: daily; rest of the year by appointment

Le Musée du Lac Sanguinet

⊗ ⌚ ⌂ 102 place de la Mairie ⊙ Times vary, check website ⓦ musee-lac-sanguinet.fr

⑤
Courant d'Huchet

🄰 A5 🛈 Maison de la Réserve Naturelle du Courant d'Huchet; 05 58 48 73 91

The coast of Landes is dotted with watercourses, known as *courants*, that flow into the ocean. The best-known is the Courant d'Huchet, a river with vibrant plants and wildlife to enjoy around the riverbanks. Since 1908, visitors have been able to travel on the water in *galupes*, flat-bottomed boats that are propelled along using a *palot* (punt). Starting from the Étang de Léon, the lake from where the *courant* flows, *galupe* tours follow a maze of watercourses, which are inhabited by a variety of birds, including teal, herons and woodcock. The banks are covered with cypresses, hibiscus, irises, gladioli and bracken, and in summer there are ducks, otters, wild boar, mink, crayfish and eels that come to spawn from the Sargasso Sea. *Galupes* owned by the Bateliers du Courant d'Huchet (*www.bateliers-courant-huchet.fr*) travel between Étang de Léon and the sea daily from April to October; the trip covers some 10 km (6 miles) and takes around two hours, with longer options in high summer.

STAY

Wood'n Sea Surf Lodge
Close to the best surfing spots in the area, this relaxed lodge has both dorms and private ensuite rooms.

🄰 A5 ⌂ 6 rue de Baye, Capbreton ⓦ woodnsea-lodge.com

€ ⓔ ⓔ

Hotel & Spa Villa Seren
Overlooking Hossegor Lake, this modern and stylish hotel has an outdoor heated pool.

🄰 A5 ⌂ 1111 avenue du Touring Club, Hossegor ⓦ villaseren.fr

ⓔ ⓔ ⓔ

Les Echasses Golf & Surf Eco Lodge
Chic cabins surround a private forested lake, minutes from the beach.

🄰 A5 ⌂ 701 route des Bruyères, Saubion ⓦ ecolodge-leschasses.com

ⓔ ⓔ ⓔ

6

Pays d'Orthe

🅰 B5 ℹ️ 147 avenue des Évadés, Peyrehorade; www.tourisme-orthe-arrigans.fr

South of the Landes lies the Pays d'Orthe, a region that has sat at the crossroads of travellers' routes through southwestern France since prehistoric times. The seat of the Orthe family from the 11th century until the French Revolution, the area has a wealth of magnificent châteaux and religious buildings. The *bastide* town of Hastingues, on the pilgrim route to Compostela overlooking a bend in the river, was founded by the English in the 13th century. Its fortified gate once formed part of the town's original defensive ramparts.

The **Centre d'Exposition Saint-Jacques-de-Compostelle**, situated in a layby on the A64 motorway just south of Hastingues, documents the pilgrimage to Santiago de Compostela. East of Hastingues is the **Abbaye d'Arthous**, founded by Premonstratensians in the 12th century and remodelled in the 17th and 18th centuries. The Romanesque church

↑ Sorde-l'Abbaye's abbey on the Gave d'Oloron river; its boathouse opens onto the former millrace

here, built in about 1167, has Gothic elements, including pointed arches in its south aisle and capitals with superb carvings. A ceramics festival with potters from the locality, as well as from further afield, takes place in the gardens each summer. Inside, the **Musée d'Histoire** has interesting exhibits.

Saint-Étienne-d'Orthe, north of Hastingues, is the gateway to the alluvial plains of the river Adour, now a vast nature reserve. This stretch of land is home to a number of protected species, including white storks, European pond turtles and Landes ponies.

Centre d'Exposition Saint-Jacques-de-Compostelle

🅰 Service area on the A64; also accessible from Hastingues 📞 05 59 41 56 00 🕐 Daily

Abbaye d'Arthous

🅰 785 route de l'abbaye, Hastingues 🕐 Times vary, check website 🌐 arthous. landes.fr

←

Statue of St James at the Centre d'Exposition Saint-Jacques-de-Compostelle

Musée d'Histoire

♻️🕐 🅰 785 route de l'abbaye 🕐 Times vary, check website 🌐 arthous.landes.fr

---

7

Sorde-l'Abbaye

🅰 B6 📧ℹ️ Mairie; 05 58 73 04 83

The spot where Sorde-l'Abbaye now stands has been continuously inhabited since prehistoric times. The Falaise du Pastou, a cliff opposite the Gave d'Oloron, contains four rock shelters (not open to the public) dating from the Magdalenian period (around 12,000 BC). For thousands of years, a natural fault in the cliff here provided a passage between France and Spain. From the early Middle Ages, it was regularly used by pilgrims on their way to Compostela, and the village became an important stopping point. In the Bourg-Vieux, the town's historic centre, is the **Abbaye Saint-Jean**, now a World Heritage Site. Benedictine monks, who settled here from around 975, founded it in the Middle Ages. Destroyed during the Wars of Religion, and rebuilt in the 17th century, and again by a Maurist community a hundred

Sorde-l'Abbaye is a picturesque starting point for kayaking and canoeing down the Gave d'Oloron, which rises in the Pyrénées. Trips range from easygoing paddles to more challenging rapids.

years later, the abbey was abandoned during the French Revolution. A medicinal herb garden has been recreated in front of it, which looks down onto the river. Next to the monastery buildings, now in ruins, is a Romanesque church with elements dating from the late Middle Ages, such as the mosaic floor in the choir, the apse, doorway and carved capitals. There is also an underground boathouse with a vaulted ceiling, which opens onto the river. This cellar, the only one of its kind in France, was used for storing cereals.

East of the monastery stands the 16th-century abbot's house, built on the site of a Gallo-Roman villa.

Now privately owned, the house is not open to visitors, but the remains of 4th-century baths and mosaic floors can be seen. As an interesting aside, Sorde-l'Abbaye is now the largest producer of kiwi fruit in France.

Abbaye Saint-Jean
Place de l'Église
05 58 73 09 62 Mar & Nov: Mon–Fri; Apr & Sep–Oct: Tue–Sun; Jul & Aug: daily

---

8

Capbreton

A5 Avenue Georges-Pompidou; www.capbreton-tourisme.com

Separated from Hossegor *(p192)* by an inlet of the sea, Capbreton became an important port in the Middle Ages and was also a stop on the coastal route of the pilgrimage to Santiago de Compostela. In the 16th and 17th centuries it was known as the "town of a thousand captains", dispatching its whaling and cod-fishing fleets to Newfoundland. Subsequently it lost business to rising Bayonne and sank into decline until Napoléon III ordered the Estacade to be built in 1858. This wooden pier with its lighthouse remains a beloved symbol of the town and a favourite place for

← Capbreton's long wooden pier, stretching out to its weathered lighthouse

promenades. Nowadays Capbreton is still a fishing port as well as a popular tourist destination.

Nearby, the **Marais d'Orx** is a nature reserve covering 8 sq km (3 sq miles). Every year, thousands of migratory birds of over 200 species, including the common spoonbill, stop here on their annual journey south.

Marais d'Orx
1005 route du Marais d'Orx Daily reserve-naturelle-marais-orx.fr

TOP
4 **BEACHES IN LANDES**

Biscarrosse Plage
Surf the waves or feast on seafood at little eateries along this wide beach west of Biscarrosse *(p192)*.

Lac de Sanguinet
A freshwater lake perfect for families, with bouncy castles and pedal boats *(p193)*.

Mimizan Plage
A long stretch of coast-line with plenty of beach houses for rent if you want to stay awhile *(p192)*.

Plage Santocha
Dotted with WWII blockhouse ruins, this Capbreton beach is a surfer's paradise, with lessons available for amateurs.

⑨ Pomarez

A B5 🚉🚌 **ℹ** 28 rue Saint-Pierre, Amou; www.landes-chalosse.com

Although Pomarez is an old-established river port, few traces of its early history remain. It is now known as a major centre for _course landaise_ (bull-leaping).

Although Pomarez, on the Adour, is an old-established river port, few traces of its early history remain. It is now known as a major centre for _course landaise_ (bull-leaping), a non-violent sport which has an enthusiastic following in Landes. This colourful spectacle demands both courage and agility. The _écarteur_ (bull-leaper) avoids the _coursière_ (charging cow) by executing balletic moves of varying complexity. Working in teams, or _cuadrillas_, and dressed in white trousers and a bolero, they leap, dodge and make their passes, while wind bands, known as _bandas_, play. Today, a rope is attached to the cow to control it more as it charges. The animal's horns are trimmed and the performance does not end with its slaughter.

West of Pomarez lies the 17th-century **Château de Gaujacq**. The Marquis de Montespan retired to the château to seek solace following his wife's liaison with the king, Louis XIV. The château has a pretty inner courtyard, and the view from the terrace shows the spectacular sweep of the Pyrenean mountain chain. Inside there are several furnished rooms, including the dining room and the Cardinal's bedroom.

Château de Gaujacq

♿ 🅿 🏠 Gaujacq **☎** 05 58 89 01 01 🕐 Mid-Apr-Jun & first half of Sep: Thu–Sun; Jul & Aug: Tue–Sun

⑩ Montfort-en-Chalosse

A B5 🚌 **ℹ** 55 place Foch; 05 58 98 58 50

This ancient _bastide_ town lies in the heart of the Chalosse, a fertile area that produces high-quality beef, as well as ducks that are fed on maize grown on the Landes' flatlands to produce the area's famous _foie gras_. The fact that Montfort was an important stopping place on the pilgrimage route to Santiago de Compostela can be seen from its church, the Église Saint-Pierre. It has a medieval nave and its tower dates from the late Middle Ages.

The **Musée de la Chalosse** is housed in an estate dating back to the _Ancien Régime_ era, the manor house and its outbuildings providing a perfect setting for the recreation of daily life in 19th-century Chalosse.

Just under 10 km (6 miles) from Montfort-en-Chalosse is the spa village of Préchacq-les-Bains, where the sulphur-rich thermal waters are used primarily in the treatment of rheumatism.

Musée de la Chalosse

♿ 🅿 🏠 480 chemin du Sala **☎** 05 58 98 69 27 🕐 Mar-Oct: Tue–Sun

→ Colonnaded courtyard that consoled a marquis, Château de Gaujacq, Pomarez

Dax

⛰B5 🚗🚌 ℹ️11 cours Foch;
www.dax-tourisme.com

Once a lake settlement, the town of Dax stretches out along the banks of the Adour between flatlands and the Pyrénées. Under Roman rule, the town grew, as it prospered from its thermal springs. In the 19th century, the arrival of the railways made Dax the foremost spa town in France. Today, Dax's resorts and hotels continue its ancient legacy, offering therapeutic and stress-busting treatments in beautiful settings. In the town centre, with its narrow medieval streets, the Dax's famous therapeutic waters gush out of the Fontaine Chaude, also known as the Fontaine de la Nèhe.

The **Musée Jean-Charles de Borda**, named for a noted mathematician, scientist and mariner born in Dax, is housed in the Chapelle des Carmes, in the west of the town. The museum traces the town's past, from prehistory through the Middle Ages to present-day Dax. There is also an art exhibition devoted to Landais landscapes, and temporary

↑ Statue of the polymath Jean-Charles de Borda in the pretty place Thiers, Dax

exhibitions of modern art. The **Musée Georgette-Dupouy** displays paintings by this 20th-century artist. In the north, along Parc Théodore-Denis, you can find the remains of Gallo-Roman walls, as well as the town's bullring, which was erected in 1913.

The **Parc du Sarrat** is laid out with an unusual mixture of formal, Japanese and vegetable gardens. Many of the plants and trees in the gardens are rare and protected species, and visits are by guided tour only. Further south is the **Musée de l'Aviation Légère de l'Armée de Terre (l'ALAT) et de l'Hélicoptère**, a museum of light army aircraft where the exhibits include vintage army helicopters. In addition, there is also a gallery of aviation photography.

The village of Saint-Paul-lès-Dax, which lies 2 km (1.5 miles) west of Dax, has an 11th-century church with carved reliefs. Also worth visiting here is the Forges d'Ardy, an old metalworks.

However, the main reason that visitors come to this peaceful town is still its curative thermal waters. There are four thermal spa centres, including **Espace Aquatique Sourcéo**.

TOP 4 DAX SPA TREATMENTS

Pelotherapy
Uses mud from the Adour river mixed with algae from spring water.

Underwater Massage
A massage by a physiotherapist under a stream of spring water.

Floating Therapy
Feel weightless and calm in soothing salt water pools.

Arobaths
Relaxing bubble baths in pure thermal water.

Did You Know?

Dax's annual Feria in August lasts a mighty six days, filled with parades, music and dancing.

Musée Jean-Charles de Borda
♿🚫 🏠11 bis rue des Carmes 📞05 58 74 12 91 🕐Feb–Dec: Tue–Sat

Musée Georgette-Dupouy
♿ 🏠Passage de Presidial 📞05 58 56 04 34 🕐Daily

Parc du Sarrat
♿🚫 🏠Rue du Sel-Gemme 📞05 58 56 86 86 🕐Mid-Mar-Nov: Tue, Thu & Sat

Musée de l'ALAT et de l'Hélicoptère
♿🚫 🏠58 avenue de l'Aérodrome 🕐Times vary, check website 🌐musee helico-alat.com

Espace Aquatique Sourcéo
♿ 🏠355 rue du Centre Aéré 🕐Daily 🌐thermes-dax.com/sourceo

↑ Charming display of bicycle memorabilia in the chapel of Our Lady of Cyclists, Labastide-d'Armagnac

⑫

Labastide-d'Armagnac

Ⓐ C5 🚌ⓘ **Place Royale; 05 58 44 67 56**

Set in lush surroundings, this *bastide* was founded by Bertrand VI, Comte d'Armagnac, in 1291, at a time when the area was held by Edward I of England.

Around place Royale, the town's arcaded central square, are 14th–17th-century half-timbered houses. In the 15th-century Gothic church is a painted wooden *pietà*, which dates from the same period. The fortified bell tower is a sign of the town's turbulent history.

The **Écomusée de l'Armagnac** is an open-air museum that shows how Armagnac is made. It is said to be the oldest style of brandy in the world and has been exported from this area since at least the late 15th century or early 16th century.

Also of interest here is **Notre-Dame-des-Cyclistes**, an 11th-century Romanesque chapel now dedicated to cyclists, whether those following regional pilgrimages (*p226*) or general enthusiasts. This unusual chapel has a museum, created by the Abbé Massie in 1959, exhibiting former cycling champions' jerseys and bicycles ridden in the Tour de France. The annual Fête de Notre Dame takes place on Whit Monday with a celebratory Mass in the chapel, followed by a bike ride and concert.

The **Domaine d'Ognoas**, 12 km (7 miles) southwest of Labastide, is an estate of Armagnac-producing grapes. Visitors can see how Armagnac is distilled by traditional methods using the oldest distilling device in Gascony, and sample the results.

ARMAGNAC

Armagnac, a type of brandy, is sipped from a wide-bowled glass so as to ensure the release of complex fragrances. Exported since the late Middle Ages, it has probably been made since ancient Gaulish times. It was often consumed for supposed health benefits, including enlivening the spirit and emboldening the wit. See for yourself at Domaine d'Ognoas or at Chateau de Ravignan (*www.armagnac-ravignan.com*), a 17th-century castle and Armagnac producer that offers daily afternoon tastings.

Écomusée de l'Armagnac

🏠 4 km (3 miles) southeast of Labastide 📞 05 58 44 84 35 🕐 Nov–Mar: Mon–Fri; Apr–Oct: daily

Notre-Dame-des-Cyclistes

🏠 40240 Labastide-d'Armagnac 🕐 Times vary, check website 🌐 notredamedescyclistes.net

Domaine d'Ognoas

🌐 🏠 Arthez-d'Armagnac 🕐 May–Sep: daily; Oct–Apr: Thu & Fri 🌐 domaine-ognoas.com

⑬

Soustons

Ⓐ B5 🚌ⓘ **Grange de Labouyrie; www.soustons.fr**

The main village of the Marensin district, Soustons stretches out along the banks of a large freshwater lake, which is popular with water sports enthusiasts. In the centre of Soustons is a statue of François Mitterrand, the former president of France, who liked to spend time at his residence, Latché, situated 3 km (2 miles) from here. The **Musée des Traditions et des Vieux Outils** at Château de la

→ Gates and weirs regulating the confluence of two rivers in Mont-de-Marsan

Pandelle brings to life local trades such as roofing, carpentry and resin-collecting.

The Marensin, an area that lies south of Soustons, is cut by rivers and dotted with lakes. These include the **Réserve Naturelle de l'Etang Noir** and the Étang Blanc. Towards the coast, near Vieux-Boucau-les-Bains, is the resort of Port-d'Albret, clustered around a salt lake. Popular in summer, the resort can only be reached via the leafy Promenade du Mail.

Musée des Traditions et des Vieux Outils

⚜ 🏠 Château de la Pandelle, avenue du Général-de-Gaulle 📞 05 58 41 39 09 🕒 15 Jun-15 Sep: Wed-Mon

Réserve Naturelle de l'Etang Noir

🕒 🕒 Daily 🌐 reserves-naturelles.org/etang-noir

14

Mont-de-Marsan

🅰 C5 🚍 ℹ 1 place Charles de Gaulle; 05 58 05 87 37

Mont-de-Marsan, Landes' administrative centre since 1790, is set on the banks of the Midou and Douze rivers, which join to form the Midouze. Nicknamed the "Three-River Town", Mont-de-Marsan is a lively centre built on a history of trade.

The **Musée Despiau-Wlérick**, in the 14th-century Donjon Lacataye fortress, is the only museum in France that is devoted to French figurative sculpture of the first half of the 20th century. On show here is the work of artists from Mont-de-Marsan, including Charles Despiau (1874–1946) and Robert Wlérick (1882–1944). Other exhibits include works by Alfred Auguste Janniot (1889–1969), a sculptor of the Art Deco period.

On rue Victor-Hugo, the Neo-Classical Église de la Madeleine, built in the early 19th century, contains a high altar created by the Mazetti brothers in the 18th century.

Walking up towards the Douze river, visitors will see two Romanesque houses at Nos. 6 and 24 bis rue Maubec, built of the local shelly stone. An entrance on place Francis-Planté leads into the **Parc Jean Rameau**, named

after the Landes novelist and poet (1858–1942). It was created in 1793 and now contains sculptures and Japanese-style gardens.

East of the centre, in the Quartier Saint-Médard, is the 230,000 sq km (2.5 million sq ft) **Parc de Nahuques**.

Musée Despiau-Wlérick

🕒 🏠 Donjon de Lacataye, 6 place Marguerite-de-Navarre 📞 05 58 75 00 45 🕒 May-Sep: daily; Oct-Apr: Wed-Mon

Parc Jean Rameau

🏠 Place Francis Planté 📞 05 58 05 87 37 🕒 Daily

Parc de Nahuques

🏠 Avenue de Villeneuve 📞 05 58 75 65 41 🕒 Daily

💬 INSIDER TIP
Wild Swimming at the Lake

Surrounded by forest but just a short distance from Mont-de-Marsan, the Base de Loisirs du Marsan is a popular summertime spot for swimming at its white-sand beach. A free shuttle from the city centre heads to the lake in summer.

🕒 Saint-Sever

C5 🚌🛈 Place du Tour-du-Sol; www.saint-sever.fr

Founded in 993, Saint-Sever is a strategically positioned town with a number of architectural jewels. Remains of the early settlement are clustered on the Plateau de Morlanne, which, with the town's former abbey and its surrounding streets, makes up one of Saint-Sever's two main districts.

The **Abbaye de Saint-Sever**, a World Heritage Site, stands on a square lined with fine 18th-century townhouses. First established in 988, the abbey was at its full glory in the 11th and 12th centuries. Damaged by fire, earthquakes and wars, the building was restored on several occasions but was abandoned in 1790. In the 19th century, this architecturally important structure underwent some questionable restoration. Built to a Benedictine plan, the church has 150 capitals. Their colourful painted decoration has been restored.

At the Couvent des Jacobins, founded in 1280 and later remodelled, the monastery buildings are no longer open to the public, except for the west wing, which houses the **Musée des Jacobins**. Among the exhibits

in the museum of the history of the town is a copy of the *Beatus*, a commentary on the *Apocalypse of St John* (or Book of Revelations), illuminated by Stephanus Garcia. The original is in the Bibliothèque Nationale, Paris.

Abbaye de Saint-Sever
🕒 🏠 Place du Tour-du-Sol
📞 05 58 76 34 64 ⏰ Daily

Musée des Jacobins
🏠 Place de la République
📞 05 58 76 34 64 ⏰ Jul & Aug: daily

🕒 Aire-sur-l'Adour

C5 🛈 Place 19 mars 1962; www.tourisme-aire-eugenie.fr

This picturesque town on the banks of the Adour also stands on the pilgrim route to Compostela, and is the gateway to the Tursan. The site was inhabited even before the Romans arrived in 50 BC. The former bishop's palace, built in the early 17th century, now houses the town hall. Next to it stands the 14th-century Palais de l'Officialité, the old lawcourts. The Cathédrale Saint-Jean-Baptiste dates from the 12th century, with later alterations. The **Église Sainte-Quitterie-du-Mas**, on the

Colline du Mas, is a World Heritage Site. The church's large 11th-century crypt contains the tomb of the patron saint of Gascony. Other notable features are the arches of the 12th-century choir, above which is a brick-built bell tower, and the Baroque pulpit, carved in 1770.

Église Sainte-Quitterie-du-Mas
🏠 Rue du Mas 📞 05 58 71 47 00 ⏰ Jul-early Sep: daily

🕒 Grenade-sur-l'Adour

C5 🛈 14 place des Tilleuls; 05 58 45 45 98

A *bastide* town founded by the English in 1322, Grenade-sur-l'Adour has 14th- and 15th-century houses and an attractive church, with a Gothic apse, dating from the late 15th century. The **Musée de l'Histoire Landaise** holds a collection of pieces relating to popular traditions and a display of costumes.

Bascons, 6 km (4 miles) north of Grenade, is a *course landaise* (or bull-leaping) centre. It even has a museum– the **Musée de la Course Landaise** – with exhibits on the history of this popular regional sport. Displays include 19th-century posters advertising events, and a collection of early-20th-century postcards attesting to the exploits of leading competitors.

Musée de l'Histoire Landaise
🏠 20 place des Déporté 📞 05 58 76 05 25 ⏰ Wed-Fri pm

Musée de la Course Landaise
🏠 337 chemin de Guiret 📞 05 58 52 91 76 ⏰ Apr-Jun & Sep-Oct: 2:30-6:30pm Wed & Sat; Jul & Aug: 2:30-6:30 Tue-Fri

↑ Saint-Sever abbey, designated by UNESCO as part of the Santiago pilgrimage route

← The four-towered Château d'Orthe, on the river bank at Peyrehorade

18 Peyrehorade

🅰B6 🚌📶 ℹ️147 ave des Evadés; 05 58 73 00 52

Located in the far south of the Landes between two rivers, the Gave d'Oloron and Gave de Pau, Peyrehorade is the largest village in the Pays d'Orthe. It is also the youngest, as it was only established in the 14th century as a result of trade between Bayonne and Toulouse. The village is dominated by the Château d'Aspremont, built in the 13th century by the Vicomtes d'Orthe on the site of an 11th-century fortress, of which only the ruins of the keep remain. The Château d'Orthe (also known as the Château de Montréal), which now houses the town hall, is another splendid building. Dating from the 16th century, it was remodelled by Jean de Montréal in the 18th century. It is not open to the public, but with its four towers, which look down on the Gave de Pau, it is an impressive sight.

EAT

L'Art des Mets
The menu reflects the region well at this restaurant, which is set in a former wine storage house. Try the local goat cheese ravioli and the roasted lamb.

🅰C5 🕐19 rue Louis Sentex, Saint-Sever 🌐lartdesmetsaint sever.com

€€€

19 Brassempouy

🅰C5 ℹ️28 rue Saint-Pierre, Amou; www.landes-chalosse.com

Founded in the 13th century, this ancient *bastide* town is associated with the famous Venus of Brassempouy, a Stone Age figurine of a woman discovered in the Grotte du Pape, a prehistoric cave near the town, in 1894. Carved in mammoth ivory more than 20,000 years ago, this figure is the earliest representation of a human face that has so far come to light. It is on display at the Musée des Antiquités Nationales de Saint-Germain-en-Laye, near Paris. A copy of the figure can be seen in the Maison de la Dame de Brassempouy, next to the Château de Poudenx, along with other replicas of pre-historic figures from France and elsewhere dating from 35,000–15,000 BC.

Maison de la Dame de Brassempouy
♨♨ 📞05 58 89 21 73 🕐Mid-Feb-Jun & Sep-Nov: Tue-Sun; Jul & Aug: daily 🕐Dec-mid-Feb

→ The mammoth-ivory Venus of Brassempouy, sometimes called "Lady with the Hood"

A DRIVING TOUR
TOUR OF
THE TURSAN

Length 90 km (55 miles) **Starting Point** Samadet **Stopping-off points** For lunch, sample some of the Tursan's excellent home-made products at Les Halles market in Geaune

The Tursan is an area of lush green valleys, where maize – grown to fatten the many geese and ducks raised here – is the major crop. Tursan wine has been produced for centuries and, in the Middle Ages, Eleanor of Aquitaine (p53) had it exported to the English royal court. Light red, very dry white and rosé wines are made from grapes grown on 4.6 sq km (1.8 sq miles) of steep, terraced vineyards. The road over these hills follows a scenic route past wine estates, a spa town and picturesque buildings.

Larrivière's Église Notre-Dame-du-Rugby is a church dedicated to rugby. The sport is very popular throughout southwest France.

Opened in 1861, the **Eugénie-les-Bains** *spa resort is named after Empress Eugénie. Michel Guérard, who has a restaurant here, offers gourmet dishes and special health menus.*

Samadet *was once the home of the prominent Royal Faïence Factory, which made fine glazed pottery. A museum here now showcases some of the old wares.*

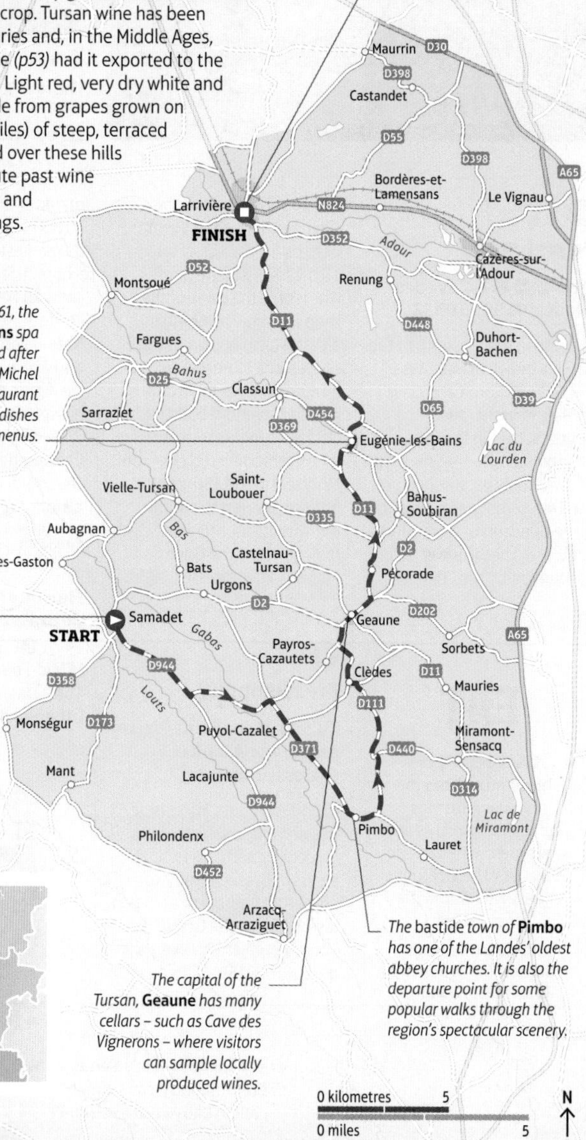

The bastide town of **Pimbo** *has one of the Landes' oldest abbey churches. It is also the departure point for some popular walks through the region's spectacular scenery.*

The capital of the Tursan, **Geaune** *has many cellars – such as Cave des Vignerons – where visitors can sample locally produced wines.*

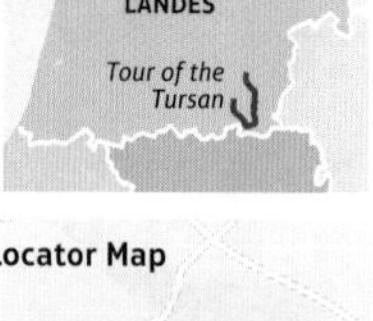

LANDES

Tour of the Tursan

Locator Map

0 kilometres 5
0 miles 5

N

↑ Vineyards of the Tursan,
a prominent wine region
in southwest France

The twin spires of Bayonne Cathedral rising above the rooftops

PAYS BASQUE

There is evidence of settlement in this part of France going back to Neolithic times. In the Middle Ages, the region was invaded by a series of peoples – including the Celts, the Romans and Germanic tribes – before becoming part of the newly created Kingdom of Navarre in the mid-9th century. In the 16th century, the region was split between France and Spain, and the inhaitants endured many years of conflict between the two nations, until the Peace of the Pyrénées brought about a reconciliation in 1659. At the end of the 18th century, the Pays Basque entered a period of economic decline, which ended only with the birth of tourism.

Despite the many changes over the centuries, the Pays Basque has held on firmly to its national identity, which is expressed as much in the use of Euskara, the Basque language, as in the region's architecture, festivals, and food specialities. The western edge of the region is bordered by the Atlantic Ocean, with a coastline of beautiful beaches to which tourists flock year after year. Inland, picturesque villages dot the wide expanses of lush, unspoiled greenery.

PAYS BASQUE

Must See

1 Bayonne

Experience More

2 Hendaye
3 Saint-Jean-de-Luz
4 Biarritz
5 Itxassou
6 Ainhoa
7 Nivelle Valley
8 Larrau
9 Hasparren
10 Bidache
11 Cambo-les-Bains
12 Saint-Étienne-de-Baïgorry
13 Bidarray
14 Espelette
15 La Bastide-Clairence
16 Saint-Jean-Pied-de-Port
17 Saint-Palais
18 L'Hôpital-Saint-Blaise
19 Ciboure
20 Sainte-Engrâce
21 Gorges de Kakuetta
22 Forêt d'Iraty
23 Mauléon-Licharre
24 Massif des Arbailles
25 Tardets-Sorholus

❶

BAYONNE

A6 Place des Basques; www.bayonne-tourisme.com

Two rivers converge on Bayonne and shape its very essence. From architecture to cuisine, the city will satisfy your appetite for the cultures of both France and neighbouring Spain. Only the summer festival interrupts the serenity of the place.

①

Nive Embankment

Starting at place de la Liberté, the Nive embankment runs past the covered market and open-air marketplace. Place de la Liberté is where the keys of the city are thrown into the crowd at the start of the city's August festivals. Quai Jauréguiberry, with its typical Bayonne houses, and rue Poissonnerie, further on, were hives of activity when Bayonne formed a major port for goods from the New World.

A popular place for a stroll in summer, the embankment is lined with restaurant terraces and is filled with music and dancing in the festival season.

②

Historic City Centre

Until the 17th century, the old city, which clusters round the Gothic Cathédrale Sainte-Marie, was crisscrossed by canals. Some streets, like rue Port-Neuf, were created when the canals were filled in. Rue Argenterie is named after the goldsmiths and silversmiths who had their workshops here, while rue de la Salie was once part of the cloth and spice merchants' quarter.

③

Musée Bonnat-Helleu

5 rue Jacques-Laffitte For restoration until 2021 museebonnat.bayonne.fr

Occupying a 19th-century building, the Musée Bonnat-Helleu contains over 5,000 works of art. These date from antiquity right up to the early decades of the 20th century. The galleries contain paintings, sculpture and ceramics,

→ An attractive gallery displaying works of art at Musée Bonnat-Helleu

↑ Aerial view of Bayonne, showing how the two rivers bisect the city

including works by Goya, Rubens, Degas and other major artists.

The museum is closed for restoration (reopening fully in 2021), but temporary exhibits and events are being held during the refurbishments – see the website for details.

④
Château-Vieux

🏠 Rue des Gouverneurs

Built in the 12th century and extended in the 17th, the castle incorporates elements of a Roman fort. It was once home to Bayonne's English governor, and two French kings, François I and Louis XIV, stayed here. It is not open to the public, but visitors can walk into the courtyard.

⑤ 🏛 🎭
Musée Basque

🏠 37 quai des Corsaires
🕑 Tue–Sun (Jul & Aug: daily)
🌐 museebasque.com

The museum is housed in the Maison Dagourette, a superbly restored 16th-century house that is listed as a historic monument. The collections, which have grown since the museum's foundation in 1922, concentrate on Basque culture. Laid out in 20 rooms, they give an insight into the folk art and customs of Pays Basque. Displays cover a number of different themes, including local farm life and sea and river trade, as well as theatre, music, dance, games and sports, with a room devoted to pelota. There are also sections on everyday clothing and traditional costume, architecture, religious and secular festivals and burial customs. Among the paintings are depictions of typical local scenes and activity. Regular temporary exhibitions are also held here.

⑥
Place Paul-Bert

In August, during Bayonne's festival season, this square in Petit Bayonne is where young cows are let loose as part of the traditional bull-running events. Nearby is the 19th-century Église Saint-André, where Mass is celebrated in Basque. Directly opposite the church is Château-Neuf, built in the 15th century during the reign of Charles VII. It forms part of the defences that were later built around the city. During the summer, the castle is the venue for large-scale temporary exhibitions mounted by the Musée Basque.

⑦
Quartier Saint-Esprit

This district on the north bank of the Adour, east of Pont Saint-Esprit, remains largely working class, with quite a cosmopolitan feel. It is where immigrants settled, especially Jews driven out of Spain and Portugal from the mid-16th century onwards, helping build up sea trade. A synagogue and a Jewish cemetery located here are two vestiges of this period.

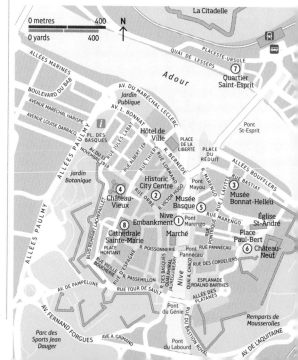

⑧ Ⓜ️

CATHÉDRALE SAINTE-MARIE

🏠 15 rue des Prébendes 🕐 8am–6:30pm Mon-Sat, 8am–8pm Sun
🌐 cathedraledebayonne.com

The impressive twin-spired cathedral over the skyline of Bayonne was in the Roman stye, and altered to Gothic through two renovations. The Cathedral of Sainte-Marie – also known as Bayonne Cathedral or the Cathedral of Notre-Dame de Bayonne – is on the famed path to Santiago de Compostela.

Built in the 12th and 13th centuries on the site of a Romanesque cathedral, the Cathédrale Sainte-Marie is one of Bayonne's most iconic emblems. This imposing, northern Gothic structure, with its tall twin spires, can be seen from afar. Located in the heart of the old city, it was an important stopping place for pilgrims travelling to Santiago de Compostela in Spain (p226). In the 19th century, it underwent extensive restoration after suffering damage during the French Revolution (p54), meaning that the church that stands today is the result of around 800 years of continuous building work and renovation. Highlights to seek out in the cathedral are the Choir – the oldest part of the cathedral – art by Nicolas-Guy Brenet and the beautiful stained glass windows.

A large-scale biblical scene painted by Nicolas-Guy Brenet (1728–92) hangs in the Chapelle Saint-Léon. Brenet executed many such works for a number of churches in France.

West door

↑ The twin spires of the cathedral beyond the shaded cloisters

In the Flamboyant Gothic style, the cloister is on the south side of the cathedral. Three of its arcaded galleries survive.

Illustration of Cathédrale Sainte-Marie, showing the interior of the church ↑

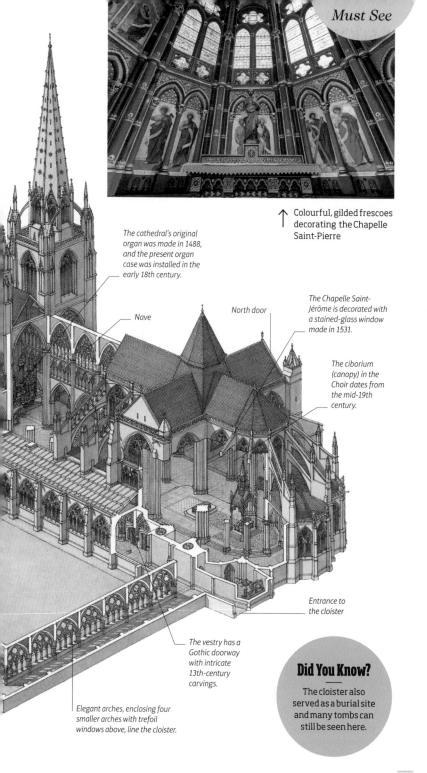

↑ Colourful, gilded frescoes decorating the Chapelle Saint-Pierre

The cathedral's original organ was made in 1488, and the present organ case was installed in the early 18th century.

Nave

North door

The Chapelle Saint-Jérôme is decorated with a stained-glass window made in 1531.

The ciborium (canopy) in the Choir dates from the mid-19th century.

Entrance to the cloister

The vestry has a Gothic doorway with intricate 13th-century carvings.

Did You Know?

The cloister also served as a burial site and many tombs can still be seen here.

Elegant arches, enclosing four smaller arches with trefoil windows above, line the cloister.

A SHORT WALK
BAYONNE

Distance 1.5 km (1 mile) **Time** 20 minutes
Nearest station Gare de Bayonne

The cultural capital of the northern Pays Basque, Bayonne grew and prospered from maritime trade and its strategic position near the border with Spain. It was long held by the English but was finally taken by the French in 1451. In the 16th century Bayonne also opened its gates to many Jewish refugees, who came here to escape persecution during the Spanish and Portuguese Inquisitions. At the confluence of the great Adour, near its estuary, and the smaller Nive, Bayonne has a remarkable architectural heritage that makes a walk around town a delight. Try to time your visit for Bayonne's well-known August festivals.

In **place de la Liberté**, the keys of the city are thrown into the crowd at the start of the city's August festivals.

Set on the Nive, at the point where it joins the Adour, this former theatre was built in 1842. It now houses the **town hall**, from whose balcony Bayonne's festivals are announced.

START

PLACE DE LA LIBERTÉ

0 metres   100
0 yards   100

N ←

Château-Vieux

The Gothic **Cathédrale Sainte-Marie** stands in the heart of Bayonne's historic centre.

↑ The *mairie* (town hall), a former theatre on place de la Liberté beside the Nive river

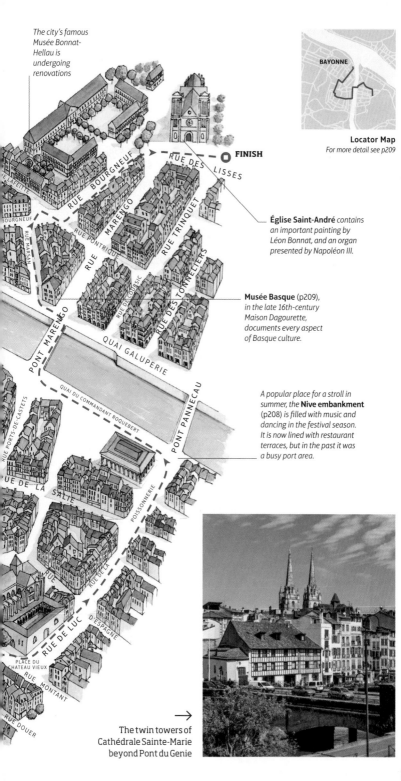

The city's famous **Musée Bonnat-Hellau** is undergoing renovations

Locator Map
For more detail see p209

BAYONNE

● **FINISH**

Église Saint-André contains an important painting by Léon Bonnat, and an organ presented by Napoléon III.

Musée Basque (p209), in the late 16th-century Maison Dagourette, documents every aspect of Basque culture.

A popular place for a stroll in summer, the **Nive embankment** (p208) is filled with music and dancing in the festival season. It is now lined with restaurant terraces, but in the past it was a busy port area.

→ The twin towers of Cathédrale Sainte-Marie beyond Pont du Genie

↑ The twin pillars of Pointe Sainte-Anne, Hendaye

EXPERIENCE MORE

2

Hendaye

🅰A6 🚃🚌 ℹ️67b, boulevard de la Mer; www. hendaye-tourisme.fr

The family resort of Hendaye, at the mouth of the Bidassoa river, has two distinct areas, Hendaye-Plage and Hendaye-Ville. The Église Saint-Vincent is notable for its 13th-century crucifix and a 17th-century altarpiece. The two distinctive

rocks of Pointe Sainte-Anne mark the entrance to the Baie de Fontarrabie.

Just 1.5 km (1 mile) from Hendaye lies beautiful **Château d'Abbadia**, built by explorer Antoine d'Abbadia (1810–97). Here, quirky Asian-inspired touches mix with Gothic design.

Château d'Abbadia
👁👁🚶 🏠Route de la Corniche 📞0559200451 🕐Apr-Oct: daily; Nov-Mar: Tue-Sun (call ahead to check opening hours)

3

Saint-Jean-de-Luz

🅰A6 🚃🚌 ℹ️20 boulevard Victor Hugo; www.saint-jean-de-luz.com

Once a pirates' stronghold, Saint-Jean-de-Luz lies in a bay with the Fort de Socoa on one side and Pointe de Sainte-Barbe on the other. For centuries the town grew rich from the fortunes of traders and pirates – who were at their most active from the 16th to the 19th centuries – and from cod, sardine and tuna fishing as

well as whaling. The harbour is still a lively place today, and this pleasant resort is popular with surfers. The coastline northeast of the town has a tempting choice of beaches: Erromardi, Lafitenia, Mayarco and Senix, shared with the neighbouring coastal resort town of Guéthary.

Place Louis-XIV, opposite the harbour and behind the tourist office, is lined with elegant residences. It is now filled with café terraces, attractively laid out in the shade of plane trees. Dominating the square is the **Maison Louis-XIV**, with an imposing façade of pale grey stone. This house was built in 1643 by Johannis de Lohobiague, a shipowner. Cardinal Mazarin (1602–61), effectively ruler of France during the minority of Louis XIV, stayed here in 1660, as did Anne of Austria and Louis XIV himself, when he came here to marry the Spanish *infanta* Marie-Thérèse to fulfil the terms of the Peace of the Pyrénées. Next door are Maison Saubat-Claret, with carved balconies, and the Hôtel de Ville (1654), which contains an equestrian statue of Louis by Bouchardon.

The handsome rue de la Republique leads from place Louise-XIV to the seafront and the Grande Plage. Having survived the fire of 1558, Maison Esquerrenea, at No. 17, is the town's oldest house. Like Maison Duplan at No. 10, it has a tower for observing ships entering the harbour. Curving around the point to the harbourside itself is the Quai de l'Infante, where the **Maison de l'Infante** can be found. This house, also known as Maison Joanoenea and built in about 1640,

belonged to the Haraneders, a shipowning family. Running parallel to the quay, rue Mazarin also has beautiful townhouses, such as Maison de l'Infante, the Maison des Trois-Canons at No. 10, and Maison de Théophile de la Tour-d'Auvergne at No. 18.

To the east of place Louis-XIV is rue Gambetta, which has beautiful houses at Nos. 18 and 20. On this street is the **Église Saint-Jean-Baptiste**. Having been destroyed by fire in 1419 and then rebuilt in several stages, this sturdy-looking church appears plain from the outside, but has a splendid 17th-century interior with a fine altarpiece. It was here that the marriage of Louis XIV and Marie-Thérèse took place on 9 June 1660.

The town of Urrugne, 5 km (3 miles) south of Saint-Jean-de-Luz, has an interesting church, the 16th-century Église Saint-Vincent. It has a Renaissance doorway, a 45-m (148-ft) bell tower, an organ gallery and lofty wooden galleries.

↑ Galleried altar in Saint-Jean-Baptiste, St-Jean-de-Luz

Maison Louis-XIV
⊛ ⊛ ⌂ Place Louis-XIV
⌚ Apr–early Nov: Wed–Mon
🅦 maison-louis-xiv.fr

Maison de l'Infante
⊛ ⊛ ⌂ Quai de l'Infante
📞 05 59 26 36 82 ⌚ Jun–mid-Nov: Mon–Sat

Église Saint-Jean-Baptiste
⌂ Rue Gambetta 📞 05 59 26 08 81 ⌚ Daily

 GREAT VIEW
On Point

It's an easy walk from Saint-Jean-de-Luz, around the bay to the Pointe de Sainte-Barbe and its little white chapel. The reward is a stunning view back across the bay to Saint-Jean-de-Luz.

→ The Église Saint-Jean-Baptiste in St-Jean-de-Luz

Stairs to the galleries

The elaborate Baroque altarpiece of 1670 features twisted columns, with vine-leaf and acanthus motifs.

Painted walls

As in many Basque churches, the interior is lined with tiered wooden galleries. Here there are three tiers on each side and four behind the organ.

Did You Know?
Marie-Thérèse had been married to Louis XIV by proxy before even arriving in France.

Entrance

Buttress

Vestry

④

Biarritz

🅰 A6 🚉🚌 🛈 1 square d'Ixelles; www.tourisme. biarritz.fr

Biarritz was just a small whaling port until the late 19th century, when seabathing came into vogue. This new trend, fuelled by the town's popularity with Napoléon III and Empress Eugénie, led to its discovery by the wider world. Expansion of the railways meant new visitors could easily access the Emperor and Empress's favourite resort, and since then, Biarritz has attracted a cosmopolitan crowd.

The resort's famous Grande Plage (Great Beach) stretches out in front of the casino, an Art Deco building dating from 1924. On the right stands the impressive Hôtel du Palais, built in the early 20th century on the site of Villa Eugénie, the former imperial residence. In the distance is the **Phare de Biarritz**. The 248 steps in this lighthouse lead up to the lantern, from where there is a lovely panoramic view. Plage Miramar, an extension of Grande Plage, is backed by luxurious Belle Époque villas. The Russian Orthodox church in avenue de l'Impératrice was built in the late 19th century. The fishing harbour, created in 1870, sits in a sheltered inlet, above which stands the Église Sainte-Eugénie.

The city's emblem is the Rocher de la Vierge, a rock formation jutting from the ocean, connected to the promenade by an iron walkway designed by Alexandre Eiffel. The rock is crowned by a statue of the Madonna.

On the esplanade itself, set in a 1935 Art Deco building, is **L'Aquarium Biarritz**, which explores the Gulf of Gascony's marine life. The pretty Villa Belza is an unusual house with a turret and a peaked roof. The Plage du Port-Vieux, south of the rocks, leads on to the Côte des Basques.

Phare de Biarritz
⊛ 📞 05 59 22 37 10 ⏰ May, Jun & Sep: daily; Jul & Aug: daily; Oct-Apr: Sat & Sun

L'Aquarium Biarritz
⊛ 📍 Esplanade du Rocher de la Vierge ⏰ Times vary, check website 🌐 aquarium biarritz.com

SHOP

Chic beachwear is always *de rigueur* in Biarritz. Find your own style of funky, individually designed and planet-friendly pieces here, many by local designers.

Baigneuses Palace
🅰 A6 📍 8 rue Lahontine 🌐 baigneusespalace. com

BTZ
🅰 A6 📍 2 place Bellevue 🌐 btz-biarritz.com

L'Étiquette Biarritz
🅰 A6 📍 54 rue Gambetta 📞 09 83 06 34 39

The Grande Plage and Casino and the fairytale Villa Belza *(inset)* ↓

↑ The Art Deco casino beside Biarritz's Grand Plage in the 1920s

HIGH SOCIETY IN BIARRITZ

In the late 19th century, when Napoléon III and Empress Eugénie were putting Biarritz on the map as a coastal resort, the Second Empire gave way to the Belle Époque. It was then that Biarritz became an upper-class resort with a lively nightlife. Full of newly built Art Nouveau and Art Deco buildings, it held great allure for many prominent people, and throughout the early 20th century, the town's casinos and nightlife drew celebrities from France and around the world.

BATHING AT BIARRITZ

Bathing at Biarritz was at its most fashionable in the first half of the 20th century. The fashion for sea bathing was born in Biarritz thanks to Napoléon III and Empress Eugénie, who reigned as "Beach Queen" until World War I and again in the interwar period. The heyday of that epoch's seaside holidays was brought to an abrupt end by the Wall Street crash of 1929 and the economic hardship of the 1930s that followed.

↑ People sunbathing in Biarritz in the early 1920s, one of Biarritz's many heyday eras

FAMOUS VISITORS

The British Royal Family became regular visitors to Biarritz's sunny shores, following the lead set by King Edward VII, who spent many summer holidays in Biarritz in the early 20th century. Empress Elizabeth of Austria, also came in search of a cure for her world-weariness. But as well as royalty, the city became a hotspot for entertainment and big screen legends. Charlie Chaplin was one of a host of internationally famous people who regularly frequented Biarritz's many luxurious hotels, such as the Hôtel Miramar, in the 1930s and 1940s. Later, the Marquess of Cueva threw extravagant parties, entertaining royalty and film stars such as Rita Hayworth, Gary Cooper, Bing Crosby and Frank Sinatra.

↑ Edward, Duke of Windsor, and Wallis Simpson during a stay at a villa in Biarritz

↑ Elaborate carpentry decorating the interior of the church at Itxassou

5

Itxassou

🅰A6 🏛ℹMairie; 05 59 29 75 36

Itxassou is set in the heart of a picturesque valley. In the Urzumu quarter of the village stands the 17th-century white-walled Église Saint-Fructueux, which is lined with galleries of turned and carved wood. The cemetery contains over 200 circular-topped funerary stones. Black cherries are a speciality of the area and are celebrated at a

---

EAT

Zuzulua

An authentic Basque restaurant and bar, right on La Nivele river, with a menu that's strong on grilled meats and seafood.

🅰A6 🅰Lieu-Dit Cherchebruit, Saint-Pée-sur-Nivelle
🕐Mon 🌐zuzulua.fr

€€€

---

festival on the first Sunday in June. Either fresh or made into jam, these cherries are delicious with a slice of local ewe's milk cheese.

1.5 km (1 mile) from Itxassou, a winding road runs alongside the Nive river and the Gorges d'Ateka-Gaitz as far as Pas-de-Roland. According to legend, Roland pierced this great rock with his sword, Durandal. Here, Artzamendi (Basque for "Bear Mountain") soars up to 926 m (3,040 ft) and is within easy reach, by car or on foot. Another gentle walk along a marked path leads up to the summit of Mondarrain, at 750 m (2461 ft), where there are ruins of a Roman fortress that was rebuilt in the Middle Ages

---

6

Ainhoa

🅰A6 🏛ℹMaison du Patrimoine; 05 59 29 93 99

Said to be one of France's prettiest villages, Ainhoa has rows of splendidly picturesque old houses with red or green woodwork. Some in the main street have carved lintels. The 14th-century church, in the main square, is lined with galleries and

---

contains a gilt altarpiece. It also has a five-tiered bell tower and circular-topped funerary stones in the graveyard. More of these traditional Basque gravestones can be found at Notre-Dame-de l'Aubépine, another church higher up at 450 m (1,477 ft). Views from here take in the Rhune peak, the Atlantic and the frontier district of Dancharia, in Navarre.

7

Nivelle Valley

🅰A6

Set against the backdrop of three peaks – the Rhune, Mondarrain and Axuria – the landscape of this valley is a mix of rolling hills, open meadows and farmland, enclosed by neat hedges.

Ascain, 6 km (4 miles) from the coast, nestles in the foothills of the Rhune. The village was immortalized by French naval officer and novelist Pierre Loti (1850–1923) in his novel Ramuntcho. The old Labourd-style houses painted red, white and green on the main square make a picturesque sight. Consecrated in 1626 in the presence of Louis XIII, the church has an imposing west tower. Nearby is Saint-Pée-sur-Nivelle, which has 18th-century houses and a church, the Église Saint-Pierre, with tombstones – including one from the 16th century – set in the floor. Behind the church is the **Moulin Plazako Errota**, a 15th-century mill. It is no longer in use, but contains old grain-measures that were used by Basque millers. The state-owned forest has footpaths and bicycle tracks, as well as strangely shaped pollarded oaks. The **Lac de Saint-Pée**, 2 km (1 mile) further on, via the D918, offers water sports activities.

The summit of the lofty Rhune (905 m, 2970 ft) can be reached on foot or by the **Petit Train de la Rhune**, that runs on a cog railway that dates from the 1920s. The mountainsides here are dotted with megalithic monuments dating from the Neolithic period. Visitors will also see shepherds with their sheep, as well as the little Basque ponies known as *pottoks*. Griffon vultures may be seen soaring overhead.

The old smugglers' village of Sare has some fine 17th- and 18th-century Labourd-style houses. Strolling through its various districts, visitors will come across 14 oratories dedicated to the Madonna

POTTOKS OF THE PAYS BASQUE

Since prehistoric times, the hills of the Pays Basque have been inhabited by a type of pony known as a *pottok* (pronouned "potiok"), meaning "little horse". *Pottoks* are hardy, having evolved in a harsh environment where food was scarce. They are typically bay or black and pot-bellied, with long manes, dainty legs and small hooves. These tiny horses are endangered but, in the 1970s, certain breeders began to take an interest in them. Once used for farm work or slaughtered for food, they are now protected and treated as the emblem of the Pays Basque.

and various saints, built in thanksgiving by fishermen from the 17th century.

Maison Ortillopitz, just outside Sare, is a stately 17th-century farmhouse. With half-timbered walls, a fine oak-beamed roof and thick stone walls, it is a typical *etxe*, or traditional Basque house.

The **Grottes de Sare** lie 7 km (4 miles) south of the village. Bones and flint tools that were discovered here show that these caves were inhabited in prehistoric times.

Moulin Plazako Errota
Rue de l'Église 05 59 54 11 69 Times vary, call ahead

Lac de Saint-Pée
Rue du Fronton 05 59 54 11 69 Jul & Aug: daily

Petit Train de la Rhune
Col de Saint-Ignace Mid-Mar–early Nov rhune.com

Maison Ortillopitz
La Maison Basque de Sare, Col de St Ignace Early Apr–Sep: Mon–Fri ortillopitz.com

Grottes de Sare
Times vary, check website Jan grottes desare.fr

> The summit of the lofty Rhune in the Nivelle Valley can be reached on foot or by the Petit Train de la Rhune, that runs on a cog railway that dates from the 1920s.

↑ Shaped like a natural amphitheatre, the entrance to the Grottes de Sare in the Nivelle Valley

8 Larrau

⚠ B7 **ℹ Rue Arhanpia, Tardets; 05 59 28 51 28**

Larrau, a village of slate-roofed houses, clings to the sides of the Pic d'Orhy, a mountain that figures in local legends. On the edge of the Forêt d'Iraty (p229), the village is the main centre of wood-pigeon hunting, a sport with a lively local following.

About 12 km (7 miles) south of Larrau is Col de Larrau, a pass at 1,573 m (5,163 ft). Having featured in the Tour de France, it's a major draw for mountain-bikers seeking a challenge. It's also a good place to stop on the way up to Pic d'Orhy, at 2,017 m (6,619 ft), 1.5 hours' walk away.

The Gorges d'Holzarté and Gorges d'Olhadubi, near Larrau, are two great canyons cut into the limestone by the action of water. There are dramatic views across the river valleys of both from the Passerelle d'Holzarté, a footbridge over the Gorges d'Olhadubi. Those who suffer from vertigo may find this bridge unnerving, but it is perfectly safe, and there are even picnic places where visitors can stop for lunch.

9 Hasparren

⚠ B6 **ℹ 2 place Saint-Jean; www.hasparren-tourisme.fr**

Hasparren is surrounded by rolling hills and meadows grazed by flocks of sheep, and the landscape is dotted with villages and traditional half-timbered Basque farmhouses with white walls and red shutters. Once a centre for shoemaking and leather goods, Hasparren is now an industrial yet pleasant town.

The Chapelle du Sacré-Cœur, or Chapelle des Missionnaires, was built in 1933. The walls of the nave are covered in huge frescoes depicting 48 saints, some shown with the instruments of their martyrdom. A Byzantine-style mosaic, *Christ in Majesty*, adorns the choir.

Maison Eyhartzea, in rue Francis-Jammes, at the entrance to the village, was, from 1921 until his death in 1938, the home of the poet Francis Jammes, whose work celebrates traditional life in the Basque country.

Between Cambo and Hasparren, the D22, known as the Route Impériale des Cimes (Mountaintop Road), offers panoramic views of the Nive valley, and of the Rhune, Artzamendi and Mondarrain mountain peaks. Turn off at a junction in the Pachkoenia district to return to Hasparren via Cambo-les-Bains and Bayonne-Saint-Pierre-d'Irube.

Nearby, at Ayherre, there is a panoramic view of the countryside. The Basque name for this village is *Eihera*, which means "mill". There were 14 mills, but now only one is in working order. On the edge of the village are the ruins of Château de Belzance.

About 13 km (8 miles) from Hasparren are the **Grotte d'Isturitz and Grotte d'Oxocelhaya**, caves formed by an underground stretch of the Arbéroue river. Paintings and engravings of deer and horses, as well as bones, tools and a musical instrument made of bone, were found here.

Grotte d'Isturitz and Grotte d'Oxocelhaya

♿ 🅿 **⚠ Saint-Martin-d'Arbéroue** **⏰ Times vary, check website** **🆆 grottes-isturitz.com**

10 Bidache

⚠ B6 **ℹ 1 place du Fronton; 05 59 56 03 49**

The fact that Bidache was once the seat of a dukedom gives some idea of the town's historical importance. This is also evident from the ruins of the Château de Gramont, built by the duke here in the Middle Ages. It was remodelled several times up until the 18th century and has both medieval and Renaissance elements. The Jewish cemetery in the village is one of the oldest in France dating to the 17th century.

↑ The Passerelle d'Holzarté bridge over the Gorges d'Holzarté, near Larrau

↑ Edmond Rostand's house in Cambo-les-Bains and the Great Hall *(inset)*

11 Cambo-les-Bains

🅰B6 �︎🚌 𝒊3 avenue de la Mairie; www.camboles bains.com

Well known as a spa resort, Cambo-les-Bains is set above the Nive river. Many people, including artists, writers and other famous figures in the 19th and early 20th centuries, have come here to sample the sulphur- and iron-

GREAT VIEW
Top Spot

Climb to the top of Mount Ursuia near Hasparren for sweeping views of the Basque countryside around it, the Pyrénées and the distant coast. The climb should take an easy three hours.

rich waters of its two springs. Among them were Napoléon III and the Empress Eugénie, who acquired a holiday home in Biarritz in 1856; the Spanish composer Isaac Albéniz, in 1909, and the painter Pablo Tillac, in 1921.

In clear weather, there are panoramic views of the river valley and the Pyrénées from rue du Trinquet and rue des Terrasses. The Église Saint-Laurent has a Baroque altarpiece in gilded wood, with a central panel that depicts the martyrdom of Saint Laurence. In the grave-yard are several examples of the circular-topped, Basque-style grave-stones.

Avenue Edmond-Rostand leads to the hillside where Rostand, best known for his verse-drama *Cyrano de Bergerac*, built his home: the **Villa Arnaga**, which is set in extensive gardens. Every room is decorated in a different style, including Classical elements in the study. Displays relating to the writer's life and work fill the first-floor rooms.

In early October Cambo celebrates the *gâteau Basque*,

STAY

Rosa Enia Guesthouse

A historic mansion with rooms that include a treehouse. Basque meals are lovingly served.

🅰B6 🏠Avenue du Prof Grancher, Cambo-les-Bains 📞05 59 93 67 20

€€€

a tart filled with cherries and crème pâtissière, with a festival that now attracts around 17,000 people. It was a baker here, Marianne Hirigoyen, who first thought to market this traditional Basque dessert to a wider audience, hence the connection between the delicacy and the town.

Villa Arnaga

🌐🌐 🏠Route du Docteur Camino 📞05 59 29 83 92 🕐Apr-Oct: daily

Colourful interior of
St Stephen's church,
St-Étienne-de-Baïgorry ↑

⑫

Saint-Étienne-de-Baïgorry

Ⓐ A6 🚗🚌 **ⓘ Maison Elizonde; 05 59 37 47 28**

Saint-Étienne-de-Baïgorry is a traditonal Basque town close to the border of Spain. From the central square there are fine views of Mont Buztanzelai and Mont Oilandoi, and over to Col d'Ispéguy.

Next to the Romanesque church is the Porte des Cagots, a doorway for Baïgorry's *cagots* – villagers who were once set apart from the ret of the community for a reason

that has now been lost in history. Their ghetto was in the Mitchelenea quarter, where there is a single-span bridge. Built in 1661, it is known locally as the Roman bridge.

With two medieval towers on its north side and two Renaissance parapets on the south, the **Château d'Etxauz** dominates Baïgorry. Its lord ruled here for 500 years. The castle has a small collection of items associated with Charlie Chaplin, who stayed here.

Nearby, the vineyards of Irouléguy are the only ones in the northern Pays Basque with their own **cave coopérative** (wine cooperative).

Just 8 km (5 miles) outside Banca are the remains of an 18th-century blast furnace, a vestige of the mines that were once active.

Les Aldudes has Navarre-style houses featuring red sandstone. At Salaisons des Aldudes, a meat-curing factory, visitors can learn about the Basque pork industry and sample its produce. Pierre Oteïza, the owner, has almost single-handedly revived the

art of making traditional hams from *pie noir*, a local breed of black-spotted pig.

Château d'Etxauz

♿🕐 **Ⓐ On the D949 ☎ 05 59 37 48 58 ⊙ Jul & Aug**

Cave Coopérative d'Irouléguy

♿🕐🅿 **Ⓐ On the D15 ⊙ Daily (Oct-Mar: Mon-Sat) ⓦ cave-irouleguy.com**

---

⑬

Bidarray

Ⓐ A6 **ⓘ 14 place Charles-de-Gaulle, Saint-Jean-Pied-de-Port; 05 59 37 03 57**

This village is divided into 12 districts, each with typical Basse-Navarre-style houses. On the square at the top of the hill stands a small 12th-century church with pink sandstone walls. Its graveyard contains circular-topped stones. The river Nive here is suitable for water sports, and several local centres organize activities on the river. Being

located on the GR10, a long-distance footpath running between Ainhoa and Baïgorry, also makes Bidarray a good starting point for scenic walks up the Iparla and Baygoura mountains and Mont Artzamendi.

Nearby, Ossès has fine half-timbered houses, such as Maison Harizmendi and Maison Ibarrondo, and houses with decorated lintels, such as Maison Arrosa and Maison Arrosagaray. On the square stands the Église Saint-Julien, a Renaissance-style church with a seven-sided bell tower. The interior has carved wooden galleries, a spiral staircase and a magnificent Baroque altarpiece.

Saint-Martin-d'Arrosa, 4 km (2.5 miles) away on the opposite bank of the Nive, has many traditional houses with carved lintels. The church, on the promontory here, has a gilded wooden altar and a moulded ceiling.

Irrissary, a village at the centre of the Pays Basque Nord, has a remarkable 12th-century priory hospital, which was once the seat of a commander of the Knights Templar, St-Jean de Jérusalem.

⑭
Espelette

🅰 A6 🛈 Château; 05 59 93 95 02

Famous for its sweet red Espelette peppers, celebrated with a major festival in late October, this large village is also noted as the birthplace of Father Armand David (1826–1900). David was the first westerner to learn of the existence of the great panda in China when he received a skin as a gift, and also discovered a species of deer – *Elaphurus davidianus* – which is named after him. A plaque marks Maison Bergara, where he lived. Also worth a visit is the 11th-century **Château des Barons d'Ezpeleta**, which now houses the village hall and tourist office. The church, just outside, has a painted ceiling, wooden galleries, a 17th-century altarpiece and a large bell tower. In the cemetery are ancient circular-topped funerary stones.

Château des Barons d'Ezpeleta

🅰 145 route Karrika-Nagusia 📞 05 59 93 95 02 ⏰ Mon-Fri & Sat (Jul & Aug: Mon-Sat)

⑮
La Bastide-Clairence

🅰 B6 🚌 🛈 Maison Darrieux, place des Arceaux; 05 59 29 65 05

This beautiful *bastide* town, on the border with Gascony, was founded in 1312 by the king of Navarre. Its location very near Béarn allowed it to control traffic on the Adour river. In the Middle Ages, the village grew as a result of its weaving and leatherworking industries, as well as trade. The town still has its original

medieval grid layout, with two main thoroughfares at right angles to six smaller streets, and half-timbered houses and arcades.

The medieval Église Notre-Dame stands in a courtyard with gravestones set into it. Further up the hill is a graveyard with about 60 headstones. This was the cemetery of a community of Sephardic Jews who came to the area from Portugal during the 17th century.

Located 3 km (2 miles) from La Bastide-Clairence is the Benedictine abbey of Nôtre-Dame-de-Belloc. It was founded in 1875 and is inhabited by a community of monks who work the land and who publish books in Basque. The graveyard has a few circular-topped gravestones.

↑ La Bastide-Clairence, nominated as one of France's loveliest villages

16

Saint-Jean-Pied-de-Port

A B6 🏛️🚆 **ℹ** 14 place Charles-de-Gaulle; www.saintjeanpieddeport-paysbasque-tourisme.com

As the final stopping place for pilgrims before the climb over the mountain pass to Roncesvalles, Saint-Jean-Pied-de-Port has been an important commercial town on the pilgrimage routes to Santiago de Compostela since the Middle Ages Known as the Garden of Navarre, this town switched between sovereigns many times until 1589, when, under Henri IV, it became part of France.

Entry into the old town is from place Charles-de-Gaulle, through Porte de Navarre, a fortified gate with arrow-slits and battlements. Steps lead up to the wall-walk near the 17th century Citadelle,. The attractive medieval Église Notre-Dame-du-Bout-du-Pont has pink sandstone columns and pillars. Maison Mansart, also built in pink sandstone, houses the town hall.

Rue de la Citadelle is lined with beautiful stone houses,

with carved lintels and eaves over richly decorated beams. One of the finest of these houses is Maison Arcanzola, built in 1510, with brick and half-timbered walls in its upper storey. Further up is the Prison des Évêques. In the 19th century it was used as a short-term prison, but the building dates from the times that the town was the seat of a bishopric – three times between 1383 and 1417. Porte Saint-Jacques, the gateway at the end of rue de la Citadelle, is a World Heritage Site, and pilgrims still pass through it.

Crossing the Nive by the picturesque Pont Notre-Dame to the rue d'Espagne quarter on the opposite bank, you will come to the ramparts. There is a covered market here, held on Mondays.

Around 28 km (17 miles) away, beyond Arnéguy and Valcarlos, in Spain, is Roncesvalles (Roncevaux in Spanish). The town lies below Col de Roncevaux (or Puerto d'Ibañeta), a pass at an altitude of 1,507 m (4,946 ft). It has an 18th-century hostel, and the medieval Chapelle de Sancti Spiritus and Église de Santiago. The town is 800 km (500 miles) from Santiago

Compostela and, for the pilgrims arriving there, the most arduous part of their journey was over.

17

Saint-Palais

A B6 🚆 **ℹ** 14 place Charles-de-Gaulle; www.saintpalais-tourisme.com

Founded in the 13th century, the *bastide* town of Saint-Palais later became the capital of the kingdom of Navarre. As it stands at the crossroads of several pilgrimage routes, many markets were held here. It is also where the region's first Estates General met in the 16th century.

The town has some lovely old houses, particularly Maison des Têtes, which is

↓ The Nive river, passing peacefully through St-Jean-Pied-de-Port

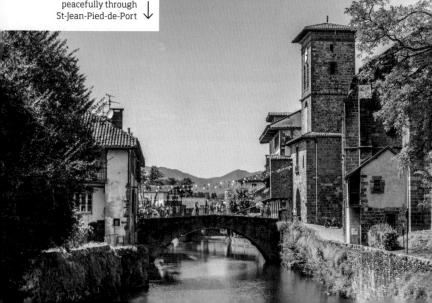

decorated with carvings of heads, set within medallions. The **Musée de Basse-Navarre et des Chemins de Saint-Jacques**, in the courtyard of the town hall, documents local history and the history of pilgrimages to Compostela. The town also has **Ona Tiss**, one of the few remaining traditional Basque linen-weaving workshops.

Every year, on the first Sunday following 15 August, Saint-Palais hosts the Force Basque festival, in which eight local teams compete in traditional Basque trials of strength, including tug of war, cart-lifting, splitting tree trunks and racing with huge sacks of grain slung across their shoulders. Parades and music add to the festivities.

The 16th-century **Château de Camou**, 5 km (3 miles) north of Saint-Palais, has models of Renaissance inventions. Ostabat, 12 km (7 miles) south of Saint-Palais, stands at the junction of several pilgrimage routes and is an important stopping place for pilgrims.

Musée de Basse-Navarre et des Chemins de Saint-Jacques

✆✆ 🏠 1 route de Gibraltar 📞 05 59 65 71 78 🕓 Jul & Aug: daily

Ona Tiss

✆ 🏠 23 rue de la Bidouze 🕓 Mon-Thu 🌐 onatiss.fr

↑ The rough stone exterior of the Église de L'Hôpital-Saint-Blaise contrasts with a magnificent interior

Château de Camou

✆✆ 📞 05 59 65 84 03 🕓 By appointment only, call ahead

---

⑱ L'Hôpital-Saint-Blaise

🅰 B6 ℹ Mairie; 05 59 66 11 12

This tiny village, located 13 km (8 miles) northeast of Mauléon-Licharre, lies very close to the border with Béarn (p232).

It was once the seat of a commander of the Knights Templar, and had a hostel where pilgrims would stay and rest, before continuing on their journey up to Col du Somport, via Oloron-Sainte-Marie (p244) or Saint-Jean-Pied-de-Port.

The striking 12th-century Église de L'Hôpital-Saint-Blaise is in the Romanesque style with Moorish elements. These are particularly noticeable in the stone latticework of the windows and in the capitals of the doorway. Moorish influence is also apparent inside the church: the stone-built dome has groin vaults that intersect to form an eight-pointed star. The interior also has a Baroque altarpiece and traditional Basque-style galleries. Both these features date from a later period than the church itself.

Église de L'Hôpital-Saint-Blaise

✆✆ 🏠 Le Village 📞 05 59 66 07 21 🕓 Daily

BASQUE LINEN

Basque linen is traditionally woven with stripes, which served to identify different families' linen at the village washhouse. Originally woven from flax on wooden handlooms, Basque linen is now made of both flax and cotton, using factory methods. Traditional patterns include variations on the Basque cross, and the ground may be a solid colour, rather than just the traditional white. Linen cloth had a wide range of uses, from table-cloths and napkins to curtains. The largest pieces were used to decorate the interior of Basque houses. Today only a few workshops – Jean Vier in Saint-Jean-de-Luz, Ona Tiss in Saint-Palais and Lartigue (p244) in Oloron-Sainte-Marie, in Béarn – keep this ancient skill alive.

PILGRIMAGE ROUTES OF SOUTHWEST FRANCE

The four main pilgrimage routes to the Spanish city of Santiago de Compostela all run through southwest France. Since the discovery of the supposed tomb of the apostle St James at Compostela in 813, many have embarked on the journey to visit it. James is believed to have preached in Spain, and it is thought that his body was taken there after his martyrdom in Jerusalem in the 1st century AD. After crossing the Pyrénées from France into Spain, pilgrims still had 800 km (500 miles) to travel before reaching the Cathedral of Santiago. The routes they used were added to UNESCO's World Heritage List in 1993 – one of only two pilgrimages to gain this status (the other being in Japan).

JACQUETS AND JACQUAIRES

In France, pilgrims travelling to Santiago de Compostela are known as *jacquets* (men) or *jacquaires (women)*. The paths vary according to their point of departure - with the four main ones being Tours, Vézelay, Le Puy-en-Velay and Arles - but all pilgrim routes converge in Pays Basque. Because of the spectacular scenery and the towns and the villages that they pass through, these routes are still very popular to this day.

THE MARK OF THE PILGRIM

Scallop shells are a symbol of St James, and are therefore a common emblem of the pilgrimage. Many pilgrims carry a shell tied to their backpack. The symbol can also be seen carved into doorways of pilgrim-friendly hostels, on route markers along common pilgrimage paths, and even on street signs in cities such as Bordeaux, through which routes pass.

↑ Today's pilgrims carry a passport that is stamped to record their progress and the places they have stopped

A map based on a 17th-century design, showing the various pilgrimage routes in France →

← Pilgrims walking ascending into the Pyrénées into Spain

← Accounts of and guides to the pilgrimage routes date back to the 12th century

LOCATIONS TO VISIT

① Porte Saint-Jacques
This gateway in Saint-Jean-Pied-de-Port (p225) is one of the many monuments on the route to Santiago de Compostela that are now listed as UNESCO World Heritage Sites.

② Religious Buildings
Many churches, such as that shown here at L'Hôpital Saint-Blaise (p224), are also World Heritage Sites. They testify to the strength of Christian faith in southwest France, as in the rest of Europe, during the Middle Ages.

③ Stèle de Gibraltar
In the picturesque village of Ostabat-Asme, near Saint-Palais, is the Stèle de Gibraltar monument. This column marks the symbolic convergence point of the pilgrim routes from Tours, Le Puy-en-Velay and Vézelay, all of which passed through this small town.

④ Pilgrim Sculpture
On the Spanish side of Col du Somport, this sculpture marks the route from Arles in France that later converges with four other pilgrim routes at Puente la Reina. From there, a single route known as the Camino Francés (French Way), continues straight to Santiago de Compostela.

19

Ciboure

A6 5 place Camille Jullian; www.ciboure.fr

Just south of Saint-Jean-de-Luz, on the other side of the Nivelle river, is Ciboure. The town has many fine examples of traditional Basque architecture, with its whitewashed houses, red woodwork and balconies. The Couvent des Récollets on Quai Pascal-Elissalt was built in 1610 and, with the cloisters, it was used as a prison and tribunal during the French Revolution. You can peek at it through locked gates. On the quayside is a 17th-century house with a Dutch-style gabled façade: this is where the composer Maurice Ravel was born. It now contains private apartments.

The 16th-century Église Saint-Vincent, in rue Pocalette, has a fortified octagonal bell tower. The church's interior has wooden galleries in three tiers, an impressive altarpiece and pictures from the Chapelle des Récollets.

The lighthouse here was built in 1936 to a design by architect André Pavlovsky. The Fort de Socoa, built in the 1600s to defend the whaling port, stands at the tip of the harbour wall.

INSIDER TIP
Local Cheese

Ossau-Iraty, an unpasteurised ewe's-milk cheese, is made in an area between the Forêt d'Iraty and the Pic du Midi d'Ossau. It has its own AOP and is often eaten as a dessert with black cherry jam.

20

Sainte-Engrâce

B7 Mairie; 05 59 28 60 83

In the heart of the upper Soule, at 630 m (2,068 ft), the shepherds' hamlet of Sainte-Engrâce lies on the border with Béarn and near Navarre, a province of the Spanish Basque country. It consists of about 100 farmsteads, and "districts" spread out over a wide area of unspoiled countryside. At the confluence of the Gorges de Kakuetta and Gorges d'Ehujarre, it seems to stand guard over the great amphitheatre of hills all around. The 12th-century Romanesque abbey church is dedicated to Santa Gracia, after whom the village is named, a young Portuguese woman who was put to death around 300, when Christians were being persecuted in Moorish Zaragoza. The original chapel on the site was built to house a relic of the saint – her arm, which was miraculously recovered. The chapel was later attached to the monastery at Leyre, in Navarre. It has a wooden pulpit and 21 capitals carved with a wealth of biblical scenes. The wrought-iron rood screen and Baroque altarpieces are noteworthy. The graveyard has several circular-topped Basque gravestones.

21

Gorges de Kakuetta

B7 Sainte-Engrâce 15 Mar-15 Nov: 8am-7pm daily sainte-engrace.com/index.php

First explored by Édouard-Alfred Martel in 1906, these narrow gorges near Sainte-Engrâce were carved out of the rock by the action of water over thousands of years. You

↑ Slippery conditions underfoot in the Gorges de Kakuetta

can walk all the way round the canyon in a 6.5-hour trek. You can also walk for 2 km (1 mile) right up into the gorge along metal walkways. Sturdy walking boots are strongly recommended.

The drop from the clifftops on either side to the bottom of the canyon is about 300 m (985 ft). Some of the narrow passages, including the Grand Étroit, which is one of the most magnificent in France, are no more than a few metres wide, but walking them is a thrilling experience.

↑ Ciboure's sheltered harbour, protected by the seawall and Fort de Socoa

The moist conditions in these deep gorges allow lush vegetation to thrive. After walking for about an hour, you will come to a 20-m (65-ft) waterfall, whose source has still not been discovered. About 200 m (655 ft) further on, the walk comes to an end when you reach the Grotte du Lac, a cave with spectacular stalactites and stalagmites.

22

Forêt d'Iraty

🅐 B7 ℹ️ 05 59 28 51 09

Straddling the border between France and Spain, the Forêt d'Iraty covers more than 170 sq km (65 sq miles). On the French side, altitudes range from 900 to 1,500 m (2,950 to 4,900 ft). The heavy annual rainfall results in luxuriant growth. Both pines and beech trees thrive here – this is Europe's largest beech forest. Like the Massif des Arbailles (p231), the terrain is dotted with the remains of ancient megalithic monuments.

The area also has many peat bogs. Because ancient plant matter is preserved by the airless conditions in the bogs, they act as a record of evolutionary change over thousands of years. The bogs are also home to most of the

TOP 4 HIKES IN FORET D'IRATY

Pic d'Orhy
At a height of 2,017 m (6,617 ft), this is an intermediate hike best done during summer.

Occabé
A well-marked trail leads to stone circles at this summit of 1,456 m (4,777 ft).

Urbeltza River
Follows an old road along the river to a waterfall and historic church ruins.

Pikatua-south
This fantastic winter route can be done in half a day but requires crampons and other winter climbing gear.

forest's wildlife, including wild boar, deer, foxes and squirrels. At Col de Bagargiak, there are several marked paths for circular walks of 1.5 to 4 hours, or for cross-country skiing in winter. The GR10, a long-distance footpath, crosses the northern part of the area. You can also drive through Iraty on the D18 from Larrau to Saint-Jean-Pied-de-Port.

㉓
Mauléon-Licharre

B6 **10 rue J B Hengas; www.soule-paysbasque.com**

Capital of the Soule, the smallest and the most sparsely populated of all the provinces of the Pays Basque, Mauléon-Licharre, also known as Mauléon-Soule, stretches out along the banks of the Saison river. In Mauléon, the upper part of the town, stands the 12th-century **Château Fort de Mauléon**. This small fortress, perched on an outcrop of rock that towers over the valley, contains dungeons and old cannons.

The old *bastide* town of Mauléon was built in the 13th century, when Edward I of England ruled Aquitaine. Licharre, the lower town to the west, was the province's administrative centre. At the far end of the allées de la Soule, a long esplanade fronts the Hôtel de Montréal, a 17th-century building that now houses the town hall, a bandstand and a *fronton* (pelota court). **Château d'Andurain de Maytie**, built in the 16th and 17th centuries, has a shingle and slate keel roof. Still inhabited by the descendants of Arnaud de Maytie, this residence has Renaissance-style decoration, including listed carved mantelpieces as well as antique furniture and rare books.

The town is renowned for its espadrilles, with several firms – some going back for generations – producing fine-quality, hand-sewn ranges of the traditional rope-soled slipper. Styling itself "the espadrille capital of the Pays Basque", it even holds an espadrille festival, on 15 August each year, with folk-dancing and pelota contests.

Gotein-Libarrenx, 4 km (2.5 miles) from Mauléon-Licharre, has a 16th-century church, which contains an 18th-century altarpiece. Its bell tower, with three steeples each topped by a small cross, is typical of the Soule region.

Ordiarp, 7 km (4 miles) further on towards Col d'Osquich, was a stopping place for pilgrims on the route to Santiago de Compostela. It has several medieval houses and a 12th-century church where Mass is held in Basque. Next to the town hall stands the **Centre d'Évocation des Chemins de Saint-Jacques**. It documents the Romanesque art and architecture that relates to the history of pilgrimages to Santiago de Compostela and the Basque region.

At Trois-Villes, 11 km (7 miles) away, is the **Château d'Eliçabéa**. Built in 1660 and surrounded by gardens, it belonged to the Comte de Tréville, captain of Louis XIII's musketeers. It features in Alexandre Dumas' famous novel *The Three Musketeers* (1844). The route leading to

Grand salon in the Château d'Andurain de Maytie *(inset)* ↓

Les Arbailles passes a Soule-style church at Aussurucq.

Château Fort de Mauléon
♿ ⓢ 🏠 Rue du Fort 📞 05 59 28 02 37 🕐 Mid-May-mid-Jun: Sat & Sun; Apr-mid-May & mid-Jun-Sep: daily

Château d'Andurain de Maytie
♿ ⓢ 🏠 1 rue du Jeu-de-Paume 📞 05 59 28 04 18 🕐 Jul-mid-Sep: daily; mid-Sep-mid-Oct: Wed & Sat

Centre d'Évocation des Chemins de Saint-Jacques
♿ ⓢ 🏠 Bourg, Ordiarp 📞 05 59 28 07 63 🕐 Daily

Château d'Eliçabéa
♿ ⓢ 🏠 Trois-Villes 📞 05 59 28 54 01 🕐 Jul-Sep: Sat-Mon

↑ Sunset over the Forêt des Arbailles, on a limestone massif riddled with caverns

㉔
Massif des Arbailles

🅰 B6/7 ℹ Rue Arhanpia, Tardets; 05 59 28 51 28

This region covers a mountainous area of limestone rocks. Heavy rainfall there has led to the formation of around 600 rock cavities. Pitted with sinkholes, crevasses and chasms, parts of the area resemble a giant Gruyère cheese. Because the terrain is often so uneven, walkers are advised not to stray from the footpaths.

The dense Forêt des Arbailles found in this region has a magical atmosphere that has inspired many legends. The forest is said to be home to several creatures from Basque mythology, including Herensuge (a dragon) and lamina (wood sprites). From earliest times, the people of Les Arbailles have derived their livelihood from grazing sheep. Today, some local shepherds live in drystone-built huts known as cayolars and, from May to October, ewes are milked and cheeses – including the regional speciality of Ossau-Iraty cheese (p228) – are made.

The D117 leads to Ahusquy, where there is a spring whose pure, almost mineral-free waters are thought to have curative and diuretic properties. A steep scramble up the mountainside leads to a public drinking fountain at the source, should you wish to sample them. Ahusquy is a gateway to the Forêt des Arbailles, which is dotted with megalithic monuments, such as the Cercle de Pierre de Potto and the Dolmen d'Ithé.

In addition to livestock, this unspoiled natural environment is inhabited by deer and feral goats, and its cliffs are home to peregrine falcons, eagle owls, vultures and woodpeckers.

㉕
Tardets-Sorholus

🅰 B7 🚌 ℹ Rue Arhanpia; 05 59 28 51 28

The origins of Tardets-Sorholus go back to 1289, when it was founded as a bastide town. The central square, its focal point, is lined with 17th-century arcaded houses. In the town hall district is a fronton where games of pelota are played. Some of the houses along the banks of the Saison river have wooden galleries. The Soule-style farmhouses in the surrounding foothills are similar to the slate-roofed buildings of Béarn.

Around 8 km (5 miles) northeast of Tardets-Sorholus is the 16th-century Chapelle de la Madeleine. From here visitors can enjoy stunning views of the Soule and the Pyrenean mountain chain. A Latin inscription inside the church mentions an ancient Basque deity.

> **In the Massif des Arbailles, shepherds live in drystone-built huts known as *cayolars* and, from May to October, ewes are milked and cheeses, including Ossau-Iraty, are made.**

BÉARN

Béarn has a long and turbulent history to match the rest of Aquitaine. After Roman settlement it was later incorporated into Spanish territory. By the 9th century, Béarn was under Gascon rule and, by 1290 had become an independent territory, despite treaties claiming it as part of France. Inheritance led to its inclusion in the kingdom of Navarre. In 1620 it was finally brought under the French Crown and, after the French Revolution, Béarn was linked with the Pays Basque to create a new *département* which was renamed the Pyrénées-Atlantiques in 1970. The modern world seemed barely to touch Béarn in the early 20th century. However, it changed enormously in postwar France thanks to the discovery of gas at Lacq, the cultivation of maize and the expansion of the capital, Pau. Improvements to the road network also helped to open up this breathtakingly beautiful, unspoiled region to visitors.

With the rugged Pic du Midi d'Ossau in the east and low-lying plains to the west, Béarn has a very varied landscape. Its cultural identity is clearly expressed by the use of its own language, Gascon, and by gastronomic specialities such as *garbure* (a vegetable soup), ewe's milk cheese, and local wines.

BÉARN

Must Sees
1 Pau
2 Ossau Valley

Experience More
3 Soussouéou Valley
4 Morlanne
5 Salies-de-Béarn
6 Orthez
7 Oloron-Sainte-Marie
8 Lescar
9 Navarrenx
10 Barétous Valley
11 Bétharram
12 Nay
13 Aspe Valley
14 Monein
15 Lembeye
16 Morlaàs

Elegant buildings on Pau's Boulevard des Pyrénées →

1

PAU

🅐C6 ✈🚊🚌 ℹ Place Royale; www.pau-pyrenees.com

To discover the capital of old Béarn, a city of history and beauty, start your visit at place Georges-Clémenceau. From here parks, museums, regal chateaus and lively street life unfold. The historic district, with its Basque-style houses and cobbled streets is a delight to explore. Steep passages and bridges span Pau's hilly terrain; from Boulevard des Pyrénées and the funicular train, mountain views are legendary.

The capital of Béarn and seat of the royal court of Navarre, Pau is the birthplace of Henri IV of France and of the Bourbon dynasty. In the first half of the 19th century, the city's gentle climate attracted many visitors, including a number of wealthy English people, who came to spend their winters here. Soon luxurious villas were being built and splendid municipal gardens were laid out. In 1856, the first golf course to be built on the continent of Europe opened in Pau, which also has an Anglican church, the Église Saint-Andrew, on the corner of rue O'Quin and rue Pasteur.

1

Villa Saint-Basil's

🅐61 avenue Trespoey 🅒05 59 84 73 87 🕑2:30–4pm

Gathered in the Quartier Trespoey are several grand houses, almost all of them privately owned. However, the ground floor of Villa Saint-Basil's, built between 1885 and 1888 and set in beautiful parkland, is open to visitors during *journées de patrimoine*. Other privately owned villas north of the castle, beyond rue Gaston-Fébus, can be seen from the outside.

2

Quartier du Château and Quartier du Hédas

The old parts of the medieval and Renaissance town cluster around the castle *(p238)*. Remodelled in the 18th century, the quarter has cobbled streets and several townhouses, including the Hôtel de Peyré, also known as Maison Sully, at 2 rue du Château. Its door knocker, in the shape of a basset hound, is said to be lucky.

Quartier du Hédas, the city's oldest district, has fine 16th-century townhouses in rue René-Fournets and at place Reine-Marguerite on rue Maréchal-Joffre.

💬 INSIDER TIP
Nightlife Revived

For the best nightlife in Pau, head to the revived Quartier du Hédas. The former notorious alleys in the area, once used for sword duels, are now lined with cafés and bars that stay open till the wee hours.

Parc du Château, and in clear weather offers both glorious views of the Château gardens below and of the highest peaks of the Pyrénées, which are snowcapped all year round. Opposite 20 boulevard des Pyrénées, there is even an orientation table that names and gives heights of the visible peaks.

The boulevard is lined with the terraces of cafés, restaurants and bars, which become lively on summer evenings, spilling out on the pavement. The funicular, installed in 1908, carries passengers from place Royale to the railway station. Nearby is the Église Saint-Martin, next to a tree-lined square, with an impressive Neo-Gothic exterior.

examples of painting from the Dutch, Flemish, Spanish, Italian, French and English schools of the 15th to the 20th centuries. Among the museum's most famous works are *Portraits dans un Bureau de La Nouvelle-Orléans* (1873) by Degas, and works by Rubens, Greco, Rodin and Morisot. Major temporary exhibitions are also regularly held at the museum.

③ Boulevard des Pyrénées

This pedestrian promenade was laid out in the late 19th century by Adolphe Alphand, a pupil of the great town planner Baron Haussmann.

About 1,800 m (1 mile) long, it lies on a natural terrace between Parc Beaumont and

④ Musée des Beaux-Arts

🏠 Rue Mathieu-Lalanne
📞 05 59 27 33 02 🕐 10am–noon (to 12:30pm Sat & Sun), 2–6pm Mon & Wed–Fri

Occupying a beautiful 1930s building, a stone's throw from the Palais Beaumont and boulevard des Pyrénées, this museum displays some fine

STAY

Hôtel Villa Navarre
Surrounded by a lush estate, this grand villa was built in 1865 and has luxurious and spacious rooms, plus an indoor pool and fine restaurant with mountain views.

🏠 59 avenue Trespoey
🌐 villanavarre.fr

€€€

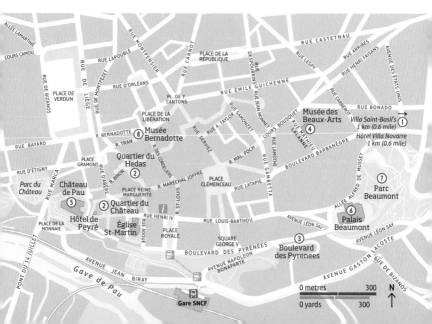

Château de Pau

📍 Rue du Château
🕐 Times vary, check website 🌐 chateau-pau.fr

A fairytale castle that birthed a king, the château in the heart of Pau was originally a fortress built to ward off the French and English before becoming home to Henry IV. Louis-Philippe ordered a complete restoration in 1838

↑ The Château de Pau, perched on a hill above the town

Did You Know?

The tapestries in Château de Pau are some of the finest in all of France.

The Salle aux Cent Couverts was once the castle's guardroom. The room takes its name from the table, round which 100 diners can be seated.

The castle contains a 17th-century tapestry designed by Raphael.

The courtyard entrance is a three-arched portico. The buildings on either side have Renaissance-style windows.

Jeanne d'Albret's bedchamber is hung with 18th-century tapestries of mythological allegories.

The king's bedchamber has some of the richest furnishings.

The turtle shell used in decorations in the Chambre du Roi de Navarre is supposed to have served as Henri IV's cradle.

Statue of Gaston Fébus

Salon de famille

that survived the Revolution (*p54*). Today it stands regally in the style of Versailles.

As it lay between his territory in Ariège and his court at Orthez, Gaston Fébus – who held the title of Comte de Foix-Béarn – chose Pau as a strategically located base. The original castle, built in 1370, was a fortress with a triple line of defences. During the Renaissance, it became the residence of the viscounts of Béarn, allies of the Albrets, rulers of Navarre, a Spanish kingdom. The birthplace of Henri IV, future king and France's first Bourbon monarch, it served as the centre of a Protestant state created by Henri's mother, Jeanne d'Albret (*p244*). Later, the castle became a shrine to Henri, and in the 19th century, Louis-Philippe, himself a Bourbon, ordered a major programme of restoration, which was continued by Napoléon III.

A tour of the château lets visitors get up close to a

—— *Chapel*

beautiful piece of French history, and reveals many more works of art inside, including some of the finest Flemish and Gobelins tapestries in France.

---

⑥

Palais Beaumont

🏠 **Allée Alfred de Musset**
📞 08 05 02 20 15 🕐 7:30am-7pm daily

This winter palace, with a Neo-Classical south façade and decorative plasterwork, was built in 1900 to cater for foreign visitors and has since been restored. Set in the stunning parkland of Parc Beaumont, it also has a casino and a conference centre.

---

⑦

Parc Beaumont

🏠 **Allée Alfred de Musset**

The variant species of flora growing in the delightful Parc Beaumont, from Californian

redwoods to Himalayan cedars, is ample testament to the gentle climate of Pau – just about anything grows here. There is also a lovely rose garden, a lake and waterfall feature, and the open-air Théâtre de Verdure.

---

⑧

Musée Bernadotte

🏠 **8 rue Tran** 📞 05 59 27 48 42 🕐 10am-noon & 2-6pm daily

The birthplace of Jean-Baptiste-Jules Bernadotte, one of Pau's greatest sons, is now a museum, documenting his phenomenal career.

Having joined the French army as a private in 1780, Bernadotte rose through the ranks to become a Maréchal d'Empire in 1804. With the help of Napoléon, he was created a royal prince of Sweden in 1810, succeeding to that country's throne in 1818, as Charles XIV.

> **The variant species of flora growing in the delightful Parc Beaumont is ample testament to the gentle climate of the Béarn region.**

↑ Façade of the Palais Beaumont, the historic winter palace in Parc Beaumont

→ Skiers on the slopes at Gourette, a resort in the Col d'Aubisque mountains

2

OSSAU VALLEY

C7 ⚑ Place de Laruns, Laruns; www.ossau-pyrenees.com

A bird's-eye view of the Ossau Valley makes it clear the Ice Age left its mark at the heart of Béarn. The peaceful valley, filled with nature's wonders, beckons hikers, skiers, birdwatchers, anglers and adrenaline seekers. Unspoiled vistas stretch beyond sight, as untouched as when glaciers and volcanoes lived here.

Beginning south of Pau, the Ossau Valley lies at right angles to the Pyrénées and runs right up to Col du Pourtalet on the border with Spain. Glaciers covered this whole area in the last Ice Age. The lower part of the valley stretches between the towns of Arudy and Laruns. In the upper valley, villages are sited in basins, amid deep gorges and broad plateaus encircled by rocky outcrops. The highest peak in this majestic landscape is the 2,884-m- (9,465-ft-) high Pic du Midi d'Ossau. The collapsed cone of an extinct volcano, it serves as the emblem of the Haut Béarn. The Ossau Valley has a strong cultural identity, reflected in traditional song and dance and the continuing use of the Gascon dialect.

①
Castet
📞 05 59 05 79 51 (Mairie)

This attractive village takes its name from the castle here, the village's only fortification. Built on a rocky outcrop in the 13th century, it was dismantled by the valley's inhabitants in 1450, and all that remain are two towers. There is also a Romanesque church, the Église Saint-Polycarpe, which stands on a promontory overlooking the village. A road leads down to the harbour, beside a lake on the Gave d'Ossau. Here there are marked pathways and an "espace naturel" devoted to the wildlife living in and around these waters.

②
Arudy
📞 05 59 05 79 51 (Mairie)

Arudy is famous for its fine marble. This ranges from a blueish-grey variety, the most common, to the rarest, which is veined with red or a mix of several colours. The Église Saint-Germain, dating from the 16th and 17th centuries, has a pointed dome and capitals carved with bears and cows, the emblems of Ossau.

③
Bielle
📞 05 59 82 60 36 (Mairie)

As the town where the *jurats* (lay judges) sat, Bielle was the valley's political capital. It remained autonomous until the French Revolution in 1789.

Did You Know?

In summer, flocks of sheep graze on the high altitude pastures at Haut Ossau, watched over by shepherds.

The records of the community's legal business were stored in a triple-lock chest, now displayed in the Église Saint-Vivien. The tympanum of this 16th-century church is carved with the symbols of Ossau. The town's richly decorated 15th–18th-century houses include Maison Trille and the former convent, which has a square pavilion and a circular tower, with an arched doorway.

④ Falaise aux Vautours

🕐 Apr–Sep: Mon–Fri (Aug: daily) 🌐 falaise-aux-vautours.com

The cliffs at the villages of Aste and Béon are a protected nature reserve. The visitor centre at the foot of the cliffs displays details about the griffon vulture. Hides in the cliffs allow these birds to be observed at close quarters.

⑤ Laruns

🛈 Maison du Parc National à Laruns, avenue de la Gare, 05 59 05 41 59

Laruns is home to the Ossau's tourist office and the Maison du Parc National. Here the valley's traditional culture is kept alive at the festival of music and dancing that takes place on 15 August each year. The Pon quarter, in the south of the town, has 16th- and 17th-century houses.

⑥ Route de l'Aubisque

This pass, which leads through stunning mountain scenery, lies beyond Laruns on the D918 to Gourette. Empress Eugénie instigated the construction of this "spa route", and encouraged the development of the health spa of Eaux-Bonnes along it.

PIC DU MIDI D'OSSAU

Standing out like a giant shark's tooth, the Pic du Midi d'Ossau soars up to a height of 2,884 m (9,465 ft). Climbing to the top is safe only for experienced mountaineers, but its lower slopes are more easily accessible and offer long, pleasant walks as well as a number of family attractions. From the lakes and passes around the peak there are spectacular views of Béarn's mountains. Hikers should never set out without a good map and suitable equipment.

⑦ Lac d'Artouste

The departure point for several good walking routes, the lake can also be reached in about 3 hours, along a footpath that starts near the hut at Soques, at the bottom of the valley.

Running along a narrow-gauge track laid out in 1924, when the dam at Artouste was being built, a little train takes visitors to Lac d'Artouste (May–Sep). This scenic journey, at an altitude of 2,000 m (6,564 ft), takes 55 minutes.

⑧ Eaux Chaudes

Laruns's municipal district includes the spa town of Eaux-Chaudes, about 6 km (4 miles) to the sourth, which was at its peak during the 19th century. The village takes its name from the seven hot springs near the baths that made it famous and that were popular in the 19th and early 20th centuries. Various health treatments are still available here.

↑ The view along the Soussouéou valley from Lac d'Artouste as summer turns to autumn

EXPERIENCE MORE

❸ Soussouéou Valley

🅰 C7 🚹 Maison de la Vallée d'Ossau; www.ossau-pyrenees.com

The breathtaking Soussouéou valley is about 10 km (6 miles) long. Information on hiking here is available from the tourist office at Laruns. If you intend to walk in the valley, drive out of Laruns on the Gabas road to the Miégebat power station; 2 km (1 mile) from there, take a left turn to Pont de Goua, a bridge by which you can park. From here a footpath leads through the undergrowth. A 30-minute walk brings you to the GR10, a long-distance path. From here, adventurous hikers can take a day's walk along this irregularly signed but well-used track to reach the Lac d'Artouste.

An alternative route up the valley is to drive through Gabas and park at the Lac de Fabrèges cable-car car park, 4 km (3 miles) further on. From here, a 12-minute ride will take you up to Col de la Sagette, where you can catch the **Train d'Artouste**, which follows a track up the side of the valley. The journey, in open carriages, takes 55 minutes, with splendid views of the Pic du Midi d'Ossau (*p241*). From the terminus, it takes about 15 minutes to reach Lac d'Artouste on foot. You can also walk down from Col de la Sagette to the Soussouéou plateau and in summer there's a chairlift known as the Télésiège de l'Ours (Bear's Chairlift).

Train d'Artouste

⊘ 🅰 Station d'Artouste, Résidence Fario ⏰ Times vary, check website 🆆 artouste.fr/billet-train-d-artouste

❹ Morlanne

🅰 C6 🚹 Carrère-du-Château; 05 59 81 42 66

This characterful village has old houses in a style typical of northern Béarn. The village's main street runs from Maison Domecq, a 15th-century abbey, to **Château de Morlanne**. It was originally built in the Middle Ages, but the building's features were restored in the 1960s. On a guided tour of the castle, visitors will see medieval furniture, and art by Fragonard, Nattier, Canaletto and Van de Velde.

Arzacq-Arraziguet, 13 km (8 miles) from Morlanne, is a *bastide* town on the pilgrim route built by the English. Its focal point is the arcaded place de la République. The parish church has a stained-glass window with a depiction of St James and a 16th-century painted wood Madonna and Child. Also here is the **Maison du Jambon de Bayonne**, a shop with a museum devoted to the history and production of Bayonne ham and other local specialities.

Château de Momas, 14 km (9 miles) away, dates from the the 14th to 16th centuries and was the residence of the lords of Momas. The present owner takes visitors on a tour of the garden here, planted with rare flowers, shrubs and vegetables.

Château de Morlanne

⊘⊘ 📞 05 59 81 60 27 ⏰ Apr-Oct: daily

Maison du Jambon de Bayonne

⊘ 🅰 Route de Samadet ⏰ Jul & Aug: Mon-Sat; Sep-Jun: Tue-Sat 🆆 maison-du-jambon-de-bayonne.com

Château de Momas

⊘⊘ ⏰ 9:30am-noon & 2:30-7pm Fri-Wed 🆆 chateaudemomas.com

> ## Did You Know?
>
> The Train d'Artouste is the highest open-top railway in Europe.

5

Salies-de-Béarn

△ B6 ⊠ ℹ Place du Bayaà; www.tourisme-bearn-gaves.com

Salies-de-Béarn's claim to fame is its saltwater spring, which led to its development as a spa resort. The town's historic district centres around the place du Bayaà, where stands the Fontaine du Sanglier (wild boar), named after the local legend of the discovery of the salt water: a boar, wounded in the hunt, was discovered dead some time later, mired in a marsh and covered in salt crystals. Perfectly preserved, it tasted delicious – the first "Bayonne ham".

Flowers hang down the buildings lining the town's ancient narrow streets. The **Musée du Sel et Traditions Béarnaises** is a local history museum that stands among 17th- and 18th-century houses and features a salt-panner's workshop. In front of it is a *coulédé*, a stone trough where water drawn from the fountain was kept before being transferred to reservoirs. The museum showcases traditional costumes and ancient tools of forgotten trades.

Beyond Pont de la Lune are half-timbered houses on pillars and, opposite, the Maison de la Corporation des Part-prenants (people who won a legal right to use the saltwater fountain in 1587). The old town ends at the spa quarter. The grand

↑ Salies-de-Béarn town-houses, with shutters to keep out the sun

hotels here, such as the Hôtel du Parc (1893), were built during the spa's heyday at the end of the 19th century. Nearby are baths, built originally in 1857 and rebuilt in the Moorish style after a fire in 1888.

Musée du Sel et Traditions Béarnaises

⊘⊘ △ 14 rue des Puits-Salants ⏱ Times vary, check website ⍵ musee dusel64.fr

↑ Resembling a toy castle, the fortified church of Saint-Laurant, Morlanne

6

Orthez

A64 🚉🚌 ℹ 1 rue des Jacobins; 05 59 12 30 40

The emblem of Orthez, Béarn's "second capital", is the Pont Vieux, built across the Gave de Pau in the 13th century. The tower was added by Gaston Fébus, who inscribed it with a Gascon saying: *Toquey si gaouses* ("Touch it if you dare"). The **Château de Moncade** towers above the town. Built in the 13th and 14th centuries, it witnessed the flowering of Fébus's court, but was torched in 1569 during the Wars of Religion (1562–98). What remained was sold during the French Revolution, and it was finally restored in the 19th century.

On rue Bourg-Vieux is a 16th-century house with a stair-tower, mullioned windows and a formal garden. It was once the home of Jeanne-d'Albret, Queen of Navarre, who converted to Calvinism in 1560 and declared her whole territory officially Protestant in the years before the Wars of Religion against the Catholics and Protestants. Her old home now houses the **Musée Jeanne-d'Albret**, which documents the history of Protestantism in Béarn. **Maison Chrestia**, home of the Béarnese poet Francis Jammes from 1897 to 1907, illustrates his life and work.

Château de Moncade

Rue Moncade 05 59 69 36 24 Mid-Apr-Sep: Tue-Sun

Musée Jeanne-d'Albret

37 rue Bourg-Vieux Times vary, check website museejeannedalbret.com

Maison Chrestia

7 avenue Francis-Jammes 05 59 69 11 24 By appointment (call ahead)

7

Oloron-Sainte-Marie

C6 🚉🚌 ℹ Allée du Comte-de-Tréville; www.tourisme-oloron.com

Situated at the confluence of the Gave d'Aspe and Gave d'Ossau, Oloron-Sainte-Marie is the capital of Haut Béarn and the gateway to the Aspe valley *(p248)*. In the 11th century, Oloron and the neighbouring bishopric of Sainte-Marie began to expand and merge, becoming a strategic point of trade with the Spanish kingdom of Aragon, as well as a major textile-weaving centre. The two were officially united to create one city in 1858.

The most notable feature here is the magnificent 12th-century Romanesque carved doorway of Cathédrale Sainte-Marie. Covered by a porch, it is certainly the finest and best-preserved such doorway in Béarn and features on UNESCO's World Heritage List.

Basque textiles are still important to the town, although **Lartigue 1910**, in Quartier Sainte-Marie, is the only surviving weaving workshop that still uses traditional methods.

PICTURE PERFECT
Pilgrim Sculptures

Oloron's streets and parks are graced with contemporary sculptures that reference the artistic activity associated with the traditional pilgrim routes to Santiago de Compostela.

Lartigue 1910

2 avenue Georges-Messier 05 59 39 50 11 Mon-Fri (Jul & Aug: also Sat)

8

Lescar

🄰 C6 🚌 ℹ️ Place Royale;
www.pau-pyrenees.com

Lescar, historically the capital of Béarn, perches on a walled promontory that looks towards the Pyrénées. In the 12th century it became a fortified bishopric, with work on the Cathédrale Notre-Dame on place Royale commencing in 1120. A plaque set into the cathedral floor lists the tombs of some of the kings of Navarre that are buried here. Floor mosaics near the altar depict hunting scenes. The building also has fine 17th-century sculptures of Christ, the apostles and local saints. Around the cathedral stand the 14th-century Tour de l'Esquirette and two 16th-century towers, the Tour de l'Évêché and du Presbytère.

From the community centre (salle des fêtes), a short walk leads along the ramparts to the upper town. The **Musée de Lescar** here is housed in the cellars of the old Episcopal Palace. Its archeological collection explores the history of Lescar, from Iron-Age jewellery to everyday objects.

About 16 km (10 miles) from Lescar are the **Cave des Producteurs de Jurançon**, at Gan, and the Maison des Vins de Jurançon, at Lacommande.

←
The Pont Vieux, a 13th-century fortified bridge over the Gave de Pau at Orthez

At both, visitors can taste and buy local wines. The area's white wine was said to be a favourite of Henri IV, who first tasted it at his christening.

Opposite the Maison des Vins stands a rare example of a 12th-century **Commanderie**, one of the hospitals founded by crusader Gaston IV. Nearby, the interior of the Église Saint-Blaise features capitals sculpted with biblical and mythological scenes.

Musée de Lescar

♿ 🄰 Rue de la Cité 📞 05 59 81 57 10 🕒 Jul & Aug: daily

Cave des Producteurs de Jurançon

♿ 🄰 53 avenue Henri IV, Gan 📞 05 59 21 57 03 🕒 Daily, for tours and tastings

Commanderie

🄰 Rue de l'Église, Lacommande 🕒 Jul & Aug: daily; Sep-Jun: Wed, Sat & Sun

---

9

Navarrenx

🄰 B6 🚌 ℹ️ 2 place des Caserne; 05 59 38 32 85

Overlooking the Gave d'Oloron, this fortified town came under attack during the Wars of Religion and was besieged in 1569. The **Arsenal**, built in 1680, was originally the residence of the kings of Navarre. As its present name implies, it became a munitions and provisions store for the viscounts of Béarn. It is now a cultural centre.

In rue Saint-Antoine is a 16th-century house known as Maison de Jeanne-d'Albret, ruler of Béarn in 1555. The 16th-century Église Saint-Germain has arches decorated with carved and painted heads.

Some 7 km (4 miles) from Navarrenx, on the D936 to Oloron, is **Camp de Gurs**. Here Spanish republicans were interned after the Civil War and Jews held before deportation. About 16 km

↑ View with cannon from the fortified city walls of Navarrenx

(10 miles) from here, at the 17th-century Château de Laàs, is **Musée Serbat**, a decorative arts museum.

Arsenal

🄰 41 rue Saint-Germain, Navarrenx 🕒 Mid-May-mid-Oct: daily

Camp de Gurs

🄰 Impasse d'Ossau 🌐 campgurs.com

Musée Serbat

♿♿ 🄰 Bourg 🕒 Times vary, check website 🌐 musee-serbat.com

❿

Barétous Valley

Ⓐ B6 **𝒊** Place des Poilus, Arette; www.pyrenees-bearnaises.com

Near the border between Pays Basque in France and Navarre in Spain, the Barétous valley is a region of sharp contrasts. Woodland, green hillsides and *estives* (summer pastures), grazed by sheep, mix with steep gorges, the lofty Pic d'Anie and the Col de la Pierre-Saint-Martin – a long, arid limestone chasm, thought to be the deepest in the world, that is a paradise for cave explorers.

Arette, with just over a thousand inhabitants, is the valley's largest town. On 13 August 1967, it was hit by an earthquake. The Centre Sismologique here registers earth tremors in the region, and tours can be arranged through the tourist office. The Maison de Barétous, at the tourist office, has an

exhibition on life in the valley, and a feature on the Junte du Roncal ceremony.

⓫

Bétharram

Ⓐ C7 **🚌** 🚐 **𝒊** 13 place des Arcades, Saint-Pé-de-Bigorre; 05 62 41 88 10

The town's main attraction is the **Grottes de Bétharram**, a series of caves on five levels that visitors explore on foot, by boat and on a small train. An amazing array of draped, fringed and lace-like rock formations hang from the walls and ceilings of these great caverns.

Bétharram also has a Baroque chapel, the **Sanctuaire de Notre-Dame de Bétharram**, built in the 17th century. According to legend, the original chapel here was built in the 14th century after the Madonna had appeared on the banks of the Gave de Pau. A second chapel was destroyed by fire in 1569. The west front of the present chapel is of grey marble, with statues of the Four Evangelists and the Madonna and Child. The interior is opulent, with black

marble pillars, a 17th-century altarpiece, paintings and gilded wooden sculptures.

The chapel is associated with Michel Garicoïts (1797–1863), a priest who is buried here. Founder of the Society of the Priests of the Sacred Heart of Bétharram, he was canonized in 1947.

Grottes de Bétharram

◈ ◉ **Ⓐ** Chemin Leon Ross **Ⓞ** Mid-Feb-late Mar: Mon-Fri; late Mar-Oct: daily **ⓦ** betharram.com

Sanctuaire de Notre-Dame de Bétharram

◈ ◉ **Ⓐ** Avenue de Bétharram, Lestelle-Bétharram **Ⓒ** 06 43 25 48 94 **Ⓞ** Daily

⓬

Nay

Ⓐ C6 **𝒊** Maison Carrée, place de la République; 05 59 13 94 99

At the beginning of the 12th century, monks from Sainte-Christine in Gabas founded Nay (pronounced "Nye") to provide food and shelter for pilgrims travelling to the

Did You Know?

Two of Alexander Dumas's musketeers, Porthos and Aramis, hail from the Navarous valley.

The lower Baretous Valley, a lush patchwork of fields and mixed woodland

the Middle Ages, thanks to the growth of the weaving industry, reaching the height of its prosperity in the 18th century with the manufacture of Basque berets and textiles. In 1543, Nay was severely damaged by fire. The Église Saint-Vincent, a single-nave church in the Languedoc Gothic style, originally from the 15th–16th century, was remodelled when the rest of the town was rebuilt.

The **Maison Carrée,** built by Pedro Sacaze – a wealthy merchant from Aragon – is a Renaissance-style townhouse with Italian loggias and an inner courtyard. It fell into ruin in the 18th century but has been restored. The upper floors house the **Musée de l'Industrie**, which features a display on industry in Nay through the ages, with sections on local metalwork, weaving and quarrying.

Spanish city of Santiago de Compostela. This small town, on the edge of the Hautes-Pyrénées, stands on the Gave de Pau, which becomes swollen with meltwater in spring. In 1302, Marguerite de Moncade made Nay a fortified *bastide* town. It began to prosper during

JUNTE DU RONCAL

On 13 July each year, at the Col de la Pierre-Saint-Martin, the Junte du Roncal, also known as the *Tribut des Trois Génisses* (Gift of Three Heifers), commemorates a peace treaty that has been in force since 1375, between the inhabitants of the Barétous valley and those of the Roncal valley, in the Spanish province of Navarre. The mayors of each valley take an oath and, to mark it, the Béarnese present the Navarrese with three heifers. In exchange, they can graze their sheep on the *estives* (summer pastures) of their neighbours in the Roncal.

The **Musée du Béret**, located in a former industrial building, traces the history of the most recognisable of all French fashions: the beret. After learning about the stages in its manufacture, visitors can pick up their own chic beret from the many choices on offer at the museum shop. Despite being associated with Pays Basque, this famous type of headgear in fact originates in the Ossau valley *(p240)*. From the industrial revolution onwards, its manufacture was a major source of income in Nay and Oloron-Sainte-Marie *(p244)*. However, beret-making is now in decline.

Maison Carrée and Musée de l'Industrie

Ⓐ Ⓑ Ⓒ Place de la République Ⓓ 05 59 13 99 65 Ⓔ Apr–Jun & Sep–Dec: Tue–Sat; Jul & Aug: daily;

Musée du Béret

Ⓐ Ⓑ Ⓒ Place Saint-Roch Ⓓ Times vary, check website Ⓦ museeduberet.com

A guide leads visitors around the Grottes de Bétharram caverns

⑬
Aspe Valley

🅰C7 ℹ Place Sarraillé, Bedous; www.pyrenees-bearnaises.com

The Aspe valley, south of Oloron-Sainte-Marie, is washed by the Gave d'Aspe. The railway viaduct here was built in 1910 to carry the now-defunct Pau–Canfranc line. Notre-Dame-de-la-Pierre, at Sarrance, is the first site of interest along a trail that makes up the **Écomusée de la Vallée d'Aspe**, the valley's open-air museum. This stop focuses on the legend of Sarrance and its pilgrims. Visitors can then see the 17th-century church and cloister. At Lourdios Ichère, the trail's next stop, an audiovisual presentation explains the daily life of the inhabitants of this mountain village. Bedous is the valley's commercial centre. The GR65, a long-distance path known as the Chemin de Saint-Jacques, runs from Bedous to Accous. Here visitors can taste cheeses made by local farmers. The village's

↓ Herdsmen's dwellings on the lower slopes of the Aspe Valley

imposing Église Saint-Martin suffered severe damage twice in its history, first in 1569, then again in 1793. The Cirque de Lescun, at the head of the valley, is a huge green plateau dotted with barns and surrounded by high peaks. Cette-Eygun has a 12th-century church, the Église Saint-Pierre.

The **Maison du Parc National des Pyrénées** visitor centre at Etsaut has an exhibition about the Pyrenean brown bear. About 2 km (1 mile) beyond Etsaut, a track joins the Chemin de la Mâture. This stretch of the GR10 is dug into the rockface above a sheer drop. In the mid-18th century, pine trunks to be used as masts (*mâture*) for French navy ships were dragged through here. The Chapelle Saint-Jacques at Borce, last of the Écomusée exhibition stops, once took in pilgrims. Inside are 16th-century frescoes as well as graffiti by Napoléon's soldiers. The main street has picturesque 15th- and 16th-century houses with mullioned windows, Gothic doorways and bread-ovens. The striking Fort du Portalet (1860), above the Gorge d'Enfer, was used as a state prison during World War II.

Écomusée de la Vallée d'Aspe

◈◈ 🅰 Rue du Bourg, Sarrance 🕐 Times vary, check website 🆆 ecomusee.haut-bearn.fr

Maison du Parc National des Pyrénées

🅰 Rue d'en Bas, Etsaut 🄲 05 59 34 88 30 🕐 During school hols

---

⑭
Monein

🅰C6 🚌ℹ 58 rue du Commerce; 05 59 12 30 40

This town is set in the rolling hills of the Jurançon, a region that produces a renowned sweet white wine. A 19th-century building with pillars and stone arches, on place Lacabanne, houses the town hall and covered market.

Église Saint-Girons, built in 1530, is the largest Gothic church in Béarn. A thousand oak trees were needed to build its magnificent hull-shaped roof. The roof beams were originally dowled rather than nailed. Visits are by tour

↑ The ship-like heart-of-oak roof frame of the Eglise Saint-Girons in Monein

only; a *son et lumière* (sound and light) show explains the roof's unusual construction.

Église Saint-Girons

 🏠2 rue Saint-Girons 📞05 59 21 29 28 ⏱Times vary, call ahead

🔵 15
Lembeye

🅰C6 🛈37 place Marcadieu; 05 59 68 28 78

Set on a steep hillside, Lembeye was founded by Gaston VII of Béarn in 1286, and became the capital of Vic-Bilh ("Old Villages"), an area adjoining Bigorre and Gascony. Not far from place Marcadieu, near some old arcaded houses, is a fortified gate, known as Tour de l'Horloge ("Clock Tower"). Lembeye's large Gothic church has an interesting carved doorway.

About 19 km (12 miles) from Lembeye is the **Château de Mascaraàs**, with 17th- and 18th-century decoration. Visits here are by guided tour only. Some 21 km (13 miles) away is the 14th-century **Château de Montaner** – built on the order of Gaston Fébus, viscount of Béarn in the 14th century – and the **Église peinte de Montaner**, a church with remarkable 15th and 16th century frescoes.

Château de Mascaraàs

🏠Mascaraàs-Haron 📞05 59 04 92 60 ⏱Apr, May & mid-Sep-Nov: Sat & Sun; Jun-mid-Sep: Wed-Mon

Château de Montaner

🏠962 chemin Costa de Febus, Montaner ⏱Times vary, check website 🌐chateau-montaner.com

Église peinte de Montaner

🏠55 chemin Camin de la Gleisa 📞05 62 31 42 33 ⏱Times vary, call ahead

---

🔵 16
Morlaàs

🅰C6 🛈Place Sainte-Foy; 05 59 33 62 25

The capital of Béarn from 1080 to 1260, and a stopping place on several of the pilgrim routes to the Spanish city of Santiago de Compostela (*p226*), Morlaàs was once an important stronghold of Gaston Fébus, viscount of Béarn, and had its own mint.

Most of the town was destroyed during the Wars of Religion in the 16th century, and very little remains of its prestigious past other than the **Église Sainte-Foy**, dedicated to St Faith, a French martyr. This church, built in 1080, has a Romanesque doorway, restored in the 19th century, carved with a depiction of St John's vision of the Apocalypse. The capitals in the apse are carved with scenes from the life of St Foy. The church is in a similar style to other buildings on the pilgrim route, particularly those in Jaca in the Spanish province of Aragon, on the other side of the Pyrénées.

Like Orthez, Salies-de-Béarn and other towns in the area, Morlaàs is also noted for traditional furniture-making.

Église Sainte-Foy

🏠11 place Sainte-Foy 📞05 59 33 40 87 ⏱Times vary, call ahead

↑ Carved figure of St James at the church of St Foy in Morlaàs

A DRIVING TOUR
TOUR OF MADIRAN

Length 40 km (25 miles) **Starting point** Lembeye
Stopping-off points The priory in the village of Madiran, where there is a Maison des Vins

The wines produced in this region are lesser known than their counterparts further north, but they are just as exquisite. Being at the intersection of Béarn, the Gers and the Hautes-Pyrénées also makes the area a wonderful place for a driving tour to visit some of the local vineyards for a tasting. Madiran's robust, dark red wine was long used as a communion wine, but became known to the wider world thanks to pilgrims who passed through the area on their way to Santiago de Compostela. Since then, as the quality of Madiran wine has improved, it has become even better known.

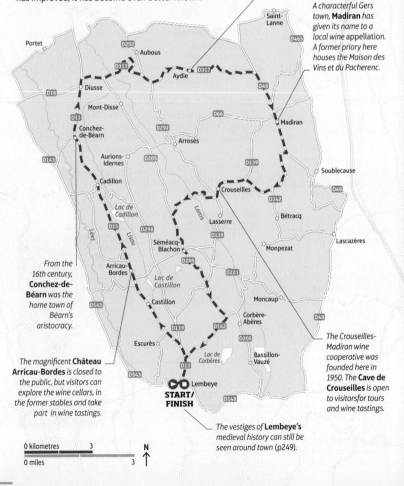

Between Béarn, Bigorre and the Landes, Aydie is a major centre for the production of Madiran wine, as well as the wines of five other estates.

A characterful Gers town, Madiran has given its name to a local wine appellation. A former priory here houses the Maison des Vins et du Pacherenc.

From the 16th century, Conchez-de-Béarn was the home town of Béarn's aristocracy.

The magnificent Château Arricau-Bordes is closed to the public, but visitors can explore the wine cellars, in the former stables and take part in wine tastings.

The Crouseilles-Madiran wine cooperative was founded here in 1950. The Cave de Crouseilles is open to visitors for tours and wine tastings.

The vestiges of Lembeye's medieval history can still be seen around town (p249).

0 kilometres   3

0 miles   3

N ↑

The Madiran vineyards around Château Arricau-Bordes

NEED TO KNOW

The Miroir d'Eau reflecting pool in Bordeaux

BEFORE YOU GO

Forward planning is essential to any successful trip. Be prepared for all eventualities by considering the following points before you travel.

AT A GLANCE

CURRENCY
Euro

AVERAGE DAILY SPEND

SAVE	SPEND	SPLURGE
€50	€100	€200+

BOTTLED WATER	COFFEE	BEER	DINNER FOR TWO
€1.50	€2.50	€5.00	€50

ESSENTIAL PHRASES

Hello	Bonjour
Goodbye	Au revoir
Please	S'il vous plait
Thank you	Merci
Do you speak English?	Parlez-vous anglais?
I don't understand	Je ne comprends pas

ELECTRICITY SUPPLY
Power sockets are type C and E, fitting C and E plugs with two or three prongs. Standard voltage is 230v/50Hz

Passports and Visas

For a stay of up to three months for the purpose of tourism, EU nationals and citizens of the US, Canada, Australia and New Zealand do not need a visa. For visa information specific to your home country, consult the French **Ministry of Foreign Affairs** website or your nearest French embassy.
Ministry of Foreign Affairs
w diplomatie.gouv.fr

Travel Safety Advice

Visitors can get up-to-date travel safety information from the **US** Department of State, the **UK** Foreign and Commonwealth Office, the **Australian** Department of Foreign Affairs and Trade and France's **Vigipirate** system.
Australia
w smartraveller.gov.au
UK
w gov.uk/foreign-travel-advice
US
w travel.state.gov
Vigipirate
w gouvernement.fr/vigipirate

Customs Information

An individual is permitted to carry the following within the EU for personal use:
Tobacco products 800 cigarettes, 400 cigarillos, 200 cigars or 1kg of smoking tobacco.
Alcohol 10 litres of alcoholic beverages above 22 per cent strength, 20 litres of alcoholic beverages below 22 per cent strength, 90 litres of wine (60 litres of which can be sparkling wine) and 110 litres of beer.
Cash If you are carrying €10,000 or more in cash (or the equivalent in other currencies) you must declare it to the customs authorities. Limits vary if travelling outside the EU, so always check restrictions before travelling.

Insurance

It is wise to take out an insurance policy covering theft, loss of belongings, medical problems and

travel cancellation and delays. To receive discounted or free emergency medical care in France, EU citizens should ensure they have an **EHIC** (European Health Insurance Card). Visitors from outside the EU must arrange their own private medical insurance.

EHIC
ⓦ gov.uk/european-health-insurance-card

Vaccinations

No specific vaccinations are required for France.

Money

Most establishments accept major credit, debit and prepaid currency cards, but it's always a good idea to carry some cash, which may be expected for purchases under €15, meals and payments in budget hotels. Contactless payments are widely accepted in all major cities.

Be aware that cash machines may charge a fee for withdrawals if your normal banking currency is not Euros.

Booking Accommodation

There is a real range of accommodation across southwest France, from budget hostels up to rooms in renovated castles and country estates. The coastal areas are busiest in July and August, so book ahead if visiting at that time. Some smaller hotels close in low season.

In the countryside, some local tourist offices can book you into accommodation on farms and in *gîtes* (holiday homes).

Travellers with Specific Needs

A number of organizations are working to improve accessibility across France. **Jaccede** has details of accessible museums, hotels, bars, restaurants and cinemas in Bordeaux, the Dordogne and the surrounding area. Rail operator **SNCF** provides information about train travel, both online and in leaflets at train stations, and also offers a booking service for free assistance on TGVs. UK-based company **Access Travel** lists wheelchair-accessible accommodation across France by area. For further information on accessibility, contact the French disability advocacy group **GIHP**.

Access Travel
ⓦ access-travel.co.uk
GIHP
ⓦ gihpnational.org
Jaccede
ⓦ jaccede.com
SNCF
ⓦ accessibilite.sncf.com

Language

French is the official language, but English is widely spoken, especially among the young. The Basque language (Euskara) is also spoken in the Pays Basque region.

Closures

Lunchtime Some shops and businesses close for an hour or two from around noon.
Mondays Some museums, small shops, restaurants and bars are closed for the day, particularly in rural areas.
Tuesdays Most national museums and monuments are closed for the day.
Sundays Most shops are closed, or open for the morning only.
Public holidays Public services, shops, museums and attractions are usually closed.
School holidays To coincide with the end of the school term, some attractions may have longer hours during the summertime, and shorter hours in late December.

PUBLIC HOLIDAYS	
1 Jan	New Year's Day
Apr	Easter Day and Easter Monday
1 May	Labour Day/May Day
8 May	Victory 1945
30 May	Ascension Day
10 Jun	Whit Monday
14 Jul	Bastille Day
15 Aug	Assumption of Mary
1 Nov	All Saints' Day
11 Nov	Armistice Day
25 Dec	Christmas Day
31 Dec	New Year's Eve

GETTING AROUND

The towns of southwest France are well connected with trains and buses, but many visitors choose to explore the region by car or bicycle.

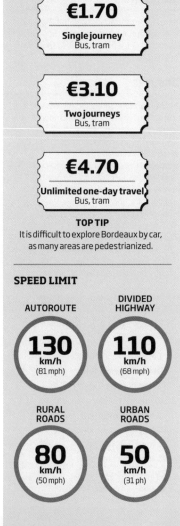

AT A GLANCE

PUBLIC TRANSPORT COSTS IN BORDEAUX

€1.70
Single journey
Bus, tram

€3.10
Two journeys
Bus, tram

€4.70
Unlimited one-day travel
Bus, tram

TOP TIP
It is difficult to explore Bordeaux by car, as many areas are pedestrianized.

SPEED LIMIT

AUTOROUTE
130 km/h
(81 mph)

DIVIDED HIGHWAY
110 km/h
(68 mph)

RURAL ROADS
80 km/h
(50 mph)

URBAN ROADS
50 km/h
(31 ph)

Arriving by Air

The biggest airport in the region is Bordeaux-Mérignac Airport, which flies to more than 100 destinations. Shuttle buses operate between Bordeaux Airport and the city centre with departures every 8–20 minutes.

Biarritz Airport, Bergerac Airport, Brive Airport and Pau Airport are smaller alternatives.

Train Travel

International Train Travel
You can travel to France from many major cities in Europe by regular rail, or on the celebrated high-speed TGVs. **Interrail** and **Eurail** sell passes to EU-residents and non-Europeans respectively, for international journeys lasting from five days up to three months. Both passes are valid directly via **TGV**, but do not include the mandatory seat reservation fee, which can be paid online in advance or at stations.
Eurail
W eurail.com
Interrail
W interrail.eu
TGV
W sncf.com

Domestic Train Travel
The state-owned **SNCF** serves all regions of France. SNCF's regional TER trains cannot be booked, while the longer Intercity and night trains require reservations. All TGVs require numbered seat bookings. Tickets can be bought online at SNCF or **Loco2**, and printed out or stored on mobile phones. Machines at stations also sell tickets, which must be inserted into yellow validating machines (located on every platform) before boarding.

Railway buffs will also enjoy France's steam locomotive routes and scenic tours, including the route from Bergerac to Le Buisson and the Le Truffadou (Truffle Train) of Martel.
Loco2
W loco2.com
SNCF
W en.oui.sncf

GETTING TO AND FROM BORDEAUX-MÉRIGNAC AIRPORT

Location	Distance to Airport	Journey Time by Car
Arcachon	66 km (41 miles)	45 mins
Bayonne	180 km (111 miles)	2 hours
Bergerac	110 km (68 miles)	1.5 hours
Biarritz	200 km (124 miles)	2 hours
Bordeaux centre	10 km (6 miles)	20 minutes
Bordeaux Saint-Jean railway station	20 km (12 miles)	30 minutes
Brive-la-Gaillarde	210 km (130 miles)	2.5 hours
Margaux	26 km (16 miles)	30 minutes
Mont-de-Marsan	130 km (80 miles)	1.5 hours
Pau	220 km (137 miles)	2.5 hours
Périgueux	140 km (87 miles)	1.5 hours
Soulac-sur-Mer	100 km (62 miles)	1.5 hours

RAIL JOURNEY PLANNER

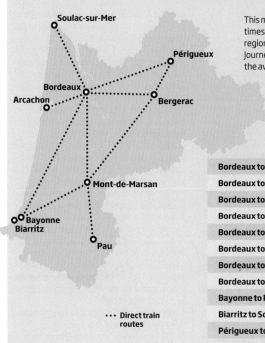

This map shows train travel times between some of the region's major towns and cities. Journey times given below are the average time for each route.

Bordeaux to Arcachon	50 min
Bordeaux to Biarritz	2 hrs
Bordeaux to Bayonne	2 hrs
Bordeaux to Bergerac	2.5 hrs
Bordeaux to Mont-de-Marsan	1.5 hrs
Bordeaux to Pau	2.5 hr
Bordeaux to Périgueux	1.5 hr
Bordeaux to Soulac-sur-Mer	1.75 hrs
Bayonne to Périgueux	4 hrs
Biarritz to Soulac-sur-Mer	4.5 hrs
Périgueux to Pau	4.5 hrs

••• Direct train routes

Long-Distance Bus Travel

SNCF operates **Ouibus**, a low-cost bus network that travels as far as Amsterdam and London and includes many stops in southwest France. **Flixbus** also has an extensive network across Europe and all over France.

Local bus companies in each region run frequent services between nearby cities.

Flixbus
W flixbus.fr

Ouibus
W ouibus.com

Public Transport

Most urban areas are served by a bus system that can be used to explore the town. Smaller villages in the countryside may have no bus system, or the schedule may be infrequent and inefficient for tourists. As such, many visitors prefer to explore the area by car.

Bordeaux

The **TBM** tram and bus network operates in and around Bordeaux, along with a network of self-service bicycles. Timetable information is available online.

You can buy tram tickets for 1, 2 or 10 journeys, as well as travel cards valid for 1 day or 7 days.

TBM
W ifotbm.com

Taxis

Official taxis are clearly identified. They can be hailed in passing, but not within sight of an official taxi stand. Billing begins from the moment of booking. Taxis are not usually seen in small rural communities, so visitors will need to find a local taxi company online and book in advance to ensure a ride.

Uber is popular throughout France, including in Bordeaux and Bergerac. **Heetch** is a late-night app-based service running in several cities, including Bordeaux.

Heetch
W heetch.com

Uber
W uber.com

Driving

With stunning views and well-maintained roads, driving may be the best way to explore the Dordogne countryside. The French love driving, and fast and spacious *autoroutes* (motorways) fan out to every region.

Congestion in the cities - particularly during July and August - may make train travel more appealing during those busy times. French cities also have many hard-to-navigate one-way streets, and parking can be difficult and expensive.

Car rental

To rent a car in France you must be aged 21 or over, have held a valid driver's licence for at least a year, and own a credit card which will be needed to pay the deposit. If visiting from the UK, you will also need to visit the **Share Driving Licence Service** on the DVLA website prior to departure to prove that you haven't exceeded 12 points on your licence. .

Rental cars with automatic transmission will need to be booked in advance. Returning a car to a different location will incur extra charges. The major car hire companies have branches in airports, and **HolidayAutos** has competitive rates in this part of France. Local companies are competitive on price but are not always able to offer one-way journeys.

HolidayAutos
W holidayautos.co.uk

Share Driving Licence Service
W gov.co.uk/view-driving-licence

Driving in France

To take your own foreign-registered car to France, you will need to carry the vehicle's registration and insurance documents, a full and valid driving licence, and a valid passport or national ID at all times. EU driving licences are valid here. If visiting from outside of the EU, or if your licence is not in French, you may need to apply for an International Driving Permit (IDP) through your government.

All French roads have national markings: A for Autoroute, N for Nationale (National Highway) and D for Département (smaller country roads). Autoroutes have blue signs, and if there is a toll this will be clearly marked. It's useful to carry cash at all times in case you use a toll road; information on rates can be found on the **Autoroutes** website. Roads that cross country borders are labelled E for European routes, and these also appear on a green sign. Rural roads appear on white signs, and are marked with C for communal or R for rural. Be aware that petrol stations can be scarce in rural areas and are often closed at night and on Sundays.

Restrictions exist across France to curb harmful emissions and improve air quality. Certain cities, including Bordeaux, now require drivers to show **Crit'Air** (clean air) stickers on windscreens. A map of low emission zones is available on the **Air Quality Certificate Service** government website, which can also be used to apply for Crit'Air stickers.

France has around 10,000 charging stations for electric cars - more than most other European countries. The **Open Charge Map** website plots charge point locations worldwide.

Air Quality Certificate Service
🆆 certificat-air.gouv.fr
Autoroutes
🆆 autoroutes.fr
Crit'Air
🆆 crit-air.fr
Open Charge Map
🆆 openchargemap.org

Parking

Parking is fairly easy throughout most of the region, but it can be hard to find spaces in Bordeaux. Traffic in the city centre is forbidden on the first Sunday of every month from 10:00am to 7:00pm in the summer and from 10:00am to 6:00pm in the winter.

Rules of the Road

Those aged 18 or over who hold a full driving licence are permitted to drive in France. An international car must display its national identification letters on a sticker (GB for the United Kingdom) unless the car has Euro-plates. Always drive on the right and remember that vehicles coming from the right have the right of way, unless signposted otherwise.

Seatbelts are compulsory, and children under ten must sit in the back seat with an appropriate booster seat. It is against the law to drive in a bus lane, to use a mobile phone (including hands-free) while driving, or to sound your horn in the city. It is also forbidden to have a Satnav or GPS system that can detect speed cameras, so disable this function on your device before your visit. French police can demand on-the-spot fines for traffic offences of up to €750.

France strictly enforces a blood alcohol content limit of 0.05 per cent. By law, drivers must carry a breathalyser – available for €1 at petrol stations – as well as a red warning triangle and a high-visibility vest.

In wet conditions, or if you have been driving for under three years, speed limits are reduced in to 110 km/h (68 mph) on *autoroutes* and 100 km/h (62 mph) on divided highways.

Cycling

Many miles of scenic cycle routes wend their way through the Dordogne region. Bicycles can be taken on some boat and ferry services, and on the the TER and Intercity trains, but non-folding bikes will incur a fee. On TGVs, bikes must be dismantled and stored in luggage spaces or carried in bags.

Bicycle Hire

In Bordeaux, **TBM** offers a self-service bike hire system with docks around the city, and with both manual and electric options. An interactive map is available via their app. You can purchase passes for 24 hours or 7 days. The first 30 minutes are free, and the fee thereafter is €2 per hour.

Visit **Freewheeling France** for more information on cycling around France, including bike-friendly accommodation, cycle routes, tours and hire.
TBM
🆆 infotbm.com/fr
Freewheeling France
🆆 freewheelingfrance.com

Bicycle Safety

Cyclists are generally well respected on French roads, so cycling here is quite safe. According to the French Highway Code, it is only compulsory for children under 12 to wear helmets, although it is advisable that adults wear them, too. It is illegal to cycle while using headphones, and cyclists are subject to an alcohol limit of 0.05 per cent, the same as drivers. Bikes must have a bell or horn and working lights, and cyclists must wear reflective vests when cycling at night.

Hitchhiking

It is forbidden to hitchhike on *autoroutes* and it is not recommended anywhere in France.

Boats and Ferries

The southwest of France is laced with an extensive network of navigable waterways formed by Aquitaine's rivers and canals. They have been used for transporting people and goods for hundreds of years and are still a great way to explore the region, as many of the most beautiful and interesting towns are accessible by water. Many cruises can be booked through **Aquitaine Navigation**, and other companies exist throughout the region to serve specific river and canal routes. Various boat trips along the coast around Arcachon are available from **Bateliers Arcachonnais**.

The city of Bordeaux lies on the Garonne river and the Bat3 (pronounced BatCoob) river shuttle, operated by TBM, travels between the two river banks several times each day. There is always a captain on board and the boats are accessible for wheelchair users. A maximum of six bicycles can also be taken on each boat.

The marina at Arcachon is the second-largest in western France. It has 2,600 moorings with 250 for visitors and there is a great deal in the area to explore by boat. Each evening, the port authority posts the weather forecast for the next few days. You will need a licence to sail a pleasure boat yourself with an engine more powerful than 6HP.
Aquitaine Navigation
🆆 aquitaine-navigatoin.com
Bateliers Arcachonnais
🆆 bateliers-arcachon.com

PRACTICAL
INFORMATION

A little local know-how goes a long way in southwest France. Here you will find all the essential advice and information you will need during your stay.

AT A GLANCE

EMERGENCY NUMBERS

EMERGENCY OPERATOR

112

POLICE

17

AMBULANCE

15

FIRE SERVICE

18

TIME ZONE
CET/CEST. Central European Summer Time runs from the last Sunday in March to the last Sunday in October.

TAP WATER
Unless otherwise stated, tap water and water from fountains in towns and villages is safe to drink.

TIPPING

Waiter	5-10 per cent
Hotel Porter	€1–€2 per bag
Housekeeping	€1 per day
Taxi Driver	Not expected
Tour Guide	€5

Personal Security

France is a safe country and visits are likely to be trouble-free. Take care of your belongings in busy tourist areas and on city buses during rush hour, as pickpockets may sometimes operate in these areas. It is also best to lock your car when leaving it, even if only for a few minutes. If travelling in a camper van or mobile home, be careful where you park at night so that you are able to seek help easily if required.

If anything is stolen, report it to the nearest police station. Get a copy of the crime report in order to make a claim on your insurance. Contact your embassy if you have your passport stolen, or in the event of a serious crime or accident.

Health

Pharmacists are an excellent source of advice when you are sick. They can diagnose minor ailments and suggest treatment. Private hospitals in major cities are more likely to have staff who speak fluent English.

All EU nationals holding an EHIC are entitled to use the French national health service.

Patients pay for treatment upfront and can reclaim most of the cost from the health authorities. The process may be lengthy so consider purchasing private travel insurance. Note that if you opt for private healthcare during your visit, this cannot be reclaimed under the EHIC scheme.

For visitors from outside the EU, payment of medical expenses is the patient's responsibility, so it is important to arrange comprehensive medical insurance.

Smoking, Alcohol and Drugs

Smoking is prohibited in all public places but is allowed on restaurant, café and pub terraces, as long as they are not enclosed. The possession of narcotics is prohibited and could result in a prison sentence. Unless stated otherwise, alcohol consumption on the streets is permitted.

France has a strict limit of 0.05 per cent BAC (blood alcohol content) for drivers and cyclists.

ID

It is a legal requirement for foreign visitors to carry ID on them when visiting France, in the form of a passport or a national identity card. In the event of a routine check, which can take place on the roads, you may be asked to show your passport. If it is not with you, the police may escort you to wherever your passport is kept, or ask you to take your ID to a police station within four hours.

Local Customs

Etiquette is important in southwest France, but there are no strict rules – simple, basic manners go a long way. On entering and leaving a shop or café, say "bonjour" and "au revoir". Be sure to add "s'il vous plait" (please) when ordering items, and say "pardon" if you accidentally bump into someone.

The French usually shake hands on meeting someone for the first time and when saying goodbye. Family, friends and colleagues who know each other well often greet each other with a kiss on each cheek. If you are unsure about what is expected, wait to see if you are offered a hand or a cheek.

Visiting Churches and Cathedrals

Dress respectfully when visiting a religious site: cover the torso and upper arms, and ensure that shorts and skirts reach at least to the knees.

Mobile Phones and Wi-Fi

For cheap calls to French numbers, it is advisable to use a French SIM card, which will work in unlocked phones.

A 5G network operates throughout France so mobile signal is strong here. Visitors on EU tariffs should be able to use their devices without being affected by data roaming charges, whereas many North American and Japanese phones aren't compatible here. It is best to check international rates with your service provider before using your phone abroad.

Free Wi-Fi hotspots are available in many public spaces. Cafés and restaurants usually allow customers to use their Wi-Fi for free.

Bordeaux also has a Wi-Fi network that is available for free across the city.

Post

Stamps can be bought at post offices and *tabacs* (corner shops). Most post offices have self-service machines to weigh your mail. Yellow post boxes are a common sight across France.
La Poste
🅦 laposte.fr

Taxes and Refunds

VAT is around 20 per cent in France. Non-EU residents can claim back tax on certain purchases over €175 if the claim is made within six months. Look out for the Global Refund Tax-Free sign, and ask the retailer for a form for a *détaxe* receipt. Present the goods receipt, détaxe receipt and your passport at customs when you leave the country to receive your refund.

Discount Cards

Entry to some museums is free on the first Sunday of each month. Under-18s and EU passport holders aged 18–26 are usually admitted free of charge to national museums, and there are sometimes discounts for students and over-60s with relevant ID.

The **Camping Card International** can provide savings of up to 20 per cent on campsite bookings. Bordeaux also offers a **CityPass** card, available for 24, 48 or 72 hours, which covers entry to local attractions, transport throughout the city and discounts on tours.
Bordeaux CityPass
🅦 visiter-bordeaux.com/en/bordeaux-citypass
Camping Card International
🅦 campingcardinternational.com

WEBSITES AND APPS

francetourism.com
　Information and inspiration for
　travelling in France
visit-dordogne-valley.co.uk
　A useful events calendar for the region
aquitainebike.com
　Information on bike tours in the region

INDEX

PHRASE BOOK

IN AN EMERGENCY

Help!	Au secours!	oh sekoor
Stop!	Arrêtez!	aret-ay
Call a doctor!	Appelez un médecin!	apuh-lay uñ medsañ
Call an ambulance!	Appelez une ambulance!	apuh-lay oon oñboo-loñs
Call the police!	Appelez la police!	apuh-lay lah poh-lees
Call the fire brigade!	Appelez les pompiers!	apuh-lay leh poñ-peeyay
Where is the nearest telephone?	Où est le téléphone le plus proche?	oo ay luh telehfon luh ploo prosh
Where is the nearest hospital?	Où est l'hôpital le plus proche?	oo ay lopeetal luh ploo prosh

COMMUNICATION ESSENTIALS

Yes	Oui	wee
No	Non	noñ
Please	S'il vous plaît	seel voo play
Thank you	Merci	mer-see
Excuse me	Excusez-moi	exkoo-zay mwah
Hello	Bonjour	boñzhoor
Goodbye	Au revoir	oh ruh-vwar
Good night	Bonsoir	boñ-swar
Morning	Le matin	matañ
Afternoon	L'après-midi	l'apreh-meedee
Evening	Le soir	swar
Yesterday	Hier	eeyehr
Today	Aujourd'hui	oh-zhoor-dwee
Tomorrow	Demain	duhmañ
Here	Ici	ee-see
There	Là	lah
What?	Quoi, quel, quelle?	kwah, kel, kel
When?	Quand?	koñ
Why?	Pourquoi?	poor-kwah
Where?	Où?	oo

USEFUL PHRASES

How are you?	Comment allez-vous?	kom-moñ talay voo
Very well, thank you.	Très bien, merci.	treh byañ, mer-see
Pleased to meet you.	Enchanté de faire votre connaissance.	oñshoñ-tay duh fehr votr kon-ay-sans
See you soon.	A bientôt.	byañ-toh
That's fine.	C'est bon	say boñ
Where is/are...?	Où est/sont...?	ooay/soñ
How far is it to...?	Combien de kilometres d'ici à...?	kom-byañ duh keelo-metr d'ee-see ah
Which way to...?	Quelle est la direction pour...?	kel ay lah deer-ek-syoñ poor
Do you speak English?	Parlez-vous anglais?	par-lay voo oñg-lay
I don't understand.	Je ne comprends pas.	zhuh nuh kom-proñ pah
Could you speak slowly please?	Pouvez-vous parler moins vite s'il vous plaît?	poo-vay voo par-lay mwañ veet seel voo play
I'm sorry.	Excusez-moi.	exkoo-zay mwah

USEFUL WORDS

big	grand	groñ
small	petit	puh-tee
hot	chaud	show
cold	froid	frwah
good	bon/bien	boñ/byañ
bad	mauvais	moh-veh
enough	assez	assay
well	bien	byañ
open	ouvert	oo-ver
closed	fermé	fer-meh
left	gauche	gohsh
right	droite	drwaht
straight on	tout droite	too drwaht
near	près	preh
far	loin	lwañ
up	en haut	oñ oh
down	en bas	oñ bah
early	de bonne heure	duh bon urr
late	en retard	oñ ruh-tar
entrance	l'entrée	l'on-tray
exit	la sortie	sor-tee
toilet	les toilettes, le WC	twah-let, vay-see
free, unoccupied	libre	leebr
free, no charge	gratuit	grah-twee

MAKING A TELEPHONE CALL

I'll try again later.	Je rappelerai plus tard.	zhuh rapeleray ploo tar
Can I leave a message?	Est-ce que je peux laisser un message?	es-keh zhuh puh leh-say uñ mehsazh
Hold on.	Ne quittez pas, s'il vous plaît.	nuh kee-tay pah seel voo play
Could you speak up a little please?	Pouvez-vous parler un peu plus fort?	poo-vay voo parlay uñ puh ploo for
local call	la communication locale	komoonikahsyoñ low-kal

SHOPPING

How much does this cost?	C'est combien s'il vous plaît?	say kom-byañ seel voo play
I would like ...	Je voudrais...	zhuh voo-dray
Do you have?	Est-ce que vous avez	es-kuh voo zavay
I'm just looking.	Je regarde seulement.	zhuh ruhgar. suhlmoñ
Do you take credit cards?	Est-ce que vous acceptez les cartes de crédit?	es-kuh voo zaksept-ay leh kart duh kreh-dee
What time do you open?	A quelle heure vous êtes ouvert?	ah kel urr voo zet oo-ver
What time do you close?	A quelle heure vous êtes fermé?	ah kel urr voo zet fer-may
This one.	Celui-ci	suhl-wee-see
That one.	Celui-là	suhl-wee-lah
expensive	cher	shehr
cheap	pas cher, bon marché	pah shehr, boñ mar-shay
size, clothes	la taille	tye
size, shoes	la pointure	pwañ-tur
white	blanc	bloñ
black	noir	nwahr
red	rouge	roozh
yellow	jaune	zhohwn
green	vert	vehr
blue	bleu	bluh

TYPES OF SHOP

antique shop	le magasin d'antiquités	maga-zañ d'oñteekee-tay
bakery	la boulangerie	booloñ-zhuree
bank	la banque	boñk
bookshop	la librairie	lee-brehree
butcher	la boucherie	boo-shehree
cake shop	la pâtisserie	patee-sree
cheese shop	la fromagerie	fromazh-ree
chemist	la pharmacie	farmah-see
dairy	la crémerie	krem-ree
department store	le grand magasin	groñ maga-zañ
delicatessen	la charcuterie	sharkoot-ree
fishmonger	la poissonnerie	pwasson-ree
gift shop	le magasin de cadeaux	maga-zañ duh kadoh
greengrocer	le marchand de légumes	mar-shoñ duh lay-goom
grocery	l'alimentation	alee-moñta-syoñ
hairdresser	le coiffeur	kwafuhr
market	le marché	marsh-ay
newsagent	le magasin de journaux	maga-zañ duh zhoor-no
post office	la poste, le bureau de poste, le PTT	pohst, booroh duh pohst, peh-teh-teh
shoe shop	le magasin de chaussures	maga-zañ duh show-soor
supermarket	le supermarché	soo pehr-marshay
tobacconist	le tabac	tabah
travel agent	l'agence de voyages	l'azhoñs duh vwayazh

SIGHTSEEING

abbey	l'abbaye	l'abay-ee
art gallery	la galerie d'art	galer-ree dart
bus station	la gare routière	gahr roo-tee-ehr
cathedral	la cathédrale	katay-dral
church	l'église	l'aygleez
garden	le jardin	zhar-dañ
library	la bibliothèque	beebleeo-tek
museum	le musée	moo-zay
railway station	la gare (SNCF)	gahr (es-en-say-ef)
tourist information office	les renseignements touristiques, le syndicat d'initiative	roñsayn-moñ tooreez-teek, sandee-ka deenee-syateev
town hall	l'hôtel de ville	l'ohtel duh veel
closed for public holiday	fermeture jour férié	fehrmeh-tur zhoor fehree-ay

STAYING IN A HOTEL

Do you have a vacant room?	Est-ce que vous avez une chambre?	es-kuh voo-zavay oon shambr
double room, with double bed	la chambre à deux personnes, avec un grand lit	shambr ah duh pehr-son avek un gronñ lee
twin room	la chambre à deux lits	shambr ah duh lee
single room	la chambre à une personne	shambr ah oon pehr-son
room with a bath, shower	la chambre avec salle de bains, une douche	shambr avek sal duh bañ, oon doosh
porter	le garçon	gar-soñ
key	la clef	klay
I have a reservation.	J'ai fait une réservation.	zhay fay oon rayzehrva-syoñ

EATING OUT

Have you got a table?	Avez-vous une table or libre?	avay-voo oon tahbl lee leebr
I want to reserve a table.	Je voudrais réserver une table.	zhuh voo-dray rayzehr-vay oon tahbl
The bill please.	L'addition s'il vous plaît.	l'adee-syoñ seel voo play
I am a vegetarian.	Je suis végétarien.	zhuh swee vezhay-tehryañ
Waitress/ waiter	Madame, Mademoiselle/ Monsieur	mah-dam, mah-demwahzel/ muh-syuh
menu	le menu, la carte	men-oo, kart
fixed-price menu	le menu à prix fixe	men-oo ah pree feeks
cover charge	le couvert	koo-vehr
wine list	la carte des vins	kart-deh vañ
glass	le verre	vehr
bottle	la bouteille	boo-tay
knife	le couteau	koo-toh
fork	la fourchette	for-shet
spoon	la cuillère	kwee-yehr
breakfast	le petit déjeuner	puh-tee deh-zhuh-nay
lunch	le déjeuner	deh-zhuh-nay
dinner	le dîner	dee-nay
main course	le plat principal	plah prañsee-pal
starter, first course	l'entrée, le hors d'oeuvre	l'oñ-tray, or-duhvr
dish of the day	le plat du jour	plah doo zhoor
wine bar	le bar à vin	bar ah vañ
café	le café	ka-fay
rare	saignant	say-noñ
medium	à point	ah pwañ
well done	bien cuit	byañ kwee

MENU DECODER

apple	la pomme	pom
baked	cuit au four	kweet oh foor
banana	la banane	banan
beef	le boeuf	buhf
beer, draught beer	la bière, bière à la pression	bee-yehr, bee-yehr ah lah pres-syoñ
boiled	bouilli	boo-yee
bread	le pain	pan
butter	le beurre	burr
cake	le gâteau	gah-toh
cheese	le fromage	from-azh
chicken	le poulet	poo-lay
chips	les frites	freet
chocolate	le chocolat	shoko-lah
cocktail	le cocktail	cocktail
coffee	le café	kah-fay
dessert	le dessert	deh-ser
dry	sec	sek
duck	le canard	kanar
egg	l'oeuf	l'uf
fish	le poisson	pwah-ssoñ
fresh fruit	le fruit frais	frwee freh
garlic	l'ail	l'eye
grilled	grillé	gree-yay
ham	le jambon	zhoñ-boñ
ice, ice cream	la glace	glas
lamb	l'agneau	l'anyoh
lemon	le citron	see-troñ
lobster	le homard	omahr
meat	la viande	vee-yand
milk	le lait	leh
mineral water	l'eau minérale	l'oh meeney-ral
mustard	la moutarde	moo-tard
oil	l'huile	l'weel
olives	les olives	leh zoleev
onions	les oignons	leh zonyoñ
orange	l'orange	l'oroñzh
fresh orange juice	l'orange pressée	l'oroñzh press-eh
fresh lemon juice	le citron pressé	see-troñ press-eh
pepper	le poivre	pwavr
poached	poché	posh-ay
pork	le porc	por
potatoes	les pommes de terre	pom-duh tehr
prawns	les crevettes	kruh-vet
rice	le riz	ree
roast	rôti	row-tee
roll	le petit pain	puh-tee pañ
salt	le sel	sel
sauce	la sauce	sohs
sausage, fresh	la saucisse	sohsees
seafood	les fruits de mer	frwee duh mer
shellfish	les crustacés	kroos-tas
snails	les escargots	leh zes-kar-goh
soup	la soupe, le potage	soop, poh-tazh
steak	le bifteck, le steack	beef-tek, stek
sugar	le sucre	sookr
tea	le thé	tay
toast	pain grillé	pan greeyay
vegetables	les légumes	lay-goom
vinegar	le vinaigre	veenaygr
water	l'eau	l'oh
red wine	le vin rouge	vañ roozh
white wine	le vin blanc	vañ bloñ

NUMBERS

0	zéro	zeh-roh
1	un, une	uñ, oon
2	deux	duh
3	trois	trwah
4	quatre	katr
5	cinq	sañk
6	six	sees
7	sept	set
8	huit	weet
9	neuf	nerf
10	dix	dees
11	onze	oñz
12	douze	dooz
13	treize	trehz
14	quatorze	katorz
15	quinze	kañz
16	seize	sehz
17	dix-sept	dees-set
18	dix-huit	dees-weet
19	dix-neuf	dees-nerf
20	vingt	vañ
30	trente	tront
40	quarante	karoñt
50	cinquante	sañkoñt
60	soixante	swasoñt
70	soixante-dix	swasoñt-dees
80	quatre-vingts	katr-vañ
90	quatre-vingt-dix	katr-vañ-dees
100	cent	soñ
1,000	mille	meel

TIME

one minute	une minute	oon mee-noot
one hour	une heure	oon urr
half an hour	une demi-heure	oon duh-mee urr
Monday	lundi	luñ-dee
Tuesday	mardi	mar-dee
Wednesday	mercredi	mehrkruh-dee
Thursday	jeudi	zhuh-dee
Friday	vendredi	voñdruh-dee
Saturday	samedi	sam-dee
Sunday	dimanche	dee-moñsh

ACKNOWLEDGMENTS

The publisher would like to thank the following for their kind permission to reproduce their photographs:

Key: a-above; b-below/bottom; c-centre; f-far; l-left; r-right; t-top

123RF.com: Boris Breytman 123tl, 123tr; delcreations 10-1b; freeprod 10ca; Philippe Halle 117tl.

4Corners: Francesco Carovillano 78-9b, 126; Günter Gräfenhain 35tr, 96-7b; Laurent Grandadam 249tl; Carlo Irek 34t; Tim Mannakee 143b; Gianluca Santoni 98-9; Luigi Vaccarella 10clb, 16, 38-9t, 60-1, 67tr, 216bl; Chris Warren 136b.

Alamy Stock Photo: ACTIVE MUSEUM / Le Pictorium / Collection 84bl; Kate After 54tr; Age Fotostock / Christian Goupi 124t, 125cra, / Felix González 80cl, / Ian Cook 173br, / J.D. Dallet 57cr, 102b, / Javier Larrea 47br, 51tr, 214t, / Kevin O´Hara 100bl, / Rafael Campillo 200bl; Agencja Fotograficzna Caro / Schwarz 49cl; Ajax News & Feature Service / COLLECTIONS / Caroline Beaumont 57tr; Jerónimo Alba 104cl, / © Bordeaux, Musée des Beaux-Arts 68tl; All Canada Photos / Ian Cook 26bl, 115tl; Andia / © Lux 32-3t, / Le Gal 248b; AOP / SCOPE-IMAGE 114bl, 118t; Art Kowalsky 8-9b; The Art Archive / Gianni Dagli Orti 227cra; Arterra Picture Library / Clement Philippe 131tl; Andy Arthur 176-7b; David Bagnall 38br; David Bertho / © XTU architects / La Cité du Vin 69crb; BIOSPHOTO / Georges Lopez 246-7t, / Laurent Lhote 35crb; Christophe Boisvieux 194tr, 249br; Andor Bujdoso 44-5t; Ed Buziak 225tr, 245tr; Cavan / Christophe Launay 30-1t; Nico Chapman 219tr; Chronicle 53tr; Classic Image 42-3t; Simon Dack 152bl; Ian Dagnall 28br, 140b, 155br; Daniel Valla FRPS 142tl; Stephane Debove 26t; David Dunbar 242tl; Keith Erskine 26crb; David Forster 155tl; Sioen Gérard 218t; Roberto Soncin Gerometta 135tr; Iurii Golub 8cla; Manfred Gottschalk 70bl; Granger Historical Picture Archive / NYC 33br, 131tr, 131cra; Sheila Halsall / Crédit Photo ASF 194bl; Hemis / Cedric PASQUINI 50cla, / Jean-Marc BARRERE 164cl, 166b, / Patrice Hauser 41crb, / Alain Felix 171tl, / Arnaud Chicurel 22cr, / Bertrand Rieger 132br, 151br, 215tr, 221cla, 222-3t, / Cédric Pasquini 12-3b, / Christophe Boisvieux 153tr, / Cintract Romain 239br, / Denis Caviglia 141tr, / Eric Bouloumié 65t, 101br, / Francis Leroy 149tr, / Franck Guiziou 89br, 90-1t, 91br, 104-5t, / Franck Guiziou / © XTU architects 69b, / Gregory Gerault 76-7t, / Jacques Pierre 145br, 244-5b, / Jean-Daniel Sudres 22crb, 24bl, 203, 223br, 230crb, 230b, 231tr, / Jean-Marc Barrère 162clb, 162b, 167tr, 178tl, 179b, 180tl, 185tr, 195b, 240t, 243b, / Jean-Paul Azam 120bl,

227cl, / Laurent Moreau 105br, / Marc Dozier 32bl, / Pasquini Cedric 51crb, / Patrice Hauser 34bl, 89tl, 140clb, 190t, / Patrick Escudero 43bl, 211tr, / Romain Cintract 50cr; Marc Hill 226crb; Historic Images 201br; Historimages Collection / Yolanda Perera Sánchez 54tl, 54br; The History Collection 52t; Robert Hoetink 143tr; Horizon Images / Motion 172-3t; Stephen Hughes 192bl; Ian Dagnall Commercial Collection 33cl; Image Professionals GmbH / Fleurent 11br, / H et M 30bl, / TravelCollection 11t; Images of Birmingham Premium 35cla; incamerastock / ICP-UK 36-7b; Tom Irvine 48-9b; Ivoha 226-7t; JBN / SCOPE-IMAGE 50clb; Jon Arnold Images Ltd / Walter Bibikow 121cra; John Keates 83br; John Kellerman 12t, 154bl, 165cra; David Kilpatrick 247bl; Piotr Krześlak 31br; Lebrecht Music & Arts 102ca; Hervé Lenain 81tr, 92cl, 144tr, 168tl, 168-9b, 170-1b, 198tl; K.D. Leperi 103tr; Look / Brigitte Merz 227bl; Julien De Marchi 148b; Martin Thomas Photography 128-9t; mauritius images GmbH / Klaus Neuner 83tr, / Walter Bibikow 93tr; MIKEL BILBAO GOROSTIAGA- TRAVELS 39crb; Jim Monk 71tl; Tim Moore 146-7b; Perry van Munster 210bl, 212bl, 216crb; Jean-Bernard Nadeau 65cra; Niday Picture Library 56tl; nobleIMAGES / David Noble 42br; Eva Ozkoidi 36-7t; Per Karlsson - BKWine.com 85cra, 50cl; Photononstop / Daniele Schneider 43c, 88bl, 90bl, 100-1t, 138t, 139b, 193t, 197tr, 229t; PjrTravel 66cra; PRISMA ARCHIVO 130bl; Profimedia.CZ a.s. / Kulinarni studio BAUER MEDIA 47c; Reciprocity Images 134bl; Fabrice Restier 51cr; robertharding / Adam Tall 31clb, / Alex Treadway 35b, / Ellen Rooney 13t; Ageev Rostislav 55bl; SAGAPHOTO.COM / Olivier Roux 94t, / Stéphane Gautier 208br; Science History Images / Photo Researchers 56crb; Kumar Sriskandan 19tl, 37cl, 39bl, 156-7, 160cra, 160-1; Neiliann Tait 49br; Paul Tavener 116bl; Claude Thibault 219bl; VPC Photo 53br; wanderworldimages 37crb.

AWL Images: Spani Arnaud 150-1t; Bertrand Gardel 66-7b; Hemis 174-5; Doug Pearson 12cl.

Bridgeman Images: Archives Charmet 227tr.

Château Lamothe Bergeron: Andy Julia 28tl.

Depositphotos Inc: ademyan 20, 204-5.

Dorling Kindersley: Philippe Giraud 182bl.

Dreamstime.com: Steve Allen 92b; Leonid Andronov 252-3; Annapustynnikova 45b; BarbaraCerovsek 58-9; Eric Cowez 96tl; Delstudio 46bl, 51cla; Pierre Jean Durieu 227clb (Stèle de Gibraltar); Sergey Dzyuba 213br, 238tl; Kevin Eaves 57br, 243tr; Iakov Filimonov 77cra; Freeprod 2-3; Freesurf69 11cr; Hans Geel 57cra; Javarman 123cra; Oleksandr Korzhenko 21, 196b,

Main Contributors Lisa Voormeij,
Mike MacEacheran, Deborah Bine,
Sophie Blackman, Gabrielle Innes,
Suzanne Boireau-Tartarat, Pierre Chavot,
Renée Grimaud, Wilfried Lecarpentier,
Santiago Mendieta, Marie-Pascale Rauzier

Senior Editor Alison McGill

Senior Designer Tania Da Silva Gomes

Project Editor Robin Moul

Project Art Editor William Robinson

Designers Kitty Glavin, Kanika Kalra,
Jordan Lambley, Bandana Paul, Stuti Tiwari
Bhatia, Priyanka Thakur

Factchecker Emma Gibbs

Editors Louise Abbott, Jackie Staddon,
Ruth Reisenberger

Proofreader Darren Longley

Indexer Hilary Bird

Senior Picture Researcher Ellen Root

Picture Research Harriet Whitaker,
Sumita Khatwani, Rituraj Singh,
Manpreet Kaur, Vagisha Pushp

Illustrators François Brosse,
Rodolphe Corbel, Éric Geoffroy,
Emmanuel Guillon, Jean-Sylvain Roveri

Cartographic Editor James Macdonald

Cartography Rajesh Chhibber,
Animesh Pathak and Simonetta Giori.
Original cartography Cyrille Suss.

Jacket Designers Maxine Pedliham,
William Robinson

Jacket Picture Research Susie Watters

Senior DTP Designer Jason Little

DTP Rohit Rojal

Producer Kariss Ainsworth

Managing Editor Rachel Fox

Art Director Maxine Pedliham

Publishing Director Georgina Dee

First edition 2006

Published in Great Britain by Dorling Kindersley Limited,
80 Strand, London, WC2R 0RL

Published in the United States by DK Publishing,
1450 Broadway, Suite 801, New York, NY 10018

A CIP catalog record for this book
is available from the British Library.

A catalog record for this book is available
from the Library of Congress.

ISSN: 1542 1554
ISBN: 978 0 2414 0934 3

Printed and bound in China.

www.dk.com

**The information in this
DK Eyewitness Travel Guide is checked regularly.**
Every effort has been made to ensure that this book
is as up-to-date as possible at the time of going to
press. Some details, however, such as telephone
numbers, opening hours, prices, gallery hanging
arrangements and travel information, are liable to
change. The publishers cannot accept responsibility
for any consequences arising from the use of this
book, nor for any material on third party websites,
and cannot guarantee that any website address
in this book will be a suitable source of travel
information. We value the views and suggestions
of our readers very highly. Please write to: Publisher,
DK Eyewitness Travel Guides, Dorling Kindersley,
80 Strand, London, WC2R 0RL, UK, or email:
travelguides@dk.com